Fodor's EXPLORING

BOSTON &
NEW ENGLAND

FODOR'S TRAVEL PUBLICATIONS, INC.

NEW YORK • TORONTO • LONDON • SYDNEY • AUCKLAND

WWW.FODORS.COM

Published in the United States by Fodor's Travel Publications, Inc.
Published in the United Kingdom by A.A. Publishing.

Fodor's and Fodor's Exploring Guides are registered trademarks of Fodor's Travel Publications, Inc.

ISBN 0–679–00263–4
Third Edition

Fodor's Exploring Boston & New England

Authors: **Tim Locke and Sue Gordon**
Additional material: **Sean Connolly**
Cartography: **The Automobile Association**
Cover design: **Louise Fili, Fabrizio La Rocca**
Front cover top photograph: **The Automobile Association**
Front cover silhouette: **Peter Guttman**

Printed and bound in Italy by Printer Trento srl.
10 9 8 7 6 5 4 3 2 1

How to use this book

ORGANIZATION

New England Is, New England Was

Discusses aspects of life and culture in contemporary New England and explores significant periods in the region's history.

A to Z

An alphabetical listing of places to visit. The book begins with a section on Boston, and is subsequently divided into states. Places of interest are listed alphabetically within each section. Suggested walks, drives and Focus On articles, which provide an insight into aspects of life in New England, are included in each section.

Travel Facts

Contains the strictly practical information that is vital for a successful trip.

Hotels and Restaurants

Lists places to stay and places to eat state by state. Entries are graded budget, moderate or expensive.

ABOUT THE RATINGS

Most places described in this book have been given a separate rating. These are as follows:

▶▶▶   **Do not miss**

▶▶   **Highly recommended**

▶   **Worth seeing**

MAP REFERENCES

To make the location of a particular place easier to find, every main entry in this book is given a map reference, such as 176B3. The first number (176) indicates the page on which the map can be found, the letter (B) and the second number (3) pinpoint the square in which the main entry is located. The maps on the inside front cover and inside back cover are referred to as IFC and IBC respectively.

Contents

A to Z

7

Tim Locke's love of the great outdoors and interest in landscape, architecture and places has encouraged him to travel widely in Europe, the U.S.A. and the Far East. In his native Britain he has written several books on walking, including *The Good Walks Guide* (Which Books), as well as guidebooks to scenic regions of England. He is the author of *Fodor's Exploring Britain* and contributed to *Germany* and *Thailand* in the same series.

Sue Gordon first got to know New England as an au pair in the 1960s. She now returns whenever she has the chance and has also written *CityPack Boston (A.A.).* She is also the author of *Explore Britain's Villages (A.A.),* and has contributed to several walks books, including *Walking Britain's Rivers and Canals* (HarperCollins) and *Country Walks and Scenic Drives* (Reader's Digest). Tim Locke and Sue Gordon are also guidebook editors.

My New England by Tim Locke

Those six little states that are crammed into the northeastern corner of the map of the U.S.A. must be one of the most written up and talked about areas of the world. They represent much of a great nation's historical and cultural emergence, the roots of modern America.

To me they are a never-ending source of discovery. The quintessential aspects of New England's character—its village greens, its delightful architectural variety, its covered bridges, its wooded hills to name but a few—stay in the memory of all visitors.

But the more I see of the region, the more I realize how much there is yet to explore. Boston is a great city of many facets: follow the red line of the Freedom Trail and in a few hours you have a remarkable cross-section of its history. Yet the city harbors many lesser-known gems too—my favorites include the Athenaeum (which Sue Gordon urged me to visit), with its bookish tranquillity, the surreal stained-glass Mapparium, with its extraordinary echo, and the gas-lit backstreets of Beacon Hill.

History and heritage are celebrated with flair at the great museums at Mystic, Plymouth, Sturbridge, Shelburne, Strawbery Banke and elsewhere. Yet equally memorable are some of the more modest parcels of a well-preserved past: among those that spring immediately to mind are the idiosyncratic Paper House near Rockport and the little steam train that puffs its way up to the summit of Mount Washington.

The natural scene is blessed with delightfully distinct seasons. The fall foliage presents a truly spectacular show, while the winter snows again transform the scene magically. I savor impressions of the view on a summer dawn from Mount Cadillac in Acadia National Park, looking along the indented coast of Maine and across the vast inland forests and folded hills. And of basking in a hot outdoor tub in an inn in Stowe, Vermont, with snow flakes falling gently on me in the dark, after a day's cross-country skiing in the birchwoods. Meanwhile the events calendar is busy with country fairs, bean cookouts, maple sugaring, historical re-enactments and more—encouraging a return visit at any time of year.

I find New England gives a warm welcome second to none. It is a friend for life.

New England Is

The states of Massachusetts, Connecticut, Rhode Island, New Hampshire, Vermont, and Maine constitute New England. Although relatively small in area, this is the cultural and historic cradle of the nation. There are qualities that characterize the region as a whole, but there are also subtle differences within it.

THE ELEMENTS The clichés have their own element of truth: against a blue sky, the wooden steeple of a church stands high over a village green fringed with neat, white clapboard houses. Back roads wind over covered bridges and through seemingly endless forests that in autumn burst into brilliant hues of russet, gold, and crimson. Bright orange pumpkins lie stacked in mounds by wooden barns and on farm stands. Lighthouses look out over the ocean from shores of rock and sand. Fishing boats unload the daily catch, and lobster and clam chowder appear on virtually every menu.

New England is a region of firsts, in industrialization and historical events. It has been the seedbed of intellectual and political thought for three centuries. It has magnificent art collections in museums, colleges, and universities. New England has produced—and continues to produce—many great names in music, art, and literature.

New England has a small-scale quality that is an integral part of its charm, and has been described as "America with the volume turned down." Many of the region's inhabitants greatly value their

Point Judith Light, Rhode Island

A white steeple framed by autumn foliage: quintessential New England at Sugar Hill, NH

lifestyle and are fiercely proud of their history and roots. The Yankee mentality—formed by a keen work ethic, frugality, shrewdness, and a serious, conservative outlook—is deeply ingrained.

EARLY DAYS The great ice masses that once covered this land have left their mark. Glaciers sculpted the mountains and valleys, and created a deeply indented coastline. The landscape was scoured, and the bedrock and boulder-strewn earth proved infertile for the first farmers. On this soil the first European settlers established themselves, primarily along the coast and the rivers. The Pilgrim Fathers arrived from England aboard the *Mayflower* in 1620. More than a century later, in 1775, the first shots

10

of the American Revolution at Lexington and Concord signaled the end of British colonial rule.

As settlers moved westward over the continent, New England's farmlands were gradually abandoned, and the trees, once cleared by the farmers, reestablished themselves. Today some 80 percent of New England is forested, and much of Vermont, New Hampshire, and inland Maine is also hilly or mountainous and sparsely settled.

VISITING THE REGION Boston is by far the largest city, and one that every visitor to the region should see. The Freedom Trail wends an intricate route past the city's historic sites. This is a city of superb museums, excitingly contrasting neighborhoods, and striking architecture. Visitors without a car can find plenty of rewarding excursions by public transportation.

New England's thick tree cover can mean that sweeping panoramic views are hard to come by, at least from a car. For the most spectacular views, however, you can take high-level walks in the White Mountains or Acadia National Park, or explore the coast by boat. Outdoor pursuits in the hills and mountains of northern New England are well developed and include winter sports, watersports, hiking, and fishing. The southern states of Massachusetts, Rhode Island, and Connecticut are more densely populated and have more historic sights.

The long and complex seaboard has a lasting appeal, with the sandy beaches of Cape Cod, the islands, and southern Maine among the most popular. There are many opportunities for cruises and sailing, and a number of museums commemorate New England's maritime heritage, including the vanished whaling industry. Today, whale-watching cruises are big business, and no visitor should miss the chance to join an exhilarating tour to the feeding grounds of the humpback whales.

New England's charms change with the seasons. Spring brings freshness and greenery. In summer, delicious Atlantic breezes make the coast a pleasant retreat from the heat, while autumn's foliage is deservedly famous. Winters are harsh but bring photogenic snowfalls and a Christmas-card look as sports enthusiasts put on their skis.

With so much of the area heavily forested, clapboard is universal

Explore New England and you experience a range of building styles from early colonial through to postmodernism. White clapboard is an integral feature of New England's charm and is a dominant theme outside the major cities; observe closely and you should be able to identify stylistic variations.

EARLY COLONIAL The early English colonists brought with them a tradition of building in wood and, as hardwoods were plentiful in New England, the timber-framed house became—and remains—universal. The frames were covered with cedar shingles or clapboards (which were painted in a variety of colors). Built with steep roofs, as they had been back home to help the rain run off, the earliest colonial houses had an overhanging upper story, central chimney, and small, irregular casement windows. The steeper the roof, the older the house. Quite commonly, a lean-to was added at the back under one sloping roof, the outline giving rise to the term "saltbox." Few of the very earliest houses survive, but Paul Revere's House in Boston and the House of Seven Gables in Salem, MA, both date from the late 1600s.

Colonial: the Mission House (1739) at Stockbridge, MA

GEORGIAN The classical Palladian style that was introduced to Britain from Italy reached eastern New England in the 18th century. The handsome houses in this style, many built by wealthy maritime traders, are recognizable by their strict symmetry. Still clapboarded, they typically have a hipped roof, a central door which is sometimes pilastered, and equally spaced sash windows; Portsmouth, New Hampshire (see pages 202–203) has many Palladian-style homes. Many modern clapboard houses are still built in this manner.

FEDERAL After Independence, Charles Bulfinch (see panel, page 72) introduced the neoclassical Adamesque style, known as Federal, with public buildings such as the State House in Boston and, notably, his Beacon Hill development of genteel, red-brick homes for the elite (see page 64). These stand proudly foursquare, lightly detailed, with a shallow, sometimes balustraded, hipped roof, an imposing porch, and a fan-shaped window over the door. Inside, rooms may be oval, circular, or polygonal, with cornices and fireplaces decorated with garlands and urns of flowers. Salem, Massachusetts, and Providence, Rhode Island, have some of the finest examples of the Federal style.

VICTORIAN After the mid-1820s the design of public, academic, and domestic building becomes more diversified, reflecting European influences. Boston's Quincy Market is an example of the Greek Revival style, featuring the columns and pediments of ancient Greek temples. The Gothic Revival style is easily recognized by

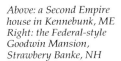

Above: a Second Empire house in Kennebunk, ME
Right: the Federal-style Goodwin Mansion, Strawbery Banke, NH

its steeply pitched gables, turrets, and intricately carved bargeboards. Italianate buildings (from 1840) include Victoria Mansion in Portland (see page 134). A variety of historical and decorative elements such as mansard roofs and ironwork balconies characterize the Second Empire style (from 1860)—Parisian buildings were a major source of inspiration. The Queen Anne style owes little to the English Queen Anne period but is characterized by contrasts of texture—often shingle and clapboard laid out decoratively—as well as of color and form; tall chimneys and round verandas are typical hallmarks. The Renaissance Revival style of the 1880s and 1890s, used for some public buildings such as Boston Public Library, is also termed "Beaux Arts." The architect of Boston's Trinity Church gave his name to the uniquely American Richardson Romanesque style, notable for its heavy stonework with chunky columns and arches. Many Victorian styles are represented in Newport's fabulously ornate mansions. Boston's Back Bay, one of history's most splendid pieces of urban planning, also makes a wonderful sampler of Victorian architecture, with bow-fronted "rowhouses" of various styles (see pages 62–3).

A Cape Cod vignette: painted clapboard, screen door, and wreath

MODERN By far the most exciting contemporary architecture in New England is to be found in Boston and Cambridge. The leading architects are international: I.M. Pei, responsible for the city's 1970s rejuvenation scheme, and the Bauhaus architect and Harvard professor, Walter Gropius.

Two houses by great 20th-century architects which are open to visitors are the Gropius House, Lincoln MA (see page 170), and Frank Lloyd Wright's Zimmerman House, Manchester NH (see page 198).

13

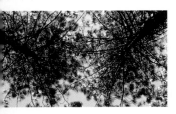

After the demise of its maritime trade and then its textile industry, the region is now one the country's main centers of technology. Tourism is of major importance, and while agriculture and fishing are of somewhat diminishing significance, the pulp and paper trade is a major growth area.

Farming meets tourism: orchards and cider mills welcome visitors

INSURANCE, INDUSTRY, EDUCATION, AND RESEARCH

Hartford, Connecticut, is the "Insurance City." The business started in the 19th century, in the heyday of New England's shipping trade, and today some of the largest U.S. insurance companies have their headquarters here.

The academic institutions of New England make a significant contribution to the economy, partly by generating business locally, but chiefly through the research and development work on which the region's electronics and communications industries depend. Connecticut has acquired the nickname of the

"Gadget State," but the manufacture of electronic components and machinery is also the economic mainstay of Rhode Island, Massachusetts (particularly along Route 128), and the southern part of New Hampshire.

TOURISM The wealthy of the Northeast recognized New England's potential as a summer playground at the end of the 19th century. Today, with the continuous popularity of snow sports, the region attracts as many visitors in winter as in summer to its mountain and coastal areas. In addition to these natural assets (and not forgetting the glory of the region's autumn foliage), the tourist industry can draw on a particularly fine maritime heritage. Tourism is New England's second largest industry, after health care.

❑ Pulp and paper mills at Rumford and Jay in Maine manufacture 1,500 tons of paper daily for books, magazines, catalogues, and business stationery, with those at Bucksport and Madawaska following not far behind. ❑

THE TIMBER TRADE A visitor to the northern areas of New England cannot fail to be impressed by the extent of the tree cover—some 80 percent in New Hampshire and Vermont, and 90 percent in Maine. It should come as no surprise that these forests make a substantial impact on the region's economy, to the tune of some $6 billion a year, although in Maine, for instance, less than 3 percent of the total forested area is actually

I Have Visited
OLD HOLLOW
IDER MILL
rbury Center
ont 0567

harvested. Maine is the second largest paper-producing state (after Wisconsin) in the U.S.A., making around 4 million tons of paper per annum. The building trade and furniture-makers also make significant use of what is a relatively new natural resource, for only a century ago most of the region's timber had been cleared for farmland. Today, both environmentalists and the trade are anxious to ensure that this rapidly expanding industry is managed well.

FARMING, FISHING, AND QUARRYING

Vermont is traditionally associated with dairy farming, and this is still an important part of the state economy, albeit a declining one. Vermont, too, specializes in turkeys, while Rhode Island is known for the breed of hen named Rhode Island Red.

There are about 2,400 dairy farms in Vermont, with an average of 70 cows

Immense quantities of potatoes are grown in northern Maine, the third largest crop in the country after Idaho and Washington. Other crops include tobacco in the Connecticut River valley, blueberries in Maine, and cranberries near Plymouth, Massachusetts, and on Cape Cod and the nearby islands.

The fishing industry is in decline. There is foreign competition in the Atlantic fishing grounds, and stocks of cod and haddock have been depleted, but fishing is still vital in ports such as Gloucester and Cape Ann in Massachusetts, and in the many lobstering ports along the coast of Maine.

New Hampshire, the "Granite State," has many granite quarries. Vermont's Green Mountains are also quarried for granite (see Barre, page 226) and for marble at Proctor (see page 235).

Lobstering in Maine alone brings in over $70 million a year

15

For anyone who considers shopping one of life's pleasures, New England has to be paradise. It is particularly famed for its antiques and crafts, for the local produce sold at farm stands and in country stores, and for its factory outlets.

For a taste of everything New England has to offer, shopaholics need to visit a factory outlet, an antiques shop or fair, a crafts gallery or show, a village store, a farm shop, and some of the one-of-a-kind shops that proliferate throughout the region. Museum shops often make good browsing territory; for example Mystic Seaport's bookshop has a huge range of maritime titles as well as the museum's own C.D.s of sea shanties. Then there is always the shopping mall: in Boston try the

The outlet store (above, one of dozens in Freeport, ME) and the village store (right) offer two very different shopping experiences. Every visitor should try them both at least once

Prudential Center and Copley Place or, for a really grand one, Chestnut Hill. (For more on shopping in Boston, see pages 82–83.)

FACTORY OUTLETS Love it or loathe it, outlet shopping is one of New England's big draws. All manner of merchandise—clothing, household goods, and gifts—is offered at these manufacturers' and distributors' outlets, either at wholesale prices or at discounts varying from 25 to 80 percent. Some bargains are older

lines being sold off while others are items made specifically for the outlets; many places have quarterly sales for which it is worth timing a visit precisely. Well-known brand names to be found include L.L. Bean (the famous mail-order clothing company), Liz Claiborne, Calvin Klein, Benetton, Black & Decker, Van Heusen, Polo/Ralph Lauren, Levi, Nautica, Sansomite—the list is endless. The outlet capitals of New England are Kittery and Freeport (also the home of L.L. Bean) in Maine (see also page 128); Fall River in southern Massachusetts; and North Conway—also known as Mount Washington Valley— in New Hampshire (particularly popular because New Hampshire has no sales tax). Worcester Common, Massachusetts, has 90 stores, all together and under cover at the heart of the city, with direct Peter Pan buses (see page 258) from Boston, including a free service on

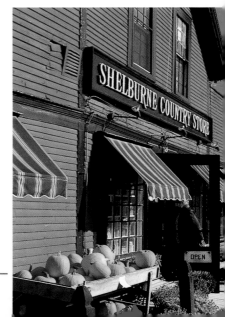

you need to know what you are about. The biggest show is held in May, July, and September in Brimfield, Massachusetts.

17

CRAFTS Visitors to New England can buy examples of traditional and contemporary crafts at a broad range of prices in shops and galleries. At any time, in any area, they will also be able to find a craft fair within easy distance. The Annual Craftsmen's Fair, the oldest in the nation, is held in the second week of August at the base of Mount Sunapee in New Hampshire. Some fairs are restricted to "juried" designers who have been judged to meet, or exceed, the highest of standards. These standards are reflected in the prices, but the quality really is outstanding. While excellent crafts can be found all over New England, it is in Vermont that the arts and crafts are particularly important. The Vermont State Craft Center at Frog Hollow has retail galleries in Burlington, Middlebury, and Manchester, and there are dozens of other outlets throughout the state.

Bargain-hunters in Boston's downtown area make for Filene's Basement, where goods are reduced according to how long they have been on display

Saturday. There are also scores of smaller complexes in many other towns.

ANTIQUES While some visitors come to New England simply for the outlets, others come purely for the antiques-hunting. Cape Cod, the Berkshires, much of Vermont, and Newport, Rhode Island, have particular concentrations of antiques shops, but it is hard to go anywhere without coming across an emporium of some sort, whether it trades in rusty farm tools or exquisite European furniture. The best bargains may be in flea markets and antiques shows (listed locally), but

In the northeast states, the weather conditions and the variety of broad-leaved trees combine perfectly to produce a sensational display of autumn color. During September and October, virtually the whole of New England is given over to "the fall."

The red maple brings the first hint of color to the hillsides

Vast areas of New England are forested and where, over the years, loggers have felled the evergreen softwoods, hardwoods have grown in their place, creating a full palette of autumn colors. Like the richest of oriental carpets, the vivid reds of the red maple, sugar maple, sweetgum, blackgum, sassafras, red oak, and scarlet oak interweave with the deep reddish-purples of the sumacs and dogwoods, the golden-yellows of the hickories, trembling aspen, and birches, and the rich bronzes and browns of beech and the other oaks.

❑ In September and October, call Fall Foliage Hotlines for a free calendar of events, a foliage guide (giving suggested leaf-peeping tours), and regularly updated reports. Connecticut: 860/270 8080. Maine: 800/932 3419. Massachusetts: 800/227 6277. New Hampshire: 603/271 2666. Rhode Island: 401/277 2601 or 800/556 2484. Vermont: 802/828 3239. ❑

THE CAUSE OF THE COLOR When the Great Bear was hunted down in the heavens, so goes the Native American legend, his blood dripped onto the forests, turning some of the leaves red, while the fat that spattered out of the hunters' cooking pot turned others yellow. A more scientific explanation has to do with the food-making process that goes on in leaves. The cells in which this takes place contain pigments, notably chlorophyll, which makes leaves green. Leaves also contain carotenoids that give them a yellow color, masked during spring and summer by the larger amount of green. When the days get shorter and the nights cooler, food-making slows down, the green goes as the chlorophyll breaks up, and yellows come to the fore. Similarly, when temperatures at night drop below 45°F, sugar made during the day is trapped, forming the pigment anthocyanin, responsible, for example, for the "fire engine" red color of the swamp or red maple.

No one can predict exactly when the leaf change will come, how long the season will be, or how bright the color. The most brilliant foliage occurs when warm, sunny days are

followed by cool nights. The season (about three weeks) starts in the northwest of New England around mid-September and progresses in a southeasterly direction.

SEEING THE SHOW Every state has its comprehensive list of fall foliage attractions for enthusiasts, known locally as "leaf-peepers," with suggested car and bicycle tours (see box). Roads such as the Kancamagus Highway in New Hampshire's White Mountains (see Drive on pages 206–7) and the Mohawk Trail in

❏ "No pen can describe the turning of the leaves—the insurrection of the tree people against the waning year. A little maple began it, flaming blood-red of a sudden where he stood against the dark green of a pine-belt. Next morning there was an answering signal from the swamp where the sumacs grow. Three days later, the hill-sides as far as the eye could range were afire, and the roads paved, with crimson and gold."
– Rudyard Kipling, *Leaves from a Winter Notebook*, 1900. ❏

19

western Massachusetts can get extremely busy, and you may be better off on the back roads (see Drives on pages 98–9 and 240–1).

In Vermont, you can combine leaf-peeping with craft shows, antiques fairs, and apple festivals, taking in some covered bridges on the way. In Maine, family outings can include visits to lighthouses and fishing villages, craft festivals and antiques fairs, farm stands and bean suppers. In New Hampshire, the Isle of Shoals Ferry runs cruises out of Portsmouth for a view from the sea, while the Lakes region offers a choice of cruises where the reflections of the trees in the water provide a double dose of color. The Massachusetts fall foliage guide suggests hot-air balloon trips and areas that are particularly good for excursions by boat or canoe. In Connecticut, cruises go down the prettiest part of the Connecticut River.

The gold of the sugar maple, most prominent around mid-October

Lobster may be the undisputed king, but seafood does not end there. And while New England is the home of maple syrup, there are many more treats for the sweet-toothed to enjoy. Orchard fruits and farm produce are of the very best.

Traditionally, New England farmers were set up for the day with a hearty breakfast of eggs with ham. Nowadays many inns and bed and breakfast establishments conjure up similarly filling fare—typically cornmeal pancakes with maple syrup, fish cakes and semi-sweet cornbread—as well as more elaborate concoctions such as fruits puréed and served on waffles with sausages or eggs with poached scallops and tarragon. In season, edible flowers sometimes put in an appearance. Later in the day, depending on the season, there may be an outdoor cookout, an ice-cream social, a clambake (see box), or a bean supper.

Baked beans, a favorite at church suppers, were invented by thrifty early colonists. Prepared in molasses, Boston baked beans, however, may be less easy to find in a restaurant than Boston cream pie, which is actually a custard-filled sponge cake covered in chocolate. Desserts tend to be very sweet and wicked. Indian pudding is a traditional recipe, a light, spicy dessert made with cornmeal and molasses. Pumpkin pie, another favorite, was also learned from the Native Americans. A more recent New England specialty is Ben & Jerry's ice cream (see page 234).

A blue lobster, a rare sight

> ❏ The clambake is a New England tradition, an outdoor event for at least 30 or 40 people. Traditionally, a deep hole is dug in wet sand, and clams, lobsters, potatoes, corn, sausages, and chicken are steamed in it over hot rocks and covered with seaweed (or, nowadays, canvas). ❏

SEAFOOD Imagine a lobster 5 feet long, as they were reported to be back in colonial times, and you can understand why the Pilgrim Fathers, setting eyes on *Homarus americanus* for the first time, thought it had been sent by the Devil. Seeing the Native Americans catching the beasts, however, and feeling pangs of hunger as they waited for their first crops to take root, the early colonists soon recognized the lobster as an important food source. Before long, it was regarded as poor-man's fodder, a far cry from the gourmet food of today. Lobster appears on menus throughout New England, but the best place to try it is from the boiling cauldrons of one of the many lobster "pounds" or "shacks" along the coast roads of Maine. A mainstay of the New Englander's diet

Corn should be eaten as fresh as fresh can be: peel back the end of each cob to check it is succulent

is chowder, notably clam, fish, or corn. Menus rarely exclude one of these delicious, thick creamy soups. Other seafoods which may not be familiar to outsiders include scrod (a flaky, tender white fish) and the strangely named large clam, the quahog (pronounced "ko-hog"), native to southeast New England.

FRUITS IN SEASON The corn season (from mid-July to early September) is short, but to be relished. Ideally, you should eat the corn within three hours of its being picked—a sweet, moist, tender treat. A favorite is the yellow and white variety called "butter and sugar." In September, just before the first frost, the orange pumpkins are harvested. Stacked against a traditional red barn, they make a sight as colorful as the autumn foliage itself.

Fall also sees the start of the Pick Your Own apple season, while farm stands sell apple cider as well as ready-picked apples. Try Paula Reds, one of the earliest, and McIntosh, Cortland, Empire, or Northern Spy.

Blueberries are a specialty of Maine, and turn up baked into anything from muffins and pancakes at breakfast to pie at dinner. Cranberries are exported all over the world from the bogs of the southeast corner of Massachusetts.

Above: Bean suppers, often held in church halls, are a New England tradition. Visitors are always welcome

Education is a way of life in New England. With a concentration of highly regarded preparatory schools and well over 250 universities and colleges, it courses through the veins of social and cultural life. As a spin off, New England leads the field in technological and medical research.

Eliot House, typical of Harvard's elegant Georgian buildings

❑ In October 1958, MIT student Oliver Smoot was carried prostrate by his classmates across what to MIT's chagrin is called Harvard Bridge. They marked off each head-to-toe length with paint and chalk. Thus the official length of the bridge is 364.4 Smoots plus one ear. The Smootmarks are regularly repainted—watch for them. ❑

compete in intercollegiate football and other sports, it is for their high academic and social standing that these elitist Ivy League colleges are so revered.

The origin of the name Ivy League is uncertain: traditional ivy-covered buildings? From "I.V.," standing for Inter Varsity? Or perhaps because initially there were just four, in Roman figures IV, members?

❑ "You can tell a Harvard man, but you can't tell him anything." ❑

THE IVY LEAGUE Four of New England's universities, Harvard, Yale, Brown, and Dartmouth, together with four other eastern universities, Pennsylvania, Princeton, Columbia, and Cornell, make up that prestigious group known as the Ivy League. In the 1870s, the colleges used to meet for football games, and in those early years they were a major force in football. In the 1920s, however, their prowess faded somewhat and, although they still

Harvard, the nation's oldest university, was founded in 1636 by the early colonists, primarily as a training ground for Puritan clergymen. Many of Harvard's first graduates in fact went on to set up other educational institutions. By 1647, towns with 50 householders had to provide primary schooling and those with 100 or more to provide secondary schools. Today, many of America's oldest and most highly regarded colleges and universities are in Massachusetts, notably the Massachusetts Institute of Technology (MIT), which was founded in 1861.

Yale, Harvard's traditional arch rival, is in New Haven, Connecticut. New England's second oldest university was founded in 1702 at Saybrook by Harvard graduates and renamed after its benefactor. It has a collegiate system modeled on that of Oxford and Cambridge universities in England, and its fine buildings recall their architecture (see pages 102–5).

Dartmouth College in Hanover, New Hampshire, the only Ivy League college in the northern part of New England, also has a beautiful campus. Founded in 1769 as a Native American charity school, Dartmouth by tradition waives tuition fees (so exorbitant as to eliminate most locals) for any resident of New Hampshire or Vermont of Native American ancestry. Consequently, the percentage of such undergraduates, although still tiny, is greater here than in other Ivy League universities. Brown University, in Providence, Rhode Island, was

❏ Fees at the Ivy League universities are currently in the region of $30,000 per year (tuition $23,000, room and board $7,000; at Harvard, fees are closer to $40,000). Compare this with a state, or public, university where fees for a state resident range from around $2,500 to about $4,500. ❏

founded in 1764 as a Baptist college by one of the leaders in the China trade, John Brown.

THE FIELD OF MEDICINE If Massachusetts is preeminent in education, it is also one of the world's major medical centers, and Boston has an illustrious tradition of leading the field in medical research. It was in Boston in 1846 that ether was first used as an anesthetic during an operation, the first kidney transplant was performed there in 1954, and open heart surgery was first performed at the Boston's Children's Hospital in 1967.

Below and opposite, top: Yale's Gothic Revival architecture

23

One of the rich and diverse strands that make up the fabric of New England is its cultural life. Classical music, jazz, and dance are a tradition, not just in Boston's concert halls and churches but throughout the region in universities and colleges, at festivals and, not least, on the village-green bandstand.

GREAT COMPOSERS One of America's first great modern composers was Charles Ives, who was born in Danbury, Connecticut, in 1874 and who graduated from Yale to become a successful insurance executive. In summer, outdoor concerts of classical music and jazz are held in Danbury at the Charles Ives Center for the Arts (see page 95). The third movement of Ives' *Three Places in New England*, "The Housatonic at Stockbridge," was suggested by a misty Sunday morning walk with his wife along the riverbank.

The New England scenery has been inspirational to many works, including Edward MacDowell's *New England Idyls* (1902) and William Schuman's *New England Triptych*. Another important New

Seiji Ozawa conducts the Boston Symphony Orchestra at Symphony Hall

England composer (although the number of his works is small because he destroyed his early compositions) was Karl Ruggles, a close friend of Charles Ives. Walter Piston, whose works include the orchestral suite *Three New England Sketches*, was born in Rockland, Maine, in 1894 and was an influential teacher at Harvard, one of his most distinguished pupils being Leonard Bernstein.

❏ For more on the BSO see page 79. For more on venues for jazz, classical, and light music in Boston, see page 85. ❏

THE HIGHLIGHTS For more than a century, the Boston Symphony Orchestra's concerts in Symphony Hall have been a vital element in

Boston life during the winter months (see page 79). The orchestra's founding spirit was Henry Lee Higginson, and it was also he who started, in July 1885, the "Popular Concerts," or "Pops," summertime concerts of light music that were to become a national tradition. The social elite flocked to Music Hall to sit at tables arranged between potted plants, partaking of refreshments and listening to "light music of the best class."

a summer evening's music in the open air.

One of Colonel Higginson's friends was Isabella Stewart Gardner, a patron of aspiring musicians, conductors, and composers, as well as painters, sculptors, actors, and writers. Her magnificent creation, Fenway Court, now the Isabella Stewart Gardner Museum, a fragrant oasis of beauty in Boston (see page 69), was a meeting place for musicians and the venue for wide-ranging programs of music, song, and dance. Following in this tradition, the museum today puts on approximately 130 public concerts each year.

Tanglewood, in western Massachusetts, is the Boston Symphony Orchestra's summer home, and the Tanglewood Music Festival is one of the cultural highlights of the Berkshires region, drawing hundreds of thousands of visitors annually to the open-sided Music Shed and the rolling lawns that surround it (see page 146). The popular Jacob's Pillow Dance Festival, held nearby at Becket from late June to August, offers 10 weeks of highly acclaimed dance programs.

Summer music on the lawns of Tanglewood

The jazz scene is traditionally a strong one, with the Charles Hotel in Cambridge a long-established haunt of afficionados. Also watch for festivals, both indoor and outdoor, and see page 85 for more suggestions for jazz venues in Boston and Cambridge.

Little changed in form or content, the concerts (held in May and June) remain a highlight of the year, and the Boston Pops is the most recorded orchestra in the world.

In 1929, outdoor concerts were introduced on the Esplanade along the Charles River in Boston. Every summer, thousands of young and old flock to the Hatch Shell with their blankets and picnic baskets for

Of the numerous regional festivals of music and dance, the recitals held in the opulent salons of some of Newport, Rhode Island's mansions have become a summer tradition.

And all over the region, the village bandstand provides many a delightful hour of informal entertainment.

Hollywood, past and present, has not failed to tap the rich vein of New England's diversity. In the field of drama, theater is as alive in small towns and villages as it is in the city of Boston.

MOVIES Among the galaxy of movies with New England associations is *On Golden Pond*, based on Ernest Thompson's 1978 play. Set on Great Pond, near Augusta, Maine, the movie was actually shot at Squam Lake, New Hampshire. *The Whales of August* is another delightful movie set in New England. *Mystic Pizza* (1988) was filmed in Connecticut, not in Mystic, but nearby Stonington, on a specially built pizzeria set. Steven Spielberg's *Amistad* (1997), telling the story of Africans captured by slave traders (see pages 101 and 105), was partly shot at Mystic, Providence and Massachusetts State House in Boston, and *Good Will Hunting* (1998) was set at Harvard.

Herman Melville's *Moby Dick*, with its settings on Nantucket, Henry James's *The Bostonians*, and John Updike's *The Witches of Eastwick*, set in Wickford, Rhode Island, are but three New England novels to have been made into movies.

PLAYS AND PLAYERS One of America's greatest playwrights,

Madeleine Potter and Christopher Reeve in The Bostonians

Eugene O'Neill (see page 47), set his final masterpiece, *Long Day's Journey into Night* (1957), in his boyhood summer home, Monte Cristo Cottage in New London, Connecticut. Today, the Eugene O'Neill Theater Center, in Waterford, champions new work by American playwrights.

World-class performers are regularly brought in for pre–New York shows in small-town theaters, particularly in Vermont. From 1938 to 1976, the Shubert Theater in New Haven, Connecticut, hosted the premières of many famous Broadway shows (see panel, page 103), and the Long Wharf Theater is one of the top regional theaters in the U.S. Goodspeed Opera House, a resplendent Victorian concoction on the Connecticut River bank at East Haddam, hosts musicals old and new. Festivals proliferate, offering strong local summertime theater programs. Those held in the Berkshires (see pages 143–147) make it a particularly popular area for theater-lovers.

Veterans Katherine Hepburn and Henry Fonda in On Golden Pond

26

New England Was

When the Pilgrim Fathers crossed the Atlantic in 1620 and founded the first permanent European colony in New England, they did so in the wake of many earlier explorers and merchant adventurers who had been probing a land that had been home to the Algonquin peoples since time immemorial.

John Cabot, an Italian navigator and explorer based in London

❏ In 1492, Native Americans in New England are estimated to have numbered about 100,000; by 1620, most were dead. ❏

It seems the ancestors of the Algonquin peoples of New England arrived in North America after the end of the last Ice Age, in a series of eastward migrations from Asia. By the time the first Europeans settled in the New World in the early 16th century, Native Americans had been inhabiting these northeastern woodlands for well over 10,000 years.

EUROPEAN EXPLORATION To the Native American way of thinking,

land—a source of food, like water—is not something that belongs to people; it is people who belong to the land. The "People of the Dawnland," the Abenaki, once inhabited an area that extended from the Maine coast westward to Lake Champlain, and from the St. Lawrence south to the Merrimack River and northern Massachusetts. This was a forested land laced with lakes and waterways, along which they traveled in their birchbark canoes to fish and hunt. The Abenaki would have been the first natives to meet with intruders, when, possibly about AD 1000, it is believed, Leif Eriksson arrived from Scandinavia with his dreaded Vikings. Over the following centuries, a number of further forays were made across the Atlantic, many seeking the entrance to the fabled Northwest Passage across Canada. By the 1400s, fishermen from Scandinavia, Portugal, Spain, France, and Britain were coming regularly to enjoy rich pickings in the continent's then teeming offshore waters.

The excitement aroused by Christopher Columbus's voyages to the Caribbean between 1492 and 1504 tempted more and more Europeans. In 1497, King Henry VII of England authorized John Cabot to set sail from Bristol; exactly where he landed is uncertain, but Nova Scotia seems likely. Cabot staked an English claim to North America by hoisting the flag and returned home with promising

reports, but little else. In 1524, France sent the Florentine Giovanni da Verrazano (who reported a frosty welcome from the Abenaki), then, in the 1530s and 1540s, Jacques Cartier, who explored the St. Lawrence River. In 1568, David Ingram captured the imagination of all with tales of "a magic city of Norumbega," glittering with "pillars of crystal and silver."

> ❏ The term "New England" was coined by John Smith, English founder of the Jamestown colony in Virginia, when he wrote *A Description of New England* (1616). ❏

ATTEMPTS TO SETTLE The Spanish, British, and French continued to look for potential sites for settlement and began to trade with the Native Americans for furs. By the turn of the 17th century, fisheries had been established and rival trading posts were in operation. Beaver hats were by now all the rage in Europe, and fur trading was serious business. In 1605, the area was mapped by Frenchman Samuel de Champlain, who gave his name to the large lake that is situated on Vermont's northwestern boundary.

Attempts to establish settlements in the region, however, failed, and relationships between Europeans and Native Americans became increasingly prickly. George Popham established a

colony at Sagadahoc, but it did not survive the harsh New England winter of 1607–8. A French Jesuit colony was set up on Mount Desert Island, but in 1613 it was burned down by the English.

TRADING IN DISEASE The concept of hunting animals, not for food and clothing but in order to sell their fur, was alien to Native Americans, but they were tempted by the Europeans' metal, which would improve their fishhooks, snowshoes, and canoe paddles, and welcomed their kettles and guns. However, traders also brought with them European viruses, to which the natives had no immunity, and which would in places wipe out practically the entire population. By the time the Pilgrims landed in 1620, the Native Americans were devastatingly weakened.

Pilgrims John Alden and Mary Chilton are the first ashore

29

The successful establishment of the English colony at Plymouth in 1620 encouraged a flood of settlers. They came with the hopes and ideals of 17th-century England, but their vision of a new world was not easily realized.

After a bad first winter, the Plymouth colony was soon settled and expanding, though closely dependent on contact with England and relying heavily on the advice of Native Americans for fishing, hunting, and growing crops (see pages 180–181 for more on the Pilgrims). In 1630, another group of Puritans, under the leadership of John Winthrop, founded the Massachusetts Bay Colony on a spot they named Boston, after their hometown in Lincolnshire, England. Quickly successful, it soon completely overshadowed Plymouth.

The meeting of Puritan and Native American was a meeting of two utterly different philosophies of life, yet at first, at least, they got along all right. Peace treaties made between the colonists and most of the neighboring Native Americans held firm. Gradually, however, relations began to deteriorate. Not only had the Europeans brought diseases by which, catastrophically, the native people had been crippled, they had also introduced guns and alcohol, which seriously disrupted their communities. Intertribal warfare broke out over trading, English missionaries tried to impose a foreign culture, and, as colonists needed more land, the Native Americans were increasingly confronted by that totally alien, European desire to stake a claim on territory.

WARS OF CONQUEST By the mid-17th century, the Puritans found themselves caught up in an unending round of skirmishes and shifting alliances between invader and native. In the Pequot War, the settlers, aided by the Narragansett, annihilated the Pequots around the Connecticut River. In what is called King Philip's War (1675–1676), however, the Puritans massacred the Narragansett, taking their land in Connecticut and Rhode Island. In the process,

Metacom, or "King Philip," sachem of the Wampanoags, who was finally driven to leading his people into vicious war in 1675

KING PHILIP

hundreds of settlers were killed and many towns raided. During the French and Indian War (a part of Britain's Seven Years' War with France that basically was about beaver fur), which sputtered on from the late 17th century until the final flare-up that led to French defeat in 1763, the colonists were to fight countless battles alongside British troops against the French and their Native American allies.

A STAND FOR FREEDOM

Even within their own communities, life was not all smooth sailing for the settlers. The Massachusetts Bay Puritans were not, like some of the Plymouth colonists, Separatists who had broken with the Anglican Church. These were Puritans who were themselves dissenters in that

John Winthrop: by 1670 his Boston colony had grown to 1,200

they hoped to reform the Church, yet condemned any who showed signs of deviating from the (very) straight and narrow path of strict Puritanism. Men and women such as Thomas Hooker, William Coddington, and Anne Hutchinson left to found new settlements. In 1636, a minister, Roger Williams, was banished for advocating freedom of religious thought. He went on to found Rhode Island, where church and state were always separate and religious freedom paramount.

The Puritans were equally assertive in their public administration. Even when others joined them, power remained firmly in their hands and, with England absorbed in the Civil War, they were left to their own devices. When Charles II acceded to the throne in 1660, however, he found he did not like the extent to which the colony was running its own affairs. He therefore introduced the Navigation Acts, aimed at making New England merchants trade only with Britain, and ended the Puritans' monopoly of the vote. With suffrage, the merchants (who ignored the Acts) rapidly grew both wealthy and powerful. They no longer needed, or wanted, the close contact with England; soon they would want to be their own masters.

❏ When history is told by the victor, language is easily tainted by prejudice. Thus Native Americans had warriors, Europeans soldiers; Native American victories were massacres, European victories were battles; Native Americans had chiefs, Europeans generals and kings. ❏

During the early 1700s, New England was growing fat on its growing international trade. Resentment mounted at the mother country's attempts to muscle in on this wealth, with events escalating in the 1760s to the inevitable shot famously "heard round the world."

"NO TAXATION WITHOUT REPRESENTATION" Britain emerged supreme from the French and Indian War in 1763, but it also emerged practically bankrupt. King George III decided the wealthy American colonies should pay for their own defense and also help recoup financial losses.

A series of tax-levying acts followed, but were met with protests from a core of colonists who argued that no one should have to give financial support to a government in which he had no representation.

The Sugar Act of 1764 reinforced the 1733 Molasses Act, which aimed to end trade with the West Indies (in fact, it was so lax that smuggling, bribery, and therefore the rum industry continued to prosper). The Stamp Act of 1765 taxed printed matter, but met with riots and was repealed the following year. The colonists also responded to the 1767 Townshend Acts, which taxed tea, glass, paint, paper, and lead, by boycotting British goods. In 1770, all except the tax on tea were repealed, ironically on the same day that five colonists were killed in the Boston Massacre. The colonists continued to smuggle tea in from Dutch traders.

❏ While the Sons of Liberty were hailed as heroes, the Daughters of Liberty enforced boycotts of British goods by serving herbal teas, using maple syrup instead of sugar, and wearing homespun cloth instead of imported silks. ❏

The "Boston Massacre," as portrayed by Paul Revere. The British resemble an execution squad firing on innocents at short range. Note the Custom House is labeled "Butcher's Hall"

Disguised as Mohawks to escape detection, the Sons of Liberty tip East India Company tea into the harbor

THE BOSTON TEA PARTY The Tea Act of December 1773 was seen as giving the British East India Company a monopoly on tea sales to the colonies. It so fueled resentment at the British government's power to legislate and levy taxes, that when three East India ships docked in Boston loaded with 342 chests of tea, the "Sons of Liberty," a group of patriots led by Samuel Adams, John Hancock, Joseph Warren, and Paul Revere, agreed to take decisive action. Disguised as Mohawks, they boarded the ships and threw the tea into the water. Britain retorted in 1774 with the Intolerable, or Coercive, Acts. Boston Harbor was closed.

THE OPENING SHOTS The American colonies united in response to these further threats to their liberty, and at the First Continental Congress plans were laid for the organization of an army (later to be led by George Washington). On April 19, 1775, the Revolutionary War began.

The British knew about a cache of arms in Concord (see pages 168–170) and sent troops to seize it. As they left Boston, Paul Revere (see page 55) made his famous ride to Lexington, on the road to Concord, to warn the Sons of Liberty there that the British were coming. There were minor scuffles in Lexington, but when the British reached Concord they met with organized resistance from the colonial Minutemen, and the "shot heard round the world," as described by Emerson in his *Concord Hymn*, was fired.

In May, Ethan Allen and his Green Mountain Boys captured Fort Ticonderoga on Lake Champlain from the British. In June, around Boston, the British won the Battle of Bunker Hill in Charlestown, but only with heavy losses, and when George Washington fortified Dorchester Heights (with arms captured from Fort Ticonderoga), they decided to quit.

The British left Boston in March 1776, never to return.

33

❏ The Battle of Bunker Hill actually took place on what in 1775 was known as Breeds Hill; Bunker Hill was nearby. In spite of the mix-up of names, the battle's name stuck and Breeds Hill was subsequently renamed Bunker Hill. ❏

The Battle of Bunker Hill, one of a series of paintings by John Trumbull (1756–1843) recording events in the Revolutionary War

The history of New England is inextricably bound up with the sea. Whether it be through fishing, whaling, trading, or ship-building, it is the sea that has shaped the region's economy, its society, and its traditions.

FISHING Even before the Europeans first established colonies on New England's shores, they were coming to fish the region's coastal waters, greedy for cod, haddock, and pollack. For 200 years, fishing was to be the mainstay of New England's trade with Europe. It declined during World War II, but there is still activity in harbors such as Gloucester, Provincetown, New Bedford, and Boston, and in the lobstering ports of Maine.

Marine art is a proud tradition

WHALING Today we look on whaling with revulsion, but during the mid-

19th century it was a brave, romantic enterprise—and also very prosperous. Right whales had long been caught by Native Americans and colonists in the inshore waters, but in 1712

Ship's figurehead: the wood-carver's skill on show at Mystic Seaport, Connecticut

Captain Christopher Hussey caught a sperm whale which, with its oil, spermaceti, and ambergris, proved a much more valuable species. So began the Yankee enterprise that every year sent hundreds of whaling ships across the oceans of the world, to return with the oil that would light the lamps of America and Europe until the discovery of kerosene in the mid-1800s. Other exported whale products were spermaceti for candles, bones for corset stays, and ambergris for perfume. Today, this legendary era is vividly recalled in whaling museums in New Bedford, Nantucket, and Mystic.

FOREIGN TRADE If whaling brought wealth in the 18th century, so, too, did the infamous Triangle Trade involving slaves from Africa, molasses from the West Indies, and rum from the colonies' distilleries, a trade that thrived on smuggling and bribery. After Independence in 1776, trade was opened up with China,

❏ Maine supplied the timber for the masts of 80 percent of British Admiral Nelson's fleet. ❏

A shipowners' advertisement for their "first class clipper ship"

and New England entered a golden age of commercial enterprise.

The capital of maritime New England during this "Federalist Era" was not so much Boston as Salem, Massachusetts, and the elegant houses built here by the captains, shipowners, and merchants who amassed such vast fortunes are splendid monuments to their prowess. The Peabody Museum displays the trinkets they brought home, along with their cargoes of tea and silks. Boston's Back Bay and Beacon Hill neighborhoods, Portsmouth (New Hampshire), and Newburyport (Massachusetts) also have their share of grand houses built on the China trade wealth.

SHIPBUILDING Seafaring activity supported a wide range of other businesses—ropemakers (a 1,000-ton vessel needed 12,000 feet of rope), sailmakers, caulkers, chandlers, and, of course, shipbuilders. Northern New England's plentiful forests supplied scores of shipyards, mostly along the Maine coast. The Merrimack River was also busy, and here was invented the little workboat, the dory, which fishermen would stack in nests of five or six on their seagoing boats.

Boston Wharf in the 19th century

This was the era in which insurance agents first began to make a killing. With premiums based on the dimensions and type of wood used for the different parts of the ship, the wise shipowner would follow their recommendations—hard (yellow) pine for the keel, Douglas fir for the deck planking, and so on. The Maine Maritime Museum in Bath (see page 118) is an excellent place for a study of boat-building.

The era of the clipper was brief, eclipsed by the steam-powered ship. New England's maritime trade began to decline, and rich merchants put their capital into manufacturing.

During the golden years of the China trade, it was the coastal areas of New England that generated the wealth. As maritime commerce declined and new industrial technology developed toward the end of the 18th century, the waterpower of the inland river valleys became the basis for a new wave of prosperity.

36

"Tuck" is the Algonquin word for "river with waves," and Pawtucket is "a divided river with waves"—ideal for powering mills. It was in Pawtucket, at the mouth of the Blackstone River Valley, which runs southeast from Worcester, Massachusetts, to Providence, Rhode Island, that the American Industrial Revolution was born. Craftsmen in metal, leather, and wood, as well as handloom weavers and fullers, had worked in Massachusetts since the days of the early settlers, but in 1793 the first waterpowered cotton mill in America, Slater Mill, opened in a clapboard building beside the river in Pawtucket.

Samuel Slater had worked in Richard Arkwright's revolutionary spinning mills in Britain. With financial backing from Rhode Island's prosperous shipping merchants, including one of the Brown brothers, he reproduced the machine designs he had learned there and made use of the local craftsmen's skills to harness waterpower to drive the carders, spinning machines, and looms that launched New England's textile industry and transformed daily life across the country. The mill and other

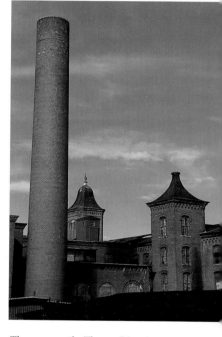

Thomson, on the Thames River in Connecticut, one of dozens of factory towns that sprang up during the 19th century to meet the growing demand for manufactured goods

❏ Some mill towns—notably Lowell—are being turned into heritage parks. Immaculately restored, they barely resemble the noisy, grimy towns of the 19th century, but they do offer an excellent insight into a turning point in the region's history. ❏

❏ The exploitation of women and the use of child and slave labor were issues of great concern to 19th-century social activists such as feminist Margaret Fuller, anti-slavery campaigner William Lloyd Garrison (see panel, page 72), and the Concord circle of thinkers and writers (see pages 46–7). ❏

buildings have been restored at the Slater Mill Historic Site in Pawtucket (see page 220).

RISE... Other merchants were quick to seize the opportunity for diversification. Alongside rivers such as the Blackstone and the Merrimack, the landscape of rolling farmland changed rapidly into a quite different scene of mills, warehouses and workers' housing, smokestacks, dams, canals, and, in time, railroads. Millbury, for instance, a town positioned to benefit from both the Blackstone River and the Blackstone canal, had no less than six wool mills in the 1830s.

The most remarkable of these mill villages was Lowell, developed by the wealthy Boston merchant Francis Cabot Lowell on the Merrimack River northwest of Boston (see page 171). Lowell had seen the appalling conditions of some factory workers in Britain and planned decent comp-any-owned housing, schools, places of worship, and recreational facilities for his workers. Women as well as men were employed, daughters of New England farmers. Letters home describe good conditions, fair treatment, and a lively social life. Lowell village became a showpiece. By 1850, it was producing 2 million yards of cloth a week and had one of the world's largest canal systems.

...AND FALL As mills grew larger and more numerous, more labor was needed. Workers were attracted off the land and immigrants flooded in from Europe. Some of the earliest were the Irish who constructed the Blackstone Canal in 1828 to transport goods from Worcester to Providence, though 20 years later this was replaced by the railroad. The mills (most of which had never operated on such caring principles as Lowell's) became overcrowded and, even in Lowell, families of Irish, Portuguese, Greeks, and others were crammed into squalid tenements. Visitors to Lowell today are moved by the conditions in which people lived and worked. Child labor was introduced and all workers were desperately exploited. Wages were cut, protests, petitions, and strikes ensued, culminating in a major strike in 1912.

Gradually, industrialists were lured by cheaper labor in the South, and by the 1920s, 50 percent of American cotton was being woven there. The Depression followed and most of New England's textile mills closed down. Industrial prosperity would only be regained with the development of the electronics industry in southern New England after World War II.

A re-creation of the long-gone days of sweat and toil at Lowell Mill

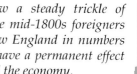

The 18th century saw a steady trickle of immigrants, but by the mid-1800s foreigners began to pour into New England in numbers significant enough to have a permanent effect on society, politics, and the economy.

BOSTON'S IRISH AND ITALIANS The Potato Famine in Ireland of 1845–1850 resulted in a flood of families seeking better prospects. Thousands went no further than Boston; there, hungry and poor, they crowded into the North End district. Initially, the Roman Catholic Irish met with prejudice from Bostonians, whose blood was basically still Puritan, and their place remained at the lower end of the social ladder. Gradually they improved their standing and proved they could hold their own in public office alongside the blue-blooded Bostonian aristocrats (with the result that the Democrats began to break the Republican hold on power).

In 1884, Hugh O'Brien became the first of many Irish mayors of Boston. In 1905 came "Honey-Fitz," as John F. Fitzgerald (grandfather of John F. Kennedy) was known, and then the colorful James Michael Curley. What Curley lacked in education he made up for in charm, and between 1920 and 1950 he was not only mayor four times, but also governor and congress-man—even though he was jailed twice, once while in office. Boston Irish politicians have become legendary, and today they make up half the city council.

Master of blarney, "Honey-Fitz," J.F.K.'s grandfather

The Irish of the North End were joined by Jews from Eastern Europe in the 1870s, who were in turn followed in the 1890s by the Italians. To this day, the area has remained an Italian quarter. In 1993 Boston elected its first Italian-American mayor, who ran unopposed for re-election in 1997.

> ❏ St. Stephen's Church in Boston's North End, Rose Kennedy's childhood church, has changed its denomination several times. In 1714, the New North Meeting House was founded on the site as a Congregationalist institution. In 1804, Charles Bulfinch designed the present building, and in 1813 it became a Unitarian church. In 1862, by which time the population of the North End was mostly Irish, the church, renamed St. Stephen's, became Roman Catholic. ❏

Hugh O'Brien, first in a long line of Boston's Irish mayors

38

A COSMOPOLITAN MIX Many Irish immigrants found employment building the railroads. In Vermont, for instance, descendants of laborers on the Rutland and Central Vermont lines today make up the Irish population in towns such as Burlington and Rutland (their railroad long since gone). Some of the Italian immigrants, from marble-producing areas of Italy, went to work in the marble quarries in Barre, Vermont, bringing skills with them in the same way as the Welshmen who went to the slate mines. The work force for southern New England's textile and shoe factories was also largely formed by European immigrants. At the turn of this century, eastern Europeans formed a significant group in Providence, Rhode Island, and Connecticut's Naugatuck Valley.

Today, the influence of immigrants on their adopted hometown often goes beyond ethnic food. Middletown, Connecticut, for instance, has had Sicilian-American mayors. Many fishing fleets were manned by Portuguese from the Azores, and those that remain—at Stonington, Connecticut, and Gloucester, Massachusetts, for example—still hold the two-day Blessing of the

❏ The Sicilians of Middletown, Connecticut, have for several generations come from just one village in southeast Sicily called Melilli. ❏

Fleet. Festivities include a parade of ships and the blessing of wreaths which are thrown into the sea.

Immigrants also came into New England from other directions. After the Civil War, French-Canadians came from Quebec, particularly to industrial cities of New Hampshire, such as Manchester, but also to Connecticut and the mill villages of Rhode Island and Massachusetts. After World War II, Jamaicans and West Indians came from the South and New York, chiefly to Boston and elsewhere in Massachusetts, Rhode Island, and Connecticut. So, too, did Hispanics, many from Puerto Rico. In Hartford, Connecticut, 20 percent of the population is Hispanic (public notices are printed in English and Spanish).

Top, opposite: the Blessing of the Fleet, Gloucester. Below: an Italian pizzeria in Boston's North End

As cities sweltered under a cloud of mid-19th-century industrial grime, New England's unsullied coast and mountains, now reached by steamship or train, began to appeal to the wealthy of the Northeast as summer homes.

Some of the hotels had their own railroads: the Profile and Franconia Notch ran from Bethlehem, NH, to the Profile House

From the 1830s, the painter Thomas Cole and other artists (see page 44) had visited the little-known White Mountains region of New Hampshire, soon to be joined by the notable writers of the day, such as Hawthorne, Emerson, and Thoreau (see pages 46–47). These early "tourists" did much to publicize areas like this and, once steamships and railroads had arrived, the stage was set for the development of New England as a playground for the wealthy new industrialists. Spas proliferated, and the rich built summer "cottages," particularly in Bar Harbor and Acadia on the Maine coast, on the islands of Martha's Vineyard and Nantucket, and, notably, in Newport, Rhode Island (see pages 216–218). It is the "grand hotel," however, that best evokes these early days of tourism.

THE FIRST RESORTS A pioneer of the summer vacation in America was Appledore House, which opened its doors in 1848 as a resort hotel on the Isles of Shoals, off Portsmouth, New Hampshire. Boston's socialites, including literary and artistic celebrities, flocked here in the new coastal steamers to spend idyllic summer months away from the stresses of urban life. Appledore's success spawned many more grand-style summer resorts on the coast and in the mountains, and by about 1880, with the benefit of a good railroad network, the tradition of summer vacationing was firmly established.

Each year, wealthy families from the eastern seaboard would arrive at the hotels on magnificent trains such as the White Mountain Express, bringing young and old, servants and governesses—and the

lifestyle enjoyed by the top echelons of urbane society.

THE GRAND HOTEL In the early 1900s, there were 19 of these "grand hotels" in the White Mountains alone. Many were self-sufficient, running their own farms, stables, and ice-cooling barns. Some had post offices (envelopes stamped by a grand hotel post office are nowadays collectors' items). Each had its resident orchestra, often made up of musicians who in the winter season played for the Boston Symphony Orchestra. Artists in residence were kept busy painting souvenirs of the landscape.

Instruction was given in dancing (the tea

❏ In the White Mountains, a daily newspaper, *Among the Clouds*, used to keep hotel guests up to date with exactly who was staying where. ❏

dance being a favorite), and various sporting facilities were offered, from croquet to boating, bathing, and fishing. The more adventurous guests would go hiking or horseback riding into the mountains; some, however, would get no further than the hotel's veranda. The veranda was an important feature of the grand hotel, built wide and long (indeed, hotels were rated by their length), with cane rocking chairs pushed well back so guests had room to promenade. Summer romances flourished, and it was important to see and be seen.

The cuisine of the grand hotel chef was legendary, and menus listed up to 70 items per meal. Guests would sit at the same table, with the same waiter, for the whole season. It was important, therefore, in order to see and be seen, not to be stuck in a corner, and for this reason the dining room in the Mount Washington Hotel was octagonal. By the 1930s, the automobile was bringing a different sort of person to the resorts, someone with less money and only a week or two to spare, looking for cheaper accommodations. It was the automobile that sounded the death knell of the grand hotel. Some were torn down, while others were gutted by fire and never rebuilt. Today, only a few remain, such as the Mount Washington in Bretton Woods and the Balsams in Dixville Notch, testaments to a gloriously romantic, sadly bygone era.

Above: wish you were here—an early postcard, of the Cannon Mountain Aerial Passenger Tramway
Left: the Mount Washington Hotel (1902) at Bretton Woods, NH, is one of the few grand hotels still operating today

41

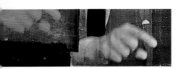

The political scene in Boston has always been active, and it is here that some of America's most influential politicians and diplomats, including five presidents, have cut their teeth.

THE ADAMS FAMILY The first member of the Adams family to come to prominence was Boston-born Samuel Adams (1722–1803). A complete failure as a businessman and tax collector, he emerged as a terrier-like political agitator, a patriot whose orchestrated propaganda stirred up anti-British feeling in the years leading to Independence.

Sam Adams's second cousin, John Adams (1735–1826), was also a patriot. A more moderate man, he helped negotiate the Treaty of Versailles, which ended the Revolution, and was appointed the first U.S. minister to Britain. On his return, he became George Washington's vice president and a leading Federalist. When Washington retired in 1796, John

Samuel Adams: an engraving of the portrait by Copley (1773)

President John Quincy Adams

Adams became the second U.S. president, with his wife, Abigail, one of the intellectual women of the day, playing a strongly supportive role. Defeated by Thomas Jefferson in 1800, John Adams spent an active retirement in Quincy, Massachusetts (see page 182).

John Adams's eldest son, John Quincy Adams (1767–1848), had accompanied his father on various diplomatic missions and, after graduating from Harvard, pursued a distinguished career as a diplomat in Europe. Returning home, he became secretary of state, and in 1824, when there was no clear majority in the presidential election, he found himself chosen in preference to Andrew Jackson. John Quincy's term of office was sullied by hostility from Jackson's supporters, and in the 1828 elections he was defeated. As a member of the House of Representatives, however, he put his energies into the anti-slavery campaign. During an impassioned speech on the subject, he had a stroke and collapsed on the floor of the House, dying two days later.

"KEEP COOL WITH COOLIDGE" The life and death of Calvin Coolidge (1872–1933), America's 30th president, was not so colorful. Born in Plymouth Notch, Vermont (see page 233), Coolidge was a quiet and cautious man of few words who worked his way up the ladder to become governor of Massachusetts. Elected Republican

The Kennedy era: Robert Rauschenburg's Retroactive (1964)

Rhode Island; see page 218), and by the time he announced his presidential candidacy in 1960 an aura of charisma surrounded the couple.

Kennedy was the youngest, and the first Roman Catholic, ever elected president. At home his main concern was social welfare, while in foreign affairs he won admiration for handling the Cuban Missile Crisis in 1962. Shortly afterward he secured the Nuclear Test Ban Treaty with Soviet leader Nikita Khrushchev and British Prime Minister Harold Macmillan. Seen by many as a symbol of hope, for America and the world, Kennedy was shot dead in Dallas on November 22, 1963.

GEORGE BUSH President from 1989 to 1993, George Bush grew up in Greenwich, Connecticut, and graduated from Yale. He served under presidents Nixon and Ford before becoming loyal vice president to Ronald Reagan. His presidency was marked by his involvement of American troops in the Gulf War. His summer home is in Kennebunkport, Maine (see page 137).

43

vice president, he became president in 1923 when Warren Harding died unexpectedly. Coolidge's two terms of office were distinguished by such government inaction that when the writer Dorothy Parker was told he had died, she is reputed to have asked "How can they tell?"

THE KENNEDY STYLE President John F. Kennedy (1917–1963) was the great-grandson of an Irish immigrant. J.F.K.'s father, Joseph P. Kennedy (1888–1969), a Harvard graduate, married Rose Fitzgerald, the daughter of mayor "Honey-Fitz" (see page 38). While Joseph made a successful career in politics and business—he was a millionaire at the age of 30—Rose bore him nine children. Four would die an early death: Kathleen, Joe, John, and Robert.

John first ran as a Democrat for Congress in 1946. In 1953, the handsome young senator married the beautiful Jacqueline Lee Bouvier (in Newport,

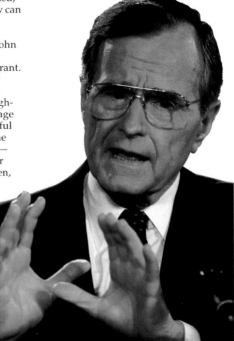

George Bush, U.S. president 1989–93

Galleries such as the Museum of Fine Arts, the Isabella Stewart Gardner Museum, the Clark Institute, and many college museums have European art, but the work of New England's own painters is also worth seeking out.

44

COLONIAL PAINTING Colonial America produced three artists of note. John Singleton Copley (1738–1815) painted portraits of Boston's elite. His *Watson and the Shark*, in Boston's Museum of Fine Arts, is a famous depiction of mankind's struggle with nature, but it is Benjamin West (1738–1820) who stands out as a historical painter during this period. Gilbert Stuart (1755–1828) was another eminent portrait painter (his George Washington appears on the dollar bill).

THE WHITE MOUNTAIN SCHOOL
Throughout the 19th century, New England artists continued to be influenced by Europe. Thomas Cole (1801–1848) was a Romantic landscape painter and a founder of the Hudson River School. He frequently traveled about the Northeast making sketches, and in 1828 visited New Hampshire's White Mountains and was instantly captivated by the scenery. Albert Bierstadt (1830–1902), another prominent member of the school, created grandiose views of the White Mountains and the Connecticut River Valley.

Top: from Boy in a Boatyard by Winslow Homer (1836–1910)

COASTAL ART COLONIES The Maine coast has been inspirational to many artists, notably Winslow Homer (1836–1910), who spent the latter part of his life at Prout's Neck. Here he painted a prodigious number of powerful seascapes. Also look for the seascapes of Fitz Hugh Lane (1804–1865). John Marin (1870–1953) was a more recent abstract landscape artist obsessive about the Maine coast. Edward Hopper (1882–1967), one of a group known as the Painters of the American Scene, also worked here, his static, silent figures set in humdrum surroundings. The area around Cushing, Maine, where Andrew Wyeth (born 1917) has his summer home, is the subject of many of his tempera and watercolor paintings. Another American Scene painter, Wyeth is best known for *Christina's World*, depicting a lonely figure in an open field.

Shipping in Down East Waters by Fitz Hugh Lane (1804–1865)

Boston Common at Twilight by Frederick Childe Hassam (1859–1935)

Appledore, an idyllic summer artists' colony on the Isles of Shoals, was immortalized by the leading American Impressionist, F. Childe Hassam (1859–1935). His *Boston Common at Twilight* is a favorite in Boston's Museum of Fine Arts. Childe Hassam also worked in Old Lyme, at the mouth of the Connecticut River, where Florence Griswold opened her house (now a museum) to an influential colony which became known as the Old Lyme Impressionists.

AMERICANS ABROAD No study of the art of 19th-century New England is complete without mention of two notable American artists whose work and influence straddled the Atlantic. These are James McNeill Whistler (1834–1903), who was born in Lowell, Massachusetts, and is perhaps best known for his paintings of London, and John Singer Sargent (1856–1925), born in Florence, Italy,

who painted portraits of Boston's prominent men and women.

THE 20TH CENTURY The two New England artists who have won the most widespread popularity in recent times must be the illustrator Norman Rockwell (see page 150) and Anna "Grandma" Moses (1860–1961), a primitive painter who created brightly colored scenes of everyday New England life (see page 226).

SCULPTORS One of America's foremost sculptors, Augustus Saint-Gaudens (1848–1907), worked, after training in Europe, in Cornish, New Hampshire (see page 195). His work includes the 1897 Shaw monument on Boston Common.

Chesterwood in Stockbridge, Massachusetts (see page 147), was the home of another notable sculptor, Daniel Chester French (1850–1931). Best known for his seated *Abraham Lincoln* in Washington, DC, French first won acclaim with his *Minute Man* statue in Concord, Massachusetts.

Writers in colonial times concentrated on religious tracts and journals, but after the Revolution, American literature quickly established a new identity, and ever since New England has nurtured writers of prominence.

❏ "As the New England summer flamed into autumn, I piled cut spruce boughs all round the draughty cottage sill, and helped to put up a tiny roofless verandah along one side of it for future needs."
– From *Something of Myself* by Rudyard Kipling (1865–1936). ❏

THE CONCORD CIRCLE Early in the 19th century, there emerged a group of thinkers and writers, centered on Concord, Massachusetts (see pages 169–170), spiritual idealists known as the New England Transcendentalists. The leading figures were essayist and poet Ralph Waldo Emerson (1803–1882) and Henry David Thoreau (1817–1862), whose classic, *Walden* (1854), is a record of two solitary, transcendentalist years spent communing with nature in a log cabin in the woods around Walden Pond. Novelist Nathaniel Hawthorne (1804–1864) also lived in Concord for a time, in the same house in which Louisa May Alcott

(1832–1888) spent some of her teenage years, a period she was to draw on in *Little Women*.

THE BERKSHIRES Nathaniel Hawthorne also lived in Lenox, western Massachusetts, where he wrote *The Scarlet Letter* (1850) and *The House of the Seven Gables* (1851), inspired by the house of that name in his birthplace, Salem. In Lenox he became good friends with Herman Melville, who was living in nearby Arrowhead completing the whaling adventure story *Moby Dick* (1851) before fading into melancholia and virtual oblivion—it was not until the 1920s that his talent was recognized. In 1902, Edith Wharton, society hostess turned novelist, built The Mount, in Lenox, where she wrote her stories of trenchant social observation (such as *Ethan Frome* and *The Age of Innocence*) in between entertaining her high-flying circle of friends, including the author Henry James.

❏ "There are three kinds of lies: lies, damned lies, and statistics."
– Mark Twain, *Autobiography* (1871). ❏

THE HARTFORD COLONY In the Nook Farm area of Hartford, Connecticut (see page 96), Samuel Clemens, alias Mark Twain, and his wife built the exuberantly Victorian house where he wrote *The Adventures of Tom Sawyer* (1876) and his masterpiece of wit and insight, *The Adventures of Huckleberry Finn* (1884). His neighbor was Harriet Beecher Stowe, a minister's wife whose *Uncle Tom's Cabin* of

Top: Tom Sawyer's band of robbers
Left: Mrs. Keeley as Topsy, Uncle Tom's Cabin

46

1852 was a widely read novel that stirred popular antislavery feeling to the extent that it is counted by some as one of the causes of the American Civil War.

❑ Kipling and his American wife, Caroline, lived for a few years in Brattleboro, Vermont, and here he wrote some of his best-known works, including the Jungle Books. Their house, Naulakha, has been restored and is available for rent (tel. 802/254 6868 for a brochure in the U.S.). ❑

POETRY AND DRAMA Henry Wadsworth Longfellow, born in 1807 in Portland, Maine, wrote many of his narrative poems, including *The Song of Hiawatha* (1855), while teaching at Harvard. Longfellow was part of an aristocratic group of New England writers closely linked with Harvard. Others were the poets Oliver Wendell Holmes and James Russell

Longfellow, one of a circle of writers associated with Harvard

Lowell. The sensitive recluse Emily Dickinson (1830–1886) is also linked with Massachusetts (see page 176), while the poems of Robert Frost (1874–1963) are so steeped in the New England countryside he is often referred to as "The Voice of New England" (see page 209).

The only American playwright to receive the Nobel Prize for Literature, Eugene O'Neill died in Boston in 1953. From a modest start with a one-act play performed in a wharfside playhouse in the Cape Cod fishing village of Provincetown, O'Neill's troubled career—much of his material was drawn from the torments of his family life—was to bring him to a position of pre-eminence among 20th-century dramatists. He is commemorated at his boyhood summer home, Monte Cristo Cottage, in New London, Connecticut.

Louisa May Alcott

47

MSGR O'BRIEN HIGHWAY

93 RUTHERFORD AVENUE

MAIN

CITY SQUARE

CHARLESTOWN

CAMBRIDGE STREET

OTIS STREET

THORNDIKE STREET

SPRING STREET

HURLEY STREET

CHARLES STREET

6TH STREET

5TH STREET

Lechmere

CambridgeSide Galleria

CHARLES RIVER DAM

Charles River

Museum of Science

Mugar Omni Theatre

Science Park

Hayden Planetarium

Science Park

NASHUA STREET

JOHN

North Static FleetCenter (Sports Museum of New England)

ROGERS STREET

BINNEY STREET

2ND STREET

1ST STREET

CAMBRIDGE

COMMERCIAL AVENUE

CAMBRIDGE PARKWAY

MUNROE ST

3RD STREET

MARTHA ROAD

WEST END

Thomas P O'Neill Federal Building

MERRIMA

CAUSEWA

State Service Center

Bowdoi

Charlesbank Park

Massachusetts General Hospital

CHARLES STREET

Old West Church

Harrison Gray Otis House

Salto stall State Buildi

MAIN STREET

LONGFELLOW BRIDGE

Basin

Charles River

Charles/MGH

Coburn's Gaming House

CAMBRIDGE

Smith Court Residences

Abiel Smith School

Colum

Massachusetts Institute of Technology

MEMORIAL DRIVE

Lewis Hayden House

PHILLIPS ST

African Meeting House

State House

Boston Athenaeum

BEACON HILL

REVERE ST

John J Smith Ho

PINCKNEY ST

DERNE ST

JOY ST

BOWDOIN

Phillips School

Park Church

EMBANKMENT ROAD

Hatch Memorial Shell

Charles Street Meeting House

CHESTNUT

LOUISBURG SQ

ACORN ST

CHARLES ST

MT VERNON ST

George Middleton House

Nichols House Museum

BEACON STREET

Shaw Memorial

PARK ST

Park Street

James J Storrow Memorial Embankment

Cheers Pub

Frog Pond

Downtown Crossing

STORROW

MEMORIAL DRIVE

BACK STREET

Gibson House

Public Garden

Boston Common

i

WASHINGTON ST

JAMES J

BEACON STREET

MEMORIAL STREET

BERKELEY STREET

ARLINGTON STREET

Arlington St Church

Arlington

Boylston Colonial Theater

TREMONT ST

Chinatown

THEATRE DISTRICT

ESS

FAIRFIELD ST

MARLBOROUGH STREET

BACK BAY

AVENUE STREET

NEWBURY STREET

COMMONWEALTH

EXETER ST

DARTMOUTH STREET

BOYLSTON STREET

Transportation Building

PARK SQ

STUART ST

Shubert Theater

Wilbur Theater

NE Medical Center

Fenway Park

GLOUCESTER STREET

CLARENDON STREET

New Old South Church

COPLEY SQUARE

Trinity Church

JAMES AVE

ST

Boston Architectural Center

BOYLSTON ST

Boston Public Library

Copley

John Hancock Observatory

STUART ST

Chinese Cultural Institute

OAK

TYLER

Hynes Convention Center

MASSACHUSETTS

Prudential Center Skywalk

TURNPIKE

90

AVENUE

MARGINAL ROAD

HUDSON

Institute of Contemporary Art

AVENUE

Copley Place

Back Bay/ South End

COLUMBUS AVENUE

HERALD STREET

Prudential

HUNTINGTON AVENUE

W NEWTON ST

APPLETON STREET

TREMONT STREET

BERKELEY STREET

WASHINGTON STREET

Christian Science Complex & Mapparium

WARREN AVENUE

SHAWMUT AVENUE

JOHN

Symphony Hall

Symphony

Museum of Fine Arts & Isabella Stewart Gardner Museum

Boston Beer Company

Center for the Performing Arts

JFK Library & Commonwealth Museum

A B C

5 4 3 2 1

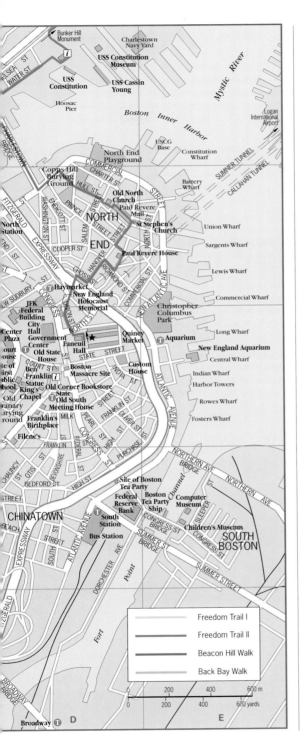

A-Z Boston

▶▶▶ CITY HIGHLIGHTS

BOSTON A TO Z CONTENTS

Boston seen from the Charles River: between Boston Common, the brownstone terraces of Back Bay and the office buildings of the financial district rises the gilded dome of the Massachusetts State House

BOSTON The cradle of American history is a city of church spires, parks, statues, and a remarkably thriving culture. To this, within the last 30 years, has been added a high-rise skyline. To most first-time visitors, the city's elements are partly familiar, partly refreshingly different. Boston also divides into strikingly contrasting neighborhoods, from the trendy elegance of the Back Bay and the old-world charm of the North End to the striking modern skyline of the financial district and adjacent Waterfront.

Boston looks pleased with life nowadays, with its elegant shops, gleaming office towers, refurbished wharves and historic buildings, and lively eateries and bars. Although it is by far New England's largest city—with a population of around 575,000—"the Hub" (referring to its position in the universe) often presents a pleasant surprise to visitors, who find it livable and manageable.

FINDING YOUR FEET Most Bostonians would tend to think of **Boston Common**▶ and the neighboring **Public Garden**▶▶ as the true heart of the city. The Common is the oldest public park in the U.S.A. and is overlooked by the State House with its dazzling gold dome. A visitor information booth nearby marks the start of the **Freedom Trail**▶▶▶ (see pages 58–61). To the east lies the main downtown district, with government buildings arranged around the huge plaza of **Government Center**. Here, too, is the renovated and ever-popular **Faneuil Hall Marketplace**▶▶▶ (pronounced Fan'el), which comprises historic Faneuil Hall, Quincy Market, and the adjacent North and South markets. Street performers entertain the shoppers and visitors, portrait artists sketch them, and food stalls feed them: the atmosphere is conducive to lingering. The historic **North End**▶▶, the Italian quarter north of here, hosts lively street festivals on weekends in July and August, has excellent bakeries and restaurants, and has sites on the Freedom Trail.

Post Office Square is at the heart of the high-rise downtown Financial District. Nearby rises Boston's first

The State House, designed by Charles Bulfinch. The dome was originally covered in copper, the work of Paul Revere

"skyscraper," the Custom House, a slender Gothic-style clocktower that graces the downtown skyline. The **Waterfront** is no longer commercial, condominiums and offices having sprouted on the old wharves. It has some fine restaurants and the **New England Aquarium**▶▶▶. Work is well under way on a project that will put the highway that crosses the Waterfront into a tunnel and transform the area into a 73-acre park. A waterside walk from the Aquarium, past Rowes Wharf and the Boston Harbor Hotel, makes the most of the Waterfront views. South of the Financial District is **Chinatown**▶, a colorful neighborhood with stores selling all manner of items and restaurants serving excellent food at bargain prices.

North and west of Boston Common are, respectively, the fashionable and delightful residential neighborhoods of **Beacon Hill**▶▶ and the **Back Bay**▶▶. South of **Copley Square**▶▶ is the main hotel district, a convenient area in which to stay; eastward lies the Theater District. The **South End** is a trendy up-and-coming area of bow-fronted Victorian townhouses, where Union Park is one of the most attractive streets. The district is full of excellent eateries, and is ethnically and socially mixed.

Southwest of the Back Bay is the Fenway, which occupies the area around Back Bay Fens, a lakeside park. It has the pick of the city's art museums—the huge **Museum of Fine Arts**▶▶▶ and the intensely personal **Isabella Stewart Gardner Museum**▶▶▶. Fenway Park, the home of the Boston Red Sox, is one of the smallest and oldest baseball parks in the major leagues.

Cambridge▶▶, on the north side of the Charles River, is actually a separate city, although it is close enough to walk to from the Back Bay over the Harvard Bridge. Harvard University (the oldest university in the U.S.A.) and the street activity and nightlife in and around Harvard Square are among Cambridge's prime attractions. Cambridge is also home to Massachusetts Institute of Technology (MIT) and boasts some of the finest restaurants in the Boston area.

Close-up on the bow-fronted houses of the South End

Boston: Getting around

The map (Boston subway / T system) shows the following stations and lines:

Oak Grove · Wonderland · Malden Center · Revere Beach · Wellington · Beachmont · Sullivan Square · Suffolk Downs · Alewife · Davis · Lechmere · Community College · Orient Heights · Harvard Avenue · Packards Corner · Pleasant Street · Porter · Science Park · North Station · Wood Island · Boston College · Fordham Road · Babcock Street · Harvard · Bowdoin · Haymarket · Airport · St Paul Street · Central · Government Center · Maverick · Boston Univ. West · Kendall · Aquarium · Boston Univ. Central · Charles/Massachusetts General Hospital · State · Boston Univ. East · Blandford St · Kent Street · St Mary's Street · Kenmore · Park St · Boylston · Cleveland Circle · Hawes Street · Arlington · Downtown Crossing · Hynes Convention Center / ICA · Copley · Fenway · Prudential · Chinatown · Longwood Avenue · Symphony · South Station · Northeastern · Riverside · Brookline Village · Mus. of Fine Arts · Longwood Medical Area · New England Medical Center · Broadway · Brigham Circle · Andrew · Fenwood Road · Back Bay/South End · JFK/Univ. of Massachusetts at Boston (For free bus to University & JFK Library) · Mission Park · Riverway · Savin Hill · North Quincy · Back-of-the-Hill · Massachusetts Avenue · Arborway · Evergreen Street · Heath St/Medical Center · Fields Corner · Wollaston · Bynner Street · Veterans Administration Medical Center · Ruggles · Quincy Center · Shawmut · Quincy Adams · Roxbury Crossing · Ashmont & Mattapan · Braintree · Forest Hills

Charles River · Boston Harbor · Dorchester Bay

©TCS V3MC/COL — Map authorised user number 9C/02/117/EXP/UDN.2

BOSTON QUIRKS

● Boston is a true peninsula; Boston Neck, which connects it to the mainland, was originally just 120 feet across. Since early times, much of the harbor has been filled in. Some 58 percent of the city is built on landfill.

● The city's first squares were modeled on those laid out in 18th-century London.

Getting around

Walking Everyone will tell you that Boston is a walking city. Distances downtown are small, and there is so much to see. New visitors will often find that they have walked nonstop for days on end before noticing their tired feet.

During the day, it is quite safe to wander around the central streets, although crossing them is another matter. Here, in what some people call the jay-walking capital of America, the tendency is to dodge the notoriously slow traffic lights and risk the traffic.

Compared to many other cities, Boston is safe for visitors, but some areas, such as the Common and the back streets of Chinatown, should be avoided at night.

Driving Don't drive in Boston unless you absolutely must. The city is notorious for having some of the country's worst drivers. You'll need good nerves to cope with the traffic, to navigate through the city's confusing maze of streets, to understand the traffic patterns where no lines are painted on the road surface, and to try to find one of those elusive parking spaces. The construction of three road tunnels may help to alleviate the traffic problem after 2006, but the building work in the mean time has exacerbated the problem. If you are planning a self-drive trip around New England, consider seriously picking the car up from somewhere out of the city that is easily reached by train or subway.

Public transportation Fortunately, public transportation in Boston is excellent, running from around 5AM to 12:30 AM. The subway train network, known as the "T," spreads across the city. The various lines are displayed on maps—and known to locals—by color. You need to buy tokens to ride the subway. Currently the cost is 85¢ for each ride on the "T" (a little more for some rides from the outer suburbs) irrespective of how many times you change lines.

The T's Visitor Passport gives unlimited travel on the T (plus discounts for certain attractions) for one, three or seven days. However this is unlikely to save you money on fares if you are only making a few rides each day; a better bet is to buy a stack of tokens first time round, thus saving time lining up at stations. Buses are slightly cheaper, but require a little more local knowledge.

From central Boston, visits to Cambridge, the Museum of Fine Arts, the Isabella Stewart Gardner Museum, and Logan Airport are best made by the "T." The color-coded lines are reasonably straightforward, even to a newcomer: remember to look for the color and destination of the train.

Guided and self-guided tours Several companies run fleets of trolleys, with guided commentary, around the hotel area and the historic parts of the city, taking in most sights on the Freedom Trail, including the remotely located Bunker Hill Monument. All the routes cover much the same ground. You can begin at any trolley stop you like. Tickets last a day, and you can get on and off where you like, then wait a few minutes for the next trolley. Additionally, Old Town Trolley Tours take in Cambridge. The same company runs a narrated J.F.K.'s Boston tour.

Boston By Foot runs guided tours from May to October; for recorded information, tel: 617/367 2345.

Boat cruises From spring until fall, Boston Harbor Cruises (tel: 617/227 4321) operate whale-watching, harbor and themed Mystery and Summertime Blues cruises from Long Wharf by the New England Aquarium. The short cruise to the Charlestown Navy Yard is the most direct and pleasant way to approach it. The longer tour into Boston Harbor passes the airport and gains views of the 17th- and 18th-century fortifications on Castle Island and there is an impressive panorama of the skyscrapers. Boston By Boat is a shuttle that takes visitors to the Children's Museum, Computer Museum, Science Museum, USS *Constitution* and Aquarium in a continuous loop. The 80-minute Boston Duck Tours, from the Prudential Center (April–November), use brightly painted World War II amphibious vehicles. In addition to making a conventional ground tour of the city, they splash into the Charles for a river trip. Tel: 617/723-DUCK.

Airport transfers See page 248.

MORE TOURS
● Trolley tours round Boston include the Chocolate and Seafood trolleys—each with appropriate samples on the way.
● Guided walks are offered by Chinatown Tours, tel: 617/764 5656.
● Take the Orange Line to Stony Brook for the Boston Beer brewery and museum, home of Samuel Adams Boston ales; tours (July and August) are on Thursdays and Fridays at 2, Saturdays at 12, 1, and 2, and Wednesdays at 2.
● For baseball fans there are tours of Fenway Park, home to the Boston Red Sox (tel: 617/236 6666).
● The Federal Reserve Bank (tel: 617/973 3451), where old banknotes are destroyed, has free tours; visitors are given a bag of shredded money.

53

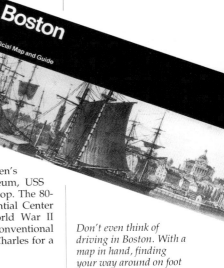

Don't even think of driving in Boston. With a map in hand, finding your way around on foot is easy

Events

For further information, contact the Greater Boston Convention and Visitors Bureau (see page 266).

January
Martin Luther King Day (January 18).
Chinese New Year (January/February), Chinatown: firecrackers, traditional music.

February
Black History Month, centered at Black Meeting House in Beacon Hill: plays, discussion, tours.
Boston Cooks, World Trade Center and Hynes Convention Center: New England's premier culinary event, with dining, wine tasting, and entertainment.

March
Seafood Show, Bayside Exposition Center.
Spring Flower Show, Bayside Exposition Center: the third largest in the world.
St. Patrick's Day Parade (mid-March): parade honoring Ireland's saint.

April
Boston Marathon (Patriot's Day), from Hopkinton to Boston: the oldest marathon in America.
Patriot's Day Parade, City Hall to Paul Revere Mall.
Swan Boats, Public Garden: season begins with ceremony and first ride.

Late April/Early May
Ducklings' Day Parade, Beacon Hill, Public Garden: make way for the mallard family and costumed relatives.

May
MayFair Book festival, Harvard Square.
Art Newbury Street: art, special exhibits, jazz, and classical music.

June
Bunker Hill Day and Parade.
Dairy Festival (first week): cows make an appearance on the Common (a colonial law mandates this); ice cream, butter-making, milking.
Cambridge International Fair, University Park, Cambridge.
Boston Globe Jazz Festival, various locations.
Harborlights Music Festival, Waterfront (June to September).

July
Boston Pops: free outdoor concerts at the Hatch Shell on the Esplanade.
Chowderfest, City Hall Plaza: sample a range of chowders produced by Boston restaurants and vote for the best.
Harborfest (week leading up to July 4): celebration of Revolutionary War events in Boston Harbor, culminating in Revolutionary Era reenactments, military parades, fireworks, concerts.

August
Boston Seaport Festival, Charlestown Navy Yard.
Caribbean Carnival, Franklin Park.
August Moon Festival, Chinatown.

September
Art Newbury Street (see May).
Boston Arts and Music Festival.
Cambridge River Festival.

October
Columbus Day Parade.
Oktoberfest, Harvard Square, Cambridge.
Head of the Charles Regatta: major rowing event (the world's largest).
Mixfest: Free pop concert in City Hall Plaza.

November
Holiday Happenings (November 19–December 24): holiday festivities, including Winter Wonderland and Sleigh Bell Parade.

December
Newbury Street Stroll.
Boston Tea Party Reenactment, Tea Party Ship.
First Night Celebration: city-wide family celebration to ring in the New Year.
Newbury Street Stroll.
Tree-lighting Ceremonies at Prudential Center and elsewhere.

Part of the July 4 celebrations in downtown Boston

"Listen, my children, and you shall hear/Of the midnight ride of Paul Revere..." So begins Longfellow's **Paul Revere's Ride,** *a ballad that was to turn a silversmith into America's favorite folk hero.*

Until Longfellow's ballad was published in 1863, Paul Revere (1735–1818) was best known as a silversmith, though he dabbled in many things (see sidebar). An ardent patriot and an experienced express rider, he frequently carried messages for the Sons of Liberty (see page 33). On April 16, 1775, Revere rode out to Lexington to warn patriot leaders Sam Adams and John Hancock that British troops in Boston were making plans to march to Concord to seize a cache of rebel arms, and to capture Adams and Hancock in Lexington on the way. A plan was made for another message to be relayed as soon as the soldiers actually left town.

In case he was unable to escape from Boston himself, Revere asked the sexton of Old North Church, Robert Newman, to signal to Charlestown, across the Charles River, by holding up one lantern in the church steeple if the troops left by land (across Boston Neck), two if by boat (across the river). On the night of April 18, the signal was duly given, and Revere got out of Boston and headed for Lexington. He was joined there by William Dawes, and as they rode on they met Sam Prescott. All three were captured by the redcoats. Only Prescott escaped and reached Concord.

The legend Most newspaper reports of the night's events did not even mention Paul Revere by name. The New York Gazette reported him dead. A century later, however, thanks to Longfellow, Revere stepped into the annals of history. But Longfellow was a poet, not a historian, and so he could play around with the facts. He has Revere waiting for the signal in Charlestown; he has him making the heroic ride alone; and he certainly does not reveal that Revere never actually reached Concord, only Prescott. But then, "Prescott" does not rhyme as easily as "Revere."

Left: Revere in middle age. Top: Revere as messenger

THE MAN
Paul Revere was born in Boston on December 21, 1735. A silversmith like his Huguenot father, he became one of the country's finest artists in silver, gold, and copper. A remarkable man of boundless energy and talent, he also turned his hand to engraving and printing, often for propaganda purposes (see below). He made spectacles, surgical instruments, and false teeth. After the American Revolution, Revere manufactured sheet copper, some being used on "Old Ironsides" (the USS *Constitution*) and on the State House dome. Revere died in 1818, age 83, and is buried in the Old Granary burial ground.

THE PATRIOT
In March 1770, a street brawl got out of hand when some youths started throwing snowballs at British troops. The soldiers panicked, opened fire, and five men were killed. Paul Revere plagiarized an engraving of the incident by Henry Pelham (to Pelham's annoyance), fueling resentment against the redcoats or "lobsterbacks," as the British troops were derisively called. The term "Boston Massacre" was coined by Sam Adams.

Bronze bell cast by Revere, a distinguished bell-maker

55

Boston could be forgiven for quietly basking in its venerable past and resting on its glorious cultural laurels. But life here is as much about computers as culture, and, in this capital of academia, the pace is intellectually challenging. Boston has its share of blue blood, but it is above all a dynamic, youthful city.

BRAHMINS AND BOSTON
The physical development of Boston is closely linked to the Brahmins. In 1795, the society portrait painter John Singleton Copley sold land on Beacon Hill to a group of entrepreneurs. On it Bulfinch built the prestigious Beacon Hill estate into which Boston's blue-blooded elite moved, leaving their homes in the old North End *en bloc*. Beacon Hill was one of three major hills to be leveled off, the soil being used to fill in the swampy "Back Bay" area along the Charles River. By about 1870, the Back Bay had been developed and many of the Brahmins then moved into its more grandiose houses.

The Christian Science Center, Prudential Center (left), and John Hancock Tower

High-rise and high-tech For many years the Custom Tower House was the only building in Boston higher than the State House dome. How different was the skyline then. In recent times, glassy skyscrapers and concrete office towers have risen rapidly one after the other to dwarf the elegant Victorian brownstone terraces of the Back Bay. The classic architectural image of Boston is the reflection of Henry Hobson Richardson's 1870s Romanesque-style Trinity Church in the glass windows of I.M. Pei's 1970s ultramodern John Hancock Tower. And since I.M. Pei and his associates completed their commission to change the face of the blighted and downward-spiraling Boston of the 1950s and 1960s, a further proliferation of thrusting office buildings has been occupied by financial and other leading institutions, and computer companies.

Boston today—together with Cambridge, across the river—is a high-tech place. Go to Harvard Square on a Friday or Saturday evening, and for every browser in the bookstores there are at least twice as many parents in the computerware shops showing their kids the latest educational software. It is not insignificant that Boston's Computer Museum (see page 68) is among the best of its kind in the world. Don't miss it—it's sensational.

In recent years, Boston and Cambridge may have become "the Hub" (as Boston is known) of the computer industry, but this does not mean that their role as leaders in medicine has in any way diminished. The place is a hotbed of research—not for nothing has the Ether Dome, the Massachusetts General Hospital's operating theater, where ether was first used as an anesthetic, been completely submerged by modern buildings (it is open to visitors, if they can find their way through to it). As for education, it sometimes feels as if virtually everyone in town is somehow connected to the 67 colleges and universities on either side of the Charles River. The start of the academic year brings chaos; the streets seem to be full of walking mattresses, as 500,000 students move into their new living quarters. It is a city full of bright and lively people.

56

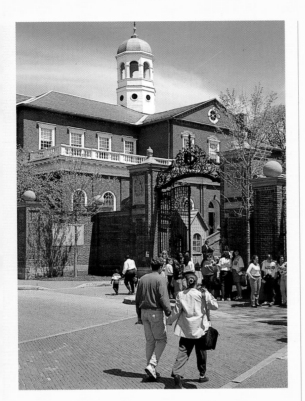

The proliferation of academic institutions on either side of the Charles River means a huge student population: left, Harvard Hall, Harvard Yard, Cambridge

THE NEW ENGLAND HOLOCAUST MEMORIAL
Six glass and steel towers, 54ft and 4ft square, stand one behind the other in the gardens alongside Union Street, right beside the Freedom Trail and in an area of the city steeped in the history of human rights. The glass panels are etched with rows of numbers, a stark reminder of the six million Jews murdered by Nazis between 1933 and 1945. The paving stones are inscribed with quotations from Holocaust survivors, and inside each tower steam rises through a grating placed over what appears to be a pit of glowing embers. The memorial is the work of architect Stanley Saitowitz.

Boston Brahmins In the midst of all this ferment, a small but deeply significant element of Boston society calmly carries on with life just the way it has always done. These are the members of Boston's top families, the "Proper Bostonians," the "Boston Brahmins," as the city's Establishment was termed by Oliver Wendell Holmes in the 19th century. They trace their ancestry back to the 18th-century merchants and many claim to be related to early Puritan settlers (not, as is popularly misconceived, to the *Mayflower* Pilgrims, who landed not in Boston but in Plymouth and were definitely not so upper crust).

Certainly all are characterized by Puritan qualities of frugality and self-restraint, and a sense of superiority. Breeding, rather than money, has always been paramount. Indeed, the intermarrying of Boston's top families is surely matched only by that of European royals. A Brahmin is born with a name such as Adams, Cabot, Lowell, Bowditch, Appleton, or Lodge, he is educated at Harvard (where else is there, after all?), he lives in the Back Bay, and has a summer home in Maine.

In the 18th and 19th centuries, it was the Brahmins who held all the power, and to a degree their blue blood continues to course through the city's veins today. Many of the financiers and businessmen in those downtown office towers are Brahmins; but perhaps it is families like the Kennedys (of Irish ancestry) and the intellectual elite who are the new generation of Brahmins?

BAR HARBOR BRAHMINS
Bar Harbor, in Maine, is where the proper Bostonian traditionally has a summer cottage. There is one page in the Bar Harbor telephone book on which every name, with just one or two exceptions, is that of a Boston Brahmin family.

Walk

The Freedom Trail: Part I

See map on pages 48–49 (yellow route).

Follow the red or brick line along the city sidewalks for colonial America's most historic walk. The route is the focus of Boston National Historical Park and passes many buildings associated with the Revolutionary War. Freedom Trail Players, in historic costume, patrol the trail to answer queries. Excellent free guided walks start every half hour (in summer months) from the park visitor center at 15 State Street opposite State subway station (and the Old State House).

Boston Common▶, at the start of the walk, is a 44-acre, undulating grass expanse, formerly used as a pasture and parade ground. Follow the Freedom Trail across the Common up to the imposing State House with its gilded dome. Continue down Park Street to

King's Chapel graveyard, where John Winthrop lies

Park Street Church (1809), where William Lloyd Garrison made his first antislavery address in 1829 and where the song *America* was first sung in 1831. Adjacent is the **Old Granary Burying Ground**, containing graves from Revolutionary days, including those of John Hancock, Samuel Adams, Paul Revere, and the five who perished in the Boston Massacre.

At the corner of Tremont and School streets, look inside **King's Chapel▶** (1754), the first Anglican church in Boston, and later the first Unitarian Church. It has especially well preserved furnishings, including white box pews and a pulpit with sounding board. A finely carved gravestone in the churchyard is that of Joseph Tapping (1678), depicting Father Time extinguishing the candle of Life.

The **Old Corner Book Store** (1712; now called the Boston Globe Store), at the corner of School and Washington streets, was a literary meeting house where the works of Longfellow, Stowe, Hawthorne, and Emerson were first published. Opposite is the **Old South Meeting House▶** (1729), a former Puritan house of worship, and at one time the largest public meeting hall in the city. Here heated meetings took place as the British sought to impose their taxes on the colony. On December 16, 1773, Samuel Adams addressed some 7,000 citizens just before the Boston Tea Party (see page 33) and pronounced the immortal words "Gentlemen, this meeting can do nothing more to save the country." Threatened with demolition in the 1870s, the building was the first in Boston to be preserved solely for its historic importance. Today, the building contains an exhibition focusing on the events leading to the Tea Party.

Farther north along Washington Street, the **Old State House▶** (1713) has changed much over the years but externally is now restored to its original appearance, with the (renewed) British lion and unicorn flanking the gable above the balcony from where the Declaration of Independence was read to the public on July 18, 1776. Today, the interior is a museum devoted to

One-time meeting place for writers and thinkers

THE GLOBE CORNER BOOKSTORE
Books & Maps for the Traveller

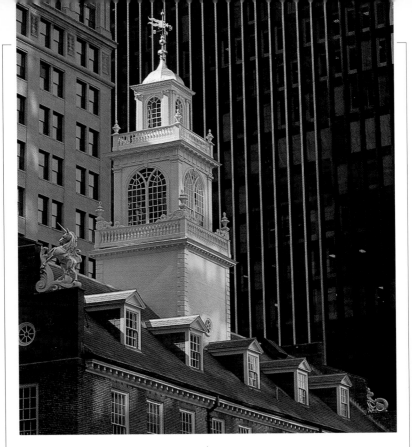

New, high-rise Boston dwarfs the Old State House; below: Faneuil Hall Marketplace

historical exhibitions about Boston, showing events preceding and following the Boston Massacre.

A neat circle of stones embedded in a pedestrian island beside the Old State House marks the site of the Boston Massacre (see page 32).

(see page 32)

Nearby **Faneuil Hall▶▶** was donated to Boston in 1742 by Peter Faneuil, the "bachelor of Boston," who died a few months after the building's completion of "an excess of good living." The building contains the meeting hall known as the "Cradle of Liberty" (*admission* free) where, over the years, revolutionary protests, women's suffrage, slavery, and every war except the 1990 Gulf War (the building was closed for renovation) have been discussed. The top floor contains regimental memorabilia of the Ancient and Honorable Artillery Company (free tours given by National Park rangers every 30 minutes from 9:30 to 4:30). Behind Faneuil Hall is **Faneuil Hall Marketplace▶▶▶**, a lively scene with shops, restaurants, and entertainers centered at Quincy Market and North and South markets.

Walk

The Freedom Trail: Part II

See map on pages 48–49 (red route).

The second part of the trail leads from Faneuil Hall Marketplace, through the old Italian quarter of North End, and past historic Charlestown Navy Yard to Bunker Hill. Some prefer to end the walk at Old North Church in the North End and take a ferry (from Long Wharf by the Aquarium), trolley, or bus to Charlestown.

From Faneuil Hall Marketplace follow the trail along Union Street past the **Union Oyster House** (opened 1826), Boston's oldest restaurant, and the **Ebenezer Hancock House** (1767), home of John Hancock's brother, the deputy paymaster-general of the Continental Army. In the gardens alongside Union Street are the six glass towers of the **New England Holocaust Memorial** (see sidebar on page 57). Nearby, the Haymarket is a great place for bargain fruit and veg-etables on Friday and Saturday.

   North End▶▶ is one of Boston's oldest neighborhoods. It has been home to wave after wave of immigrants. After the original 17th-century Puritan settlers came Irish refugees fleeing from the 1840s potato famine, then Jews from Eastern Europe. Today, the North End is the Italian quarter and has some of Boston's best restaurants.

Paul Revere House

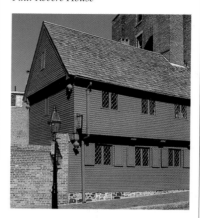

Something of a freak survival from the old town, **Paul Revere House▶** (*Open* daily, except holidays, and Mon in winter) of about 1680, on North Square, was home to patriot Paul Revere (see page 55) and is Boston's oldest building. After Revere's time, the building functioned as a cigar factory, grocery, tenement, and bank. Restored to its original appearance, the building now operates as a small museum.

   Photogenic **Paul Revere Mall** features the famous equestrian statue of Paul Revere against the magnificent steeple of **Old North Church▶▶▶** (1723), where Robert Newman, the sexton, lit two lanterns on April 18, 1775, to warn the citizens across the river of British plans to cross by sea rather than by land via Boston Neck (see page 55). The church is a magnif-icent colonial survival, with a gallery, box pews, and brass chandeliers; it is Boston's oldest church and has the tallest steeple.

   Copps Hill Burying Ground (1660) was used by the British as a vantage point for cannon while making prepa-rations for the Battle of Bunker Hill. It is Boston's second oldest cemetery and has some fascinating early epitaphs. The headstone of Daniel Malcom (to the left if entering from

The North End, once a slum, is now a neat and lively district

Hull Street and found between the broken column commemorating Prince Hall and a circular path) records "Here lies buried in a stone grave 10 feet deep. A friend to the Publick, an enemy to oppression," thus buried safe from British bullets. Though not an "official" Trail site, **North End Garage Park**, on the left side of Hull Street, is of interest as the site of the famous Brink's robbery in 1950, which netted a record $2.5 million; the FBI subsequently spent close to $29 million investigating it.

Across the bridge is **Charlestown**, founded in 1629 and named after Charles I. It was razed by the British, and no house predates 1775. Charlestown was not incorporated into Boston until 1873. The trail continues to the entrance to **Charlestown Navy Yard**▶▶ (see pages 66–67), today home of the warship the **USS Constitution**▶▶▶ and the World War II destroyer **USS Cassin Young**▶, as well as the **USS Constitution Museum**▶▶ and the Commandant's House.

Residential streets surround the **Bunker Hill Monument**▶▶, a tall obelisk that commemorates the first major Revolutionary War battle, fought on June 17, 1775. A 294-step climb is rewarded by an excellent view of the city. Musket firing takes place daily in summer, and there is an exhibition inside the lodge.

"Old North," famous for the part it played in Paul Revere's ride

The Public Garden boasts the status of the nation's oldest botanical park

Walk

Back Bay

See map on pages 48–49 (orange route).

This tour wends its way through the elegant Victorian brownstone district of the Back Bay, where almost every doorway deserves attention, and past the two great high-level viewing platforms of Boston—the Prudential and Hancock towers.

Begin at the west side of the **Public Garden**▶ ▶ (see page 73) and cross the walkway along the center of **Commonwealth Avenue**▶ ▶, often rated as one of America's finest streets. This forms the central axis of the Back Bay, an area subject to an ambitious landfill project in the late-19th century, when Parisian-style avenues were laid out on a grand scale and with an eye for symmetry.

Turn right onto Berkeley Street. At 137 Beacon Street, to the right,

Gibson House▶ (*Open* May 1–Nov 1, Wed–Sun, plus weekends Nov–Apr; tours at 1, 2 and 3) is a wonderfully preserved example of the Back Bay brownstone, in pristine Victorian condition. Continuing west on Beacon Street, turn right at Dartmouth Street to take the footbridge over the highway to **Charlesbank Park**, a riverside strip popular with bicycle riders, sunbathers, and joggers. The Hatch Shell, where outdoor concerts are held in summer, is to the right, while across the Charles River is the Massachusetts Institute of Technology (MIT).

Return by another footbridge over the highway onto Fairfield Street. Continue to Newbury Street, an inviting detour with its restaurants, sidewalk cafés, and upscale boutiques and galleries. From Fairfield Street, turn right into Boylston Street, cross over and go through the revolving doors and up the escalator into the **Prudential Center**, an enclosed mall with 75 shops and restaurants. Walk straight ahead, and at the Center Court turn right to the Prudential Tower. Take an elevator to the 50th floor for a panoramic view from the **Prudential Center Skywalk**▶ ▶ ▶ (see page 72).

Leave the Prudential Center through

Back Bay statue of local maritime writer Samuel Eliot Morison (1887–1976)

Huntington or Belvidere Arcade and turn right outside to visit the **First Church of Christ, Scientist complex** immediately ahead. The long, low Broadcasting Center to the right of a huge oblong pool houses **"A light unto my path," Bible Exhibit** (*Open* Tue–Sun. *Admission* free) that has an electronic map charting travels across the Holy Land and telephones telling the listener of assorted miracle healings. The skyscraper is the **Christian Science World Headquarters**. The **Christian Science Church▶** (1906) is modeled on St. Peter's in Rome and contains the largest pipe organ in the western hemisphere. Adjacent to the church (to its right) in a room in the

The Christian Science World Headquarters

publishing wing of the organization, the **Mapparium▶ ▶** (*Open*: Mon–Sat 9–4:30; closed Mon in winter. *Admission* free) is a stained-glass representation of the globe as mapped in 1932–1935. Looking from within the sphere (with the map appearing in concave form) you can see the whole globe in one visual sweep. The bizarre echo, with voices bouncing all around, makes this one of Boston's more offbeat experiences.

Return to the Prudential Center by escalator leading up to Belvidere or Huntington Arcade. From Center Court, take Back Bay Arcade to the Copley Bridge, a covered walkway leading over Huntington Avenue into Copley Place indoor shopping center. Walk straight through on the first floor, past the indoor waterfall, then just past the staircase go left down an escalator and cross the covered walkway into the Westin Hotel lobby. Take the escalator down to emerge in **Copley Square▶ ▶**. On its west side is the supremely dignified Renaissance Revival **Boston Public Library▶ ▶ ▶** (1894), the first public lending library in the world, while on the north side is the **New Old South Church** (1875) with its flamboyant exterior, inspired by the North Italian Gothic style. Physically the square is dominated by the huge skyscraper slab of the **John Hancock Tower and Observatory▶ ▶ ▶**, with its viewpoint 60 stories up (see page 70). Its glass reflects **Trinity Church▶ ▶ ▶** (1877), the neo-Romanesque masterpiece of Henry Hobson Richardson, with its ornate interior that includes work by John LaFarge, William Morris, and Edward Burne-Jones.

JOHN HANCOCK OBSERVATORY

The best place to see Boston

63

Beacon Hill

See map on pages 48–49 (green route).

This walk explores Beacon Hill's tight network of narrow residential streets on a sloping site. The neighborhood is a fascinating early 19th-century mixture of patrician and artisan homes. Intricate iron balconies, crisply proportioned brick façades, and carefully preserved front doors are much in evidence. Portrait artist John Singleton Copley sold land here to the Mount Vernon Proprietors, who included the great architect Charles

Harrison Gray Otis House, built in post-Revolutionary "Federal" style. A plain façade hides a supremely elegant interior

Bulfinch, and the lawyer and orator Harrison Gray Otis. Here and there you can see some of the original purple window glass imported from Hamburg in the 1820s, which discolored because of the presence of manganese oxide in the material. Another Beacon Hill quirk is that the gas lamps stay on all day.

Start from the northeast corner of the **Public Garden▶▶** (page 73) at the intersection of Charles Street and Beacon Street. Walk along Beacon Street eastward. Number 45, built in 1805, was the last of three houses on "the Hill" built for Harrison Gray Otis

by Charles Bulfinch. At number 33 lived George Parkman, the Harvard undergraduate who, in 1849, ended up in several pieces in the laboratory of a Harvard professor of medicine; the sensational trial was the major scandal of Beacon Hill.

Opposite the **State House▶▶** (see page 73), the **Robert Gould Shaw and 54th Regiment Memorial** acknowledges the role played by the first black regiment in the Civil War. Shaw, himself white, lived at 44 Beacon Street and led his regiment from here. This is the start of the Black Heritage Trail (see page 66).

Turn left into Bowdoin Street. The column by the State House marks the site of the beacon that was erected here to warn the Puritans of Indians and foreign invasion and that gave the hill its name. The district was later to become a rough-and-ready jumble of disreputable bars and brothels, popularly known as "Mount Whoredom."

Turn left onto Derne Street. From Hancock Street on the right, you can walk down to Cambridge Street and the first **Harrison Gray Otis House▶** (see page 68). If not visiting the house, continue instead along Derne Street and turn right onto Joy Street, off which is Smith Court. The **African Meeting House** here is the oldest black church building still standing in the U.S.A. and the birthplace of the antislavery movement, where William Lloyd Garrison and 12 others founded the New England Anti-Slavery Society. It houses the Museum of Afro American History. **Smith Court Residences** were typical homes of Beacon Hill's free black community, who worked as servants in the 19th century.

Return along Joy Street and turn right into Pinckney Street, which was originally built to house service workers. Author Louisa May Alcott's family lived at **number 20. Number 24** (the "house of Odd Windows") was converted by a relative of Ralph Waldo Emerson from a stable into a townhouse, and **number 54** was the home of Nathaniel Hawthorne while he worked at Boston's custom house.

Detour right onto Anderson Street

and right again onto **Revere Street**, and look for a tiny entrance on the left between numbers 25 and 29. The house with columns at the end is a false façade, with a sheer drop behind.

Retrace your steps via Anderson Street to **Louisburg Square**, laid out in 1834–1844 by Bulfinch. Louisa May Alcott spent her last two years here at number 10. America's oldest homeowners' association maintains the square itself.

Mount Vernon Street▶▶, on the south side of the square, is one of Boston's finest architectural gems: Henry James called it "the only respectable street in America." Bulfinch's second Harrison Gray Otis house (1800) is at number 85, while

The more modest houses of lanes such as Acorn Street were built as servants' quarters

the **Nichols House Museum▶** at number 55 (*Open* May–Oct, Tue–Sat 12–4:15; closed Jan, and Tue, Thu, Fri and Sun in winter), provides another opportunity to see a Bulfinch interior.

Follow Walnut Street into Chestnut Street, where abolitionist poet Julia Ward Howe resided at number 13 in 1862 and penned *The Battle Hymn of the Republic*. Turn right into Willow Street and left into **Acorn Street▶**, picturesquely cobbled and perhaps the city's most famous residential street. Finish by exploring the shops and restaurants of **Charles Street**.

Boston Beer's award-winning brew

AFRICAN AMERICAN HERITAGE
The African Meeting House, 8 Smith Court, houses the Museum of Afro-American History.The nearby Abiel Smith School, 46 Joy Street, tel: 617/742 5415, is home to the Boston African American National Historic Site and offers free guided tours of the Black Heritage Trail. Alternatively, the trail can be taken as a self-guided tour with a brochure available from the same organization or from any tourist information point.

BOSTONIAN TERMS
The Black Maria was named after Maria Lee, who owned a disreputable hotel patronized by drunks and criminals. Police made frequent calls and took the offenders into the station by a "paddy wagon," later renamed a "Black Maria" to avoid disparaging the Irish population.
   The term "gerrymandering" originated with Governor Elbridge Gerry, vice president under James Madison, who re-apportioned electoral boundaries for his own advantage.'

▶ ▶ ▶ **Aquarium** See New England Aquarium, page 72

▶ ▶ **Boston Athenaeum**　　　48C3
101/2 Beacon Street
Open: year round, Mon 9–8, Tue–Fri 9–5:30; Sep–May, Sat 9–4; free tours Tue and Thu, 3 PM with 24 hours' notice, tel: 617/227 0270. Subway: Park Street (Green and Red lines).
Originating in 1807, this private library became the preserve of wealthy Boston intellectuals. In 1845 the Athenaeum moved into this Italian *palazzo*-style building. Classical statuary and choice paintings set a rarefied atmosphere. On the top floor the high-ceilinged Reading Room of 1915 has seven pairs of recessed bays looking over the Old Granary Burial Ground, while the Oval Room contains books from George Washington's library.

▶ ▶ ▶ **Boston Public Library**　　　48B2
Copley Square
Open: year round, Mon–Thu 9–9, Fri and Sat 2–6; Oct–May, Sun 2–6. Subway: Copley (Green Line).
A true palace of literature: when Charles Follen McKim's vast Renaissance-style edifice opened in 1895, it was America's first public library. Seemingly, no expense was spared: beyond the bronze reliefs on the entrance doors designed by Daniel Chester French—depicting female personifications of Music, Poetry, Wisdom, Knowledge, Truth and Romance—the sumptuous marble foyer is revealed, its grand staircases guarded by lions sculpted by Louis Saint-Gaudens. Seek out the colonnaded courtyard, the murals by John Singer Sargent, the huge reading room and the dioramas by Albert Wiggin of printmakers at work.

▶ **Boston Tea Party Ship and Museum**　　　49E2
Congress Street Bridge (adjacent to Children's and Computer Museums)
Open: daily, except Dec 1–Mar 1
Bus: Courtesy shuttle bus from Quincy Market, at corner of State and Congress streets, in summer.
The ship moored here is a faithful replica of the brig *Beaver II*, one of the ships boarded in the Boston Tea Party protest (see page 33). You can put on quasi-Indian feather headgear and dunk a tea chest in the river, sample a cup of cold tea, and visit the small museum. It is very much an audience-participation venture: you are summoned to attend a "town meeting" such as happened (more or less) at the Old South Meeting House in 1773.

▶ ▶ ▶ **Charlestown Navy Yard**　　　49D5
Open: daily. Admission: free. Subway: North Station (Green Line), then a 10–15 minute walk; or bus 93 from Haymarket station (Green Line); or MBTA Water Shuttle from Long Wharf by Aquarium Station (Blue Line). Trolley tours pass the Navy Yard.

Charlestown Navy Yard served the United States Navy from 1800 until 1974. Some 30 acres of the yard now form part of Boston National Historical Park. It has very much the atmosphere of a shipyard, and visitors may enter only a few buildings. Tours are at 11 AM during weekends and also at 2 PM on summer weekdays. The Visitor Center gives out informative leaflets.

Now restored to its full-masted glory, the frigate **USS Constitution▶ ▶ ▶**, the most famous of all historic American warships, was built nearby in 1797 and served in three wars. In the War of 1812, British cannonballs bounced off the vessel, earning her the nickname of "Old Ironsides," as she captured two sloops-of-war and sank two frigates.

Maritime history is brought to life in the **USS Constitution Museum▶ ▶**, adjacent, for which there is an entrance fee (*Open* daily from 10). The museum displays ship models, documents, and paintings, as well as some hands-on exhibits where you can try the ship's wheel or raise the sail.

The **USS Cassin Young▶** is a World War II destroyer that was hit by kamikaze raids at Okinawa. **The Commandant's House** (*Open* Mar–Oct, 1–4) is a Federal-style building that was the home of the commanding officers of the Navy Yard from 1805 to 1976; the interior has been preserved as it was when last occupied. The **Boston Marine Society** (*Open* 10–3) situated next to the prominent octagonal Muster House of 1852 and has three rooms filled with nauticalia, including model ships and paintings of maritime scenes.

Also in the Navy Yard site, the **Bunker Hill Pavilion** (*Open* Apr–Nov) stages a 30-minute multimedia show for visitors entitled *Whites of their Eyes*, plunging you into the Battle of Bunker Hill through costumed mannequins "acting" the part.

CHANGING TIMES
More than 160 ships were built in Charlestown Navy Yard. Over the years numerous buildings have been added, including boilermaker shops, a marine railroad, New England's first granite dry dock, and America's last surviving ropewalk. The yard expanded in the Civil War, and in World War II employed nearly 50,000 people. From the 1960s, it specialized in the modernization and overhaul of old vessels.

67

SUMMER SALUTE
The USS *Constitution* traditionally takes part in the annual Harborfest celebration and enters Boston Harbor on July 4 to fire a national salute, a role resumed in 1996 after dry-dock restoration. Throughout the rest of the year, cannon firing takes place daily at sunset, when the flag is lowered.

Below: USS Cassin Young *in the Navy Yard, Charlestown.*

Having fun on the giant keyboard of the Computer Museum's walk-through computer

▶▶▶ Children's Museum 49E2
300 Congress Street
Open: daily, 10–5, plus Fri 5–9 PM, when the entrance fee is reduced; closed Mon during termtime.
Subway: South Station (Red Line).
Adults will wish they were kids again when they see this interactive museum, one of the oldest, largest, and best of its kind anywhere. Venture aboard Boats Afloat, shop at the Super Mercado, look in at the Grandparents' House, visit a Japanese home, play on a giant desktop, climb a two-story maze—and more.

▶▶ Christian Science Center and Mapparium 48A1
See page 63 and sidebar on this page.

▶▶ Computer Museum 49E2
300 Congress Street
Open: in summer daily, 10–6; in winter Tue–Sun, 10–5; closed Mon, except school holidays. Admission: half price Sun after 3.
Subway: South Station (Red Line).
The world's premier computer museum makes an excellent half-day visit for buffs and novices alike. On display are a gigantic walk-through mockup of a multimedia computer, exhibits of robots and computers through the ages, and over 160 engaging hands-on exhibits illustrating the uses and impact of computers and computer networks.

▶▶▶ Faneuil Hall Marketplace 49D3
See page 59.

▶ Federal Reserve Bank Tours
See sidebar on page 53.

▶ Fenway Park Tours
See sidebar on page 53.

▶ FleetCenter Tours 48C4
150 Causeway Street (tel: 617/624-1518)
Open: daily 11–7
Subway: North Station (Green and Orange Lines).
The FleetCenter is home to a branch of the Sports Museum of New England (see panel, page 171). Behind-the-scenes tours of Boston's state-of-the-art sports complex begin with a nostalgic look back to the days when the home of the Celtics and the Bruins was next-door Boston Garden.

▶ Harrison Gray Otis House 48C4
141 Cambridge Street
Subway: Bowdoin (Blue Line) or Charles Street (Red Line).
Dating from 1796, this fine federal house was the first of the three built on Beacon Hill for Harrison Gray and Sally Foster Otis (*Open Wed–Sun; last tour 4 PM*). It houses the Society for the Preservation of New England Antiquities (SPNEA). It can be visited on the Beacon Hill walk (see pages 64–65).

▶▶▶ Isabella Stewart Gardner Museum   48A1

280 The Fenway
Open: Tue–Sun 11–5.
Subway: Museum (Green Line).
This magnificent museum is the creation of Isabella
Stewart Gardner, the heiress of a wealthy New York family. Its exterior gives little hint of what lies within—a
Venetian-style *palazzo* crammed with priceless art treasures and ranged around an exquisite four-story courtyard in which architectural fragments are surrounded by
ferns and flowers in season. Each room has a theme and is
arranged as Mrs. Gardner left it, giving an outstanding
collection an appealing air of intimacy. As well as
numerous paintings by Italian Renaissance artists, Dutch
and Flemish masters, and French Impressionists, there
are ancient Egyptian artifacts, sculptures, ceramics,
tapestries, a lace collection, and furniture.

Concerts are held in the Tapestry Room on Saturdays
and Sundays, September to May, at 1:30 PM (tel: 617/ 734
1359) and there is an excellent small café.

▶ John F. Kennedy Library, New Museum   48C1

220 Morrissey Boulevard, Columbia Point
Open: daily, 9–5.
Subway: JFK/UMass (Red Line) for free shuttle bus.
This striking building, designed by I.M. Pei and scenically
sited on the waterfront in the southern neighborhood of
Dorchester, is the nation's memorial to J.F.K. In the New
Museum at the J.F.K. Library, the Kennedy era is re-
created with replicas of the White House Oval Office, his-
torical documents, and films on J.F.K.'s life.

See sidebar for the adjacent **Commonwealth Museum**.

A STRONG CHARACTER
Isabella Stewart Gardner
was the talk of the Back
Bay. She wore diamonds
in her hair and raised a
few eyebrows by posing
for her artist friend John
Singer Sargent. Once she
hired a boxer to perform
at a ladies' tea party. She
slept late in early-rise
Boston. After her son died
at the age of two, she suffered depression and took
a trip to Europe. She
returned to Boston a new
woman; her Back Bay
home became a fashion-
able salon, where she
held glittering galas and
balls, and she devoted
much of her time to
collecting art.

69

COMMONWEALTH MUSEUM
Next door to the J.F.K.
Library, this covers everything to do with the
Commonwealth of
Massachusetts. Changing
and permanent exhibits
feature Native Americans,
immigrants, towns and
cities, the political
system, natural history,
and labor history. (*Open*
Mon–Fri 9–5, Sat 9–3.
Admission free).

*The splendid courtyard of
the Isabella Stewart
Gardner Museum, with
its fountains, statues, and
flowers*

Nighttime view of the John Hancock Tower, an excellent observation point

LOCAL FINE ARTS
New England is well represented at the Museum of Fine Arts in the sections devoted to furniture. Among the pieces on show are a late 17th-century press cupboard from Wethersfield, Connecticut, with pillars painted black to resemble ebony, and two fine Newport chests of the mid-18th century. Silverware on display includes items by Paul Revere, and many of the museum's 19th-century pictures have a New England theme, such as Frederick Childe Hassam's *Boston Common at Twilight* and Winslow Homer's *Lookout—"all's well."*

▶▶▶ John Hancock Tower and Observatory 48B2
200 Clarendon Street (Copley Square)
Subway: Copley (Green Line) or Back Bay (Orange Line).
Boston's tallest building (built 1968–1976) is a striking 60-story slab of reflective glass designed by I.M. Pei and neatly reflecting adjacent Trinity Church. It suffered numerous teething problems just after completion when window panes repeatedly fell out and landed on the street below. On the top floor the Hancock Observatory offers, like the nearby Prudential Tower, superb panoramic views over Boston and the bay, to the highlands of Massachusetts, Vermont, and New Hampshire (*Open* Mon–Sat 9 AM–10 PM, Sun noon–10 PM. You can see out of three sides only, but a recorded narration describes the view from one side and gives a general survey of the city's history. You can also listen in on the air traffic controllers at Logan airport.

▶▶▶ Museum of Fine Arts 48A1
465 Huntington Avenue
Open: Tue, Thu, Sat, Sun 10–4:45, Wed 10–9:45.
Subway: Museum (Green Line) or Ruggles (Orange Line).
New England's largest art gallery, often referred to as the MFA, is also one of the nation's finest. It is particularly noted for its Asian collection, of worldwide importance, and its European paintings.

Most of the ground floor is devoted to a wide-ranging selection of American paintings, furniture, and decorative arts. The museum has an unrivaled collection of John Singleton Copley portraits, including John Hancock, Samuel Adams, and Paul Revere, in addition to his famous work *Watson and the Shark*. The Hudson River School landscape painters Albert Bierstadt, Fitz Hugh

Lane, and Thomas Cole; the American Impressionists Childe Hassam, Winslow Homer, Mary Cassatt, and James McNeill Whistler; and New York's Abstract Expressionists are also well represented. A series of re-created period rooms provides a good insight into daily life in New England from the 17th to the 19th centuries. For other local themes, see sidebar on page 70.

Also on the ground floor is the MFA's collection of Japanese woodblock prints, the largest in the world, and some fine Indian miniatures and Islamic ceramics. The Nubian collection includes pottery, sculpture, and fragments of furniture found in tombs and temples. The museum's Egyptian pieces include statues of King Mycerinus and Queen Kha-merer-ebty II. The rooms devoted to ancient Greece have some fine red-figure vases and the Bartlett *Aphrodite*, while among the Roman treasures are frescoes from a house in Pompeii.

The bulk of the Chinese and Japanese collection is upstairs, as is European art. Among the highlights here are J.M.W. Turner's *Slave Ship* and Constable's *Stour Valley and Dedham Church.* An outstanding selection of French masters features works by Manet, Degas, Gauguin, Van Gogh, Renoir, Cézanne, and Monet. The Firestone Silver Collection features pre-1789 French silver—rare items that escaped being melted down during the French Revolution.

The museum has a large shop and a choice of cafés, and restaurants.

▶▶▶ Museum of Science
48B5

Charles River Dam
Open: 9–5 (summer 9–7), Fri 9–9.
Subway: Science Park (Green Line).
One of the great science museums of the world, this has more than anyone could hope to see in a single day. With over 450 interactive exhibits, it is an almost unfailing hit with the children who come here in throngs. At the **Theater of Electricity**, you can watch high-voltage lightning sparks produced by the world's largest Van de Graaff generator. The **Observatory** delves into the unseen, including microscopic life and ultrasonic sounds, while **Earthworks** re-creates the process of gems growing beneath the Earth's surface. **Frontiers of Biotechnology** has interactive computers providing an introduction to genetics.

Two further attractions in the museum require separate admission; reservations are strongly advised (tel: 617/723 2500). The **Charles Hayden Planetarium** gives tours of the New England skies and offers an intergalactic journey on its multimedia "starship," as well as laser shows. The **Mugar Omni Theatre** has a wraparound domed screen, that is 76 feet in diameter and as tall as a four-story building; it also boasts state-of-the-art projection, and 84 speakers.

MUSEUM TOURS
Free tours of the Museum of Fine Arts provide an introduction to the collections. These take place on Wednesday at 6:15, Tuesday to Friday at 1:30, and Saturday at 11 and 1:30. Other themed tours depart Tuesday to Friday between 10:30 and 2:30.

71

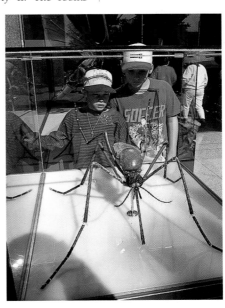

Explore the many faces of the world of nature at the Museum of Science

CHARLES RIVER CRUISES
An optional extra to a visit to the Museum of Science is to take a 50-minute narrated cruise on the Charles River. Departures are from CambridgeSide Galleria Mall in Cambridge. For information, contact the Charles Riverboat Company (tel: 617/621 3001).

72

Whale-watching with the New England Aquarium

▶▶▶ New England Aquarium   49E3
Central Wharf
Open: Jul–Labor Day, Mon, Tue, and Fri 9–6, Wed, and Thu 9–8, weekends and holidays 9–7; winter, Mon–Fri 9–5, weekends and holidays 9–6.
Subway: Aquarium (Blue Line).
A spectacular encounter with the underwater world. In 1998 the Aquarium acquired a new West Wing, with its exhibit Coastal Rhythms showing the marine and bird life of the coasts from New England shores to jungle lagoons. In the main gallery, you walk past a window onto the Aquarium Medical Center, where stranded sea creatures are treated. On the way up to the top of the ramp you will learn why fishes come in such a range of colors, shapes and patterns; you then spiral down beside a four-storey cylindrical water tank, with fish of every size—sharks among them—swimming around a replica coral reef.

Try to time your visit with a sea-lion show aboard the museum vessel *Discovery*. The Aquarium also runs whale-watching cruises and educational "Science at Sea" tours on *Doc Edgerton*; for information, call 617/973 5281.

▶ Old South Meeting House   49D3
See page 58, and sidebar opposite.

▶▶ Old State House   49D3
See pages 58–59.

▶ Paul Revere House   49D4
See page 60.

▶▶▶ Prudential Center Skywalk   48A1
Prudential Tower, Prudential Center
Open: daily, until 10 PM
Subway: Prudential (Green Line, E train).
Although scarcely Boston's best-loved building, the prominent Prudential Tower offers a superb view of the city from its Skywalk (50th) floor, 700 feet above the streets. On a really clear day, the 360° panorama stretches

to the Berkshire Hills and to high points in New Hampshire and Vermont. As you walk around the gallery, various interactive displays and sound recordings highlight significant events and personalities from Boston's history. Both the Prudential and the John Hancock Tower are on the Back Bay walk (see pages 62–3).

One of the famous and perennially popular swan boats in Boston Garden

▶▶ Public Garden   48B2

Subway: Arlington (Green Line).
Well-fed squirrels and pigeons populate this charming park, graced with statues and some 350 varieties of trees. Since 1877, pedal-powered swan boats have conveyed summer visitors across the pond, past weeping willows and beneath a scaled-down replica suspension bridge. Look for the bronze statuettes of a duck and eight ducklings, modeled on the heroes of Robert McCloskey's children's story, *Make Way for Ducklings.*

▶▶ State House   48C3

Beacon Street
Subway: Park Street (Red and Green Lines).
Prominently sited at the top of the Common, the State House is the seat of government for the Commonwealth of Massachusetts. Road distances are traditionally measured from the gold-leaf dome. The State House was originally designed by Charles Bulfinch. Subsequently extended, the building has a rich marble interior. The entrance is through the **Doric Hall**. It leads to the **Nurses Hall**, hung with a trio of paintings by Robert Reid (*Paul Revere's Ride, James Otis Arguing Against the Writs of Assistance,* and *The Boston Tea Party*), and into the circular Hall of Flags and main staircase. The **House of Representatives** contains the Sacred Cod, a wooden fish carving that is the symbol of Massachusetts. The **Senate Chamber** and **Governor's Office** are part of the original building by Bulfinch.

▶▶▶ Trinity Church   48B2

See page 63.

▶▶ USS *Constitution* Museum   48C3

See page 67.

MEETING HOUSES AND CHURCHES
Old South Meeting House, with its Wren-inspired brick façade dating to 1729, replaced an earlier wooden meeting house built by Puritan settlers. These early colonists built their churches in the plain, square, meeting-house style, with a wooden spire or cupola and, inside, wooden paneling, box pews, and galleries supported on wooden columns. Reflecting the unity of Church and State, the meeting house often also served as town hall. It was not until the 19th century that new churches were built in such European-inspired styles as Gothic or Romanesque Revival.

*Japanese print at the
Arthur M. Sackler
Museum*

74

Cambridge

Cambridge lies just across the Charles River from Boston, a short walk over the Harvard Bridge from the Back Bay. Yet it is a separate city—a commercial center as well as a famous seat of learning centered on Harvard University and the Massachusetts Institute of Technology (MIT). At night, Harvard Square comes alive with street entertainers and bustle. It is the busy atmosphere and the shopping, dining, and nightlife, rather than the physical appearance of Cambridge, that attract visitors.

Cambridge was founded in 1630 as Newtowne and became the capital of the Bay Colony, being chosen for its protected site away from the exposed Boston peninsula. Harvard University was founded in 1636, and two years later Newtowne was renamed Cambridge after the English seat of learning. Following the battles of Concord and Lexington in 1775, provincial militias grouped on Cambridge Common to form the new Continental Army under the command of George Washington. Today, Harvard University is one of the preeminent Ivy League establishments in the country (see pages 22–23).

The Massachusetts Institute of Technology was founded in 1861 as a "society of arts, a museum of arts and a school of industrial science." For the visitor it is of chief interest for its modern architecture and sculpture. In particular seek out two buildings by Eero Saarinen: the Chapel, which reveals a dramatic interior sparkling with dots of reflected light, and the Kresge Auditorium, with an eighth of a sphere forming a triangular shell over the rest of the structure.

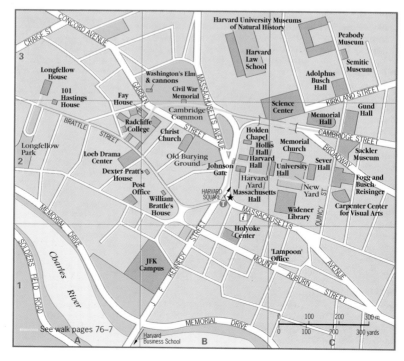

▶▶ Harvard University Museums   74C2/3

The **Fogg Art Museum**▶▶ and the **Busch-Reisinger Museum**▶▶, at 32 Quincy Street, are two museums in one, housing one of the most important and extensive art collections in the world (*Open* Mon–Sat 10–5, Sun 1–5. *Admission* free Sat 10–12). The Fogg covers art from Western Europe and the U.S., featuring Italian Renaissance works by Simone Martini and Filippo Lippi, paintings by Dutch and Flemish masters and such 19th-century Americans as Homer, Whistler and Sargent; French Impressionists and Pre-Raphaelites are also represented. The Busch-Reisinger concentrates on art from northern Europe and Scandinavia, with Bauhaus artifacts and Expressionist paintings.

The **Arthur M. Sackler Museum**▶, at 485 Broadway Street, is housed in an innovative, if controversial, candy-striped building by James Stirling known as "Stirling's Zebra." It contains beautiful and rare items from Asia and the ancient world, including Greek Attic vessels, carvings of deities, Indian and Persian miniatures, and the world's finest collection of Chinese jade.

Entrances to the Harvard University **Museums of Natural History and Peabody Museum**▶ are at 24 Oxford Street and 11 Divinity Avenue (*Open* daily, 9–4:30, Sun 1–4:30). *Admission* covers the four museums in this rambling building. Much of it is the preserve of the specialist researcher, but the public mostly comes to see the unique collection of glass flowers in the Botanical Museum, more than 700 items in all, representing giant cross sections, roots, rotting pears, and insects (see sidebar). A 30-minute tape tour guides you to the highlights. The other museums are devoted to zoology (not for stuffed-animal phobics), including fossils, dinosaurs, and the world's largest collection of spiders; archeology and ethnology, and geology, with an attractive stone and gem collection. The Peabody includes a host of ethnological artifacts, including the Hall of the American Indian.

▶▶ Longfellow House   74A3

Henry Longfellow was 30 years old when he first saw this 1759 yellow clapboard mansion at 105 Brattle Street (*Open* Wed–Sun 10–4:30, weekends in winter) and felt like a "prince in a villa" just to lodge here. It was bought for him and his wife Fanny as a wedding present from his father-in-law; the couple had a happy marriage and had six children. Here he completed his translation of Dante and penned *The Song of Hiawatha, Paul Revere's Ride*, and *Evangeline*. He entertained Dickens, Twain, Emerson, Hawthorne, and Wilde. Longfellow died here after living in the house for 45 years. His personal artifacts abound: there is a crowded study, with a book collection reflecting a passion for knowledge; a Steinway piano around which he enjoyed singing German *Lieder*, and the chair made from the "spreading chestnut tree."

HARVARD'S GLASS FLOWERS

George Lincoln Goodall, the first director of Harvard's Botanical Museum, wanted three-dimensional plant models for teaching purposes. He traveled to Dresden in 1886 to visit Leopold and Rudolf Blashka, father and son, who were specialists in supplying museums with glass sea creatures. In this way he established a year-round laboratory for scientific study. The final models were created by Rudolf to illustrate plant diseases.

75

Longfellow House, home to the poet from 1837 to 1882

JUST DESSERTS?

Millionaire ewspaper tycoon William Randolf Hearst achieved notoriety in his days at Harvard, where he kept a pet alligator and gave personalized chamber pots to his instructors before being expelled. Similar gratitude was shown in 1764 when a student took a book from the library of Massachusetts Hall on the eve of its burning. On returning the volume the next day, he was thanked by President Holyoke, and then expelled for taking the book without permission.

The nation's oldest university, Harvard has become the wealthiest, too

Walk

Harvard and Cambridge highlights

See map on page 74 (yellow route).

This is a tour of Harvard University and historic Cambridge, taking in the Common and the home of the poet Henry Wadsworth Longfellow.

From Harvard Square Red Line subway station, walk north on Massachusetts Avenue to Johnson Gate, which gives access to **Harvard Yard**, the hub of the university. The first quadrangle, **Old Yard**, contains dormitories for freshmen and the oldest campus buildings; it was here that Washington gathered his troops against the British. To the left as you enter is **Harvard Hall**, a 1764 reconstruction of the original building endowed by John Harvard and destroyed by fire. Adjacent is **Hollis Hall** (1762), whose students included Emerson and Thoreau. Dents in the steps in front of the hall were reputedly caused by the student

Leafy Harvard Yard

practice of placing cannonballs in fireplaces to radiate heat, and throwing them out in spring! On the right is **Massachusetts Hall** (1718), the oldest building of all, which numbers John and Samuel Adams among its luminaries.

In the center of Old Yard, the **John Harvard Statue** (1885), known as the "Statue of Three Lies," is not quite what it seems. A student, not Harvard, was the model, and the inscription "John Harvard, Founder, 1638" errs on two counts: Harvard was the benefactor, not the founder, and the university was founded in 1636.

Beyond **University Hall** (1816), designed by Charles Bulfinch, is **New Yard**, a quadrangle formed by Memorial Church (1931), Sever Hall (1880), and the **Harry Elkins Widener Library** (1913). The latter is the largest university library in the world and was endowed by the mother of Harry Widener, an avid collector of antiquarian books who perished aboard the *Titanic*. True to his mother's wishes, the building has been unaltered, and for a time all applicants had to undertake a swimming test (Harry could not swim). **Memorial Church** is dedicated to Harvard men who died in the two World Wars.

Leave the yard and enter Quincy Street, opposite the concrete and glass **Carpenter Center for Visual Arts** (1963), the only building in the U.S.A. designed by Le Corbusier. Turn left. Continue past the Fogg and Sackler museums to Cambridge Street, cross to the other side, and

go left past the cathedral-like **Memorial Hall** (1874), built to honor all the Harvard men killed in the Civil War. Carry straight on; cross Massachusetts Avenue at the traffic lights, then cross Cambridge Common, passing the war memorial. The Common formerly functioned as the focus for Cambridge's religious, social, and political life. Three captured British cannons stand on the grass close to where Washington took command of the 9,000 men who had gathered to form the Continental Army. Washington's Elm (not the original tree) marks the spot.

Cross Garden Street by the traffic lights. To the left the **Old Burying Ground** contains the graves of the first eight Harvard presidents, and **Christ Church** (1761) was used as a patriot barracks after its staunchly Tory Anglican congregation fled before the Revolution—its organ pipes were pilfered for use as bullets. Turn right along Garden Street, then left through the gate into **Radcliffe College**, which was founded as the Society for the Collegiate Instruction of Women in 1879, when Fay House (1807) was acquired. The college was incorporated into Harvard in 1894. Leaving Radcliffe, turn right along Brattle Street, known in the 18th century as Tory Row because of the British patriotism of its residents, to **Longfellow House**, George Washington's headquarters during the siege of Boston (see page 75). Returning along Brattle Street, see number 56, the home of Dexter Pratt, who was immortalized by Longfellow in *The Village Blacksmith* ("a mighty man is he, with large and sinewy hands"); the "spreading chestnut tree" is no longer there.

Above: there's always entertainment in Harvard Square, whether it's eating out, listening to music—or watching a game of chess

Accommodations

The upscale Lenox Hotel on Boylston Street

CITY FREEBIES
● Concerts at the Hatch Shell in summer.
● New England Conservatory concerts, some of which are held in the resplendent Jordan Hall (tel: 617/262 1120).
● Faneuil Hall Marketplace street entertainers and Faneuil Hall itself.
● Commonwealth Museum.
● Massachusetts State House.
● Ranger-led walking tour along the Freedom Trail.
● The Public Garden.
● The Harvard University Museums are free on Saturdays 10–12.
● Charlestown Navy Yard, including USS Constitution and USS Cassin Young.
● Christian Science Church and Mapparium.
● Tours of the Boston Athenaeum and Boston Public Library.

A visitor center will help with finding accommodations

Accommodations

Hotels Boston has world-class hotels right in the heart of the city. The principal hotel area begins at the Theater District, just south of Boston Common, and extends westward past the Prudential Tower toward Massachusetts Avenue. Although some of the larger streets in this area are visually uninspiring, by staying around here you are within easy walking distance of Copley Square and the Freedom Trail at Boston Common. Other convenient hotels are found in the downtown and waterfront areas, and in Cambridge.

Boston is more expensive to stay in than is rural New England. At certain periods, especially during major conventions, it can be difficult to find a room, and rates are at a premium. At times like this, consider staying out of town and visiting Boston daily by public transportation, for example from Salem or Concord (MA) using MBTA Commuter Rail—see "Canny Planning," page 259. Weekends are less busy than weekdays, and accordingly rates tend to be lower. Since the converse applies in summer resorts such as the North Shore, Cape Cod, and the islands, you can make substantial savings by visiting Boston for the weekend and making for the coast during the week. Hotel rates do not usually include breakfast, and state and local room tax are added to the charge.

Bed and breakfast If hotels are too expensive, staying at a bed-and-breakfast (B&B) provides a money-saving alternative. Several agencies organize hosted B&B accommodations, where you stay in someone's home. The most charming and convenient locations include the Back Bay, Beacon Hill, and the North End. See page 268.

You can find less expensive places by opting to stay farther out from the city. The subway and rail systems take you to most farther-flung locations, such as the suburb of Brookline, southwest of central Boston, which has inexpensive bed-and-breakfasts. For those on a tight budget, the Boston International AYH Hostel (for address and telephone number see page 268) near the Prudential Center has dormitory accommodations.

Boston has a reputation as the most musical city in the United States, a reputation that rests almost entirely on its being the home of one of the finest ensembles in the world: the Boston Symphony Orchestra.

In October 1881, the BSO, or Boston Symphony Orchestra, gave its inaugural concert, bringing to reality the dreams of the philanthropist and amateur musician Henry Lee Higginson of founding a great and permanent orchestra in his hometown of Boston. For the first 20 years or so, concerts were given in the Old Boston Music Hall, initially under the directorship of Georg Henschel and then under a series of German and French conductors.

In 1900, the orchestra moved into Symphony Hall, which to this day remains one of the world's most acoustically perfect auditoriums. Symphony Hall also became the locale for the orchestra's hugely successful "Promenade concerts," which had begun in 1885, fulfilling Higginson's ambition to provide a "lighter kind of music" in addition to more serious programs. Later called "Popular Concerts" and then "Pops," these have remained a favorite springtime tradition (see page 25) under the auspices of a separate ensemble, the Boston Pops Orchestra.

The Koussevitzky era In 1924, the Russian-born Serge Koussevitzky, a man of extraordinary talent and dynamic personality, took over as musical director. During his 25 years of illustrious leadership, the BSO began making regular radio broadcasts. From 1937 onward, it took up a summer residency at Tanglewood, in Lenox in the Berkshires (see sidebar, page 146) in western Massachusetts.

"The aristocrat of orchestras" Charles Munch followed Koussevitzky in 1949, introducing American audiences to quantities of French music. In the 1960s, promoted under Erich Leinsdorf as "the aristocrat of orchestras," the BSO made numerous recordings and tours all over the world.

With Seiji Ozawa as musical director since 1973, Higginson's "great and permanent orchestra" has consolidated its worldwide reputation, commissioning new works from composers such as Hans Werner Henze and John Cage, and presenting soloists of the highest caliber, such as Yo-Yo Ma, Pinchas Zukerman, and Itzhak Perlman.

Above and left: John Williams conducts the Boston Pops

CONCERT INFORMATION
The season at Symphony Hall runs from the beginning of October to the end of April. Contact the Subscription Office, Symphony Hall, Boston, MA 02115 (tel: 617/266 7575; fax: 617/638 9436). For the Tanglewood Music Festival, contact Symphony Hall, as above, or Tanglewood Ticket Office, Lenox, MA 01240 (tel: 413/ 637 1940). For the Pops (May, Jun, Jul 4 and holidays), tel: 617/266 1492 or 617/266 2378.

OPENING NIGHT
When Isabella Stewart Gardner opened her Venetian-style palace (see page 69) on New Year's Night 1903, her guests were entertained in the concert hall by 50 members of the Boston Symphony Orchestra. Afterward, the doors of the hall were opened and guests had their first view of the ravishing courtyard, filled with flowering plants and lit by lanterns.

"And this is the city of
Boston,
The land of the bean and
the cod,
Where the Lowells talk
only to Cabots,
And the Cabots talk only
to God."
– James Collins Bossidy,
toast at Holy Cross Alumni
dinner, 1910.

"I've never seen a Lowell
walk,
Nor heard a Cabot speak
with God,
But I enjoy good Boston
talk
And Boston beans and
Boston cod."
– R.C.H. Bruce Lockhart,
In Praise of Boston.

*Eating al fresco at
Quincy Market against
the backdrop of Faneuil
Hall*

Food and drink

As the birthplace of the humble baked bean, Boston is
nicknamed "Beantown." However, more sophisticated
fare is available. Maine lobsters, quahogs (large clams),
chowders, and scrod (white fish) also feature.

Faneuil Hall Marketplace is one of the best places to eat
cheaply. Food stalls in Quincy Market offer take-outs in
various forms—calzones, Middle Eastern pastries,
seafood, specialty milkshakes, and swordfish kebabs—
but the market starts to close down after 9:30 PM.

Options for leisurely meals include restaurants in Beacon
Hill's Charles Street and in Newbury Street. Chinatown
has some excellent eating places: some of the best offer bargain prices with functional décor to match. The North End
can boast some of the highest-quality Italian food in the
Northeast, and although Bostonians as a rule tend to eat
early, it is often possible to stop by in the early hours for a
cappuccino or bowl of pasta. Bargain-priced food stands
are set up in the streets on Friday and Saturday, when you
can have your fill of pasta, fried calamari, and mussels. The
nearby Waterfront also has several popular restaurants.

Cambridge has so much happening in the evening that to
dine out there is part of the Boston experience. A branch of
Au Bon Pain, a Boston-born sandwich bar chain, occupies
one side of Harvard Square. Popular with chess players,
this area is a good point from which to watch Cambridge
life. Cambridge is strong on ethnic eateries, with
Portuguese fare along Cambridge and Hampshire streets
and a choice of Korean, Creole, and Indian restaurants.

Boston has some excellent beers: the Boston Brewery's
Samuel Adams ale and its variants is probably the best
known. Some pub-restaurants produce their own brew: the
Commonwealth Brewing Company, Cambridge Brewery,
and the Boston Beer Works.

Boston means different things to different people. To some it means simply the Red Sox. Add the Celtics, the Bruins, and the Boston Marathon and you begin to form a picture of a rich sporting tradition.

The Red Sox The ups and downs of Boston's baseball team are inextricably entwined in the fabric of Boston life. Strong men go misty-eyed at the mention of such legendary names as Babe Ruth, Jimmie Foxx, Carl Yastrzemski, Jim Lonborg, Ted Williams (the last major leaguer to bat over 400 for a season), Dick "The Monster" Radatz or Roger "The Rocket" Clemens (both of whom regularly pitched at over 90 miles per hour).

The atmosphere at Fenway Park is phenomenal, but to attend a college or local ballpark game, along with the mayor and the cheerleaders, is every bit as thrilling.

The Celtics, the Bruins Basketball was born at the YMCA in Springfield, Massachusetts, in December 1891. The invention of a physical education teacher, Dr. James Naismith, to keep his students out of mischief in the winter months, it is the most widely played sport founded in the U.S.A. Naismith originally used two half-bushel peach baskets as targets, hence the name of the game.

Boston is home to the Boston Celtics, who won 11 of 13 titles between 1956/7 and 1968/9, making them one of the most successful teams in the National Basketball Association. If you look into almost any Boston backyard, you'll find a group of young Celtics fans in the team's green and white colors emulating a Larry Bird jump shot. The Celtics share the FleetCenter (successor to the venerable Boston Garden; see page 68) with the Bruins, Boston's popular hockey team.

And more... Other great events in the Boston sporting calendar include the Boston Marathon, held in April. The first was held in 1897 with 15 runners; now over 9,000 take part. July sees the U.S. Pro Tennis Championship, and in October about 1,000 boats take part in a day of races in the Head of the Charles Regatta.

TICKET INFORMATION
● The Boston Red Sox, Fenway Park, 4 Yawkey Way (tel: 617/267 1700, fax: 617/236 6640). The season runs from April to early October. For tours, tel: 617/236 6666
● The Boston Celtics and Bruins, Fleet Center, 150 Causeway Street—by North Station (tel: 617/523 3030 for the Celtics and 617/931 2222 for the Bruins). Celtics' season runs from October to May, Bruins' from October to April.
● New England Patriots Football Club, Foxboro Stadium, Route 1, Foxboro (tel: 508/543 1776). The National Football League is in action from August to early January.

81

Fenway Park, much revered by Red Sox fans. It was rebuilt in the 1930s by the team's greatest benefactors, Tom Yawkey and his wife

Above left: the Friday and Saturday Haymarket—lively, and colorful

Above right: altogether quieter, a bookstore near Tremont Street

BARGAIN HUNTING

Outlet shopping in New England is booming. The main places are Kittery, North Conway, Freeport, Fall River and Worcester; the last two of these can easily be reached by bus from Boston (see pages 16–17). Whether or not these places offer the best prices is a matter of debate; some contend that the best bargains are to be had at sale time at such stores as Saks Fifth Avenue and Lord & Taylor in Boston.

MORE SHOPPING IDEAS

● Music: HMV, 1 Brattle Street, Cambridge; Tower Records, 360 Newbury Street.
● Secondhand books: Brattle Bookstore, 9 West Street, Cambridge.
● Antique maps: Eugene Galleries, 76 Charles Street.

Shopping

Back Bay and Beacon Hill If a competition were held to find New England's most chic shopping street, **Newbury Street** would be among the front runners. Running parallel to Commonwealth Avenue from the Public Garden through the fashionable district of Back Bay, the street has high-class designer shops, art galleries, and boutiques (including Déjà Vu, selling used designer-label clothing for women) and makes for highly enjoyable window-shopping; Tower Records, on the corner of Mass. Avenue, is the largest in the U.S. On Beacon Hill, Charles Street is known for antiques.

The Shops at Prudential Center is a large and smart complex, connected to the Hynes Convention Center, the Sheraton Boston Hotel and, by footbridge, the Copley Place shopping center and the Westin and Marriott hotels —all enclosed. The 75 Shops at the Pru include shops for men, women, and children such as Saks Fifth Avenue, Levi's, Chico's, Britches, Talbots Kids, and Warner Brothers. There are also shoe and sports shops, gift shops, and several restaurants, including Legal Seafoods. The 100-shop, two-level **Copley Place** is high-class; here you will find Gucci, Louis Vuitton, Tiffany, a Museum of Fine Arts shop, and others. There are restaurants and a cinema.

At 338 Boylston Street, the world's largest teddy bear marks the entrance to **FAO Schwarz**, the city's main toy store. Nearby, and also in Boylston Street, the Globe Corner Bookstore has a selection of New England books and maps.

Downtown Crossing Area There are over 300 retail stores around Summer and Washington streets, including the department stores of Macy's and Filene's; **Filene's Basement** is renowned for its bargain-price clothes. **Barnes and Noble** (395 Washington Street and 607 Boylston Street) is the city's largest discount bookseller.

Other Boston Highlights Chinatown is great for browsing, with markets, restaurants, gift shops and supermarkets, as well as Vietnamese, Thai and Cambodian stores. **Faneuil Hall Marketplace** is a top attraction, with 125 shops ranging from retailers such as the Disney Store to outlets for New England crafts and souvenir stalls. Its central hall, Quincy Market, offers a variety of places to eat, including Durgin's. By total contrast, the Haymarket is a no-frills fruit and vegetables market (Fridays and Saturdays only). Italian shops in the **North End** include some outstanding food stores and bakeries around Hanover and Salem streets.

The Boston Antique Center, with more than 100 dealers, is near Haymarket subway station at 54 Canal Street.

Good **museum shops** are found at the Children's Museum, Computer Museum, Museum of Fine Arts (also at Copley Place and Faneuil Hall Marketplace), Peabody Museum in Cambridge (with a wide range of ethnic wares), and the Museum of Science.

Cambridge Harvard Square has a concentration of bookstores offering new and secondhand volumes. **WordsWorth** offers a wide range of books at discount prices. Bookshops remain open all evening and Sundays, and you are welcome to browse for hours. There are also numerous music stores and boutiques. The Harvard Coop Society (known as the Coop) on the Square is the major department store, serving the town since 1882, and has book and music sections. There are more books for sale inside the MIT Coop at Kendall Square. From the square you can take the free shuttle service to the **CambridgeSide Galleria,** which comprises more than 100 shops and restaurants, including Sears department store. For antiques, try the four-story Cambridge Antique Market (201 Msgr. O'Brien Highway, Lechmere subway); for crafts, Cambridge Artists Coop, 59A Church Street. Porter Exchange, north of Harvard Square, has several specialty stores.

More Shopping Two good places for outdoor and hiking equipment are **Eastern Mountain Sports** at 1041 Commonwealth Avenue, Boston (also winter sports gear) and **Tent City** on 272 Friend Street near North Station.

Five miles west of Boston on Route 9, the Mall at **Chestnut Hill** is a feast for the eyes, with over 100 stores, including Bloomingdales and Filene's. Concerts take place here on weekends. Take the Green Line (D train for Riverside) to Chestnut Hill station.

Farther out of town, and accessible by commuter train, **Cape Ann, Marblehead, Ipswich, Essex**, and **Newburyport** each have art galleries and antiques shops.

83

Quincy Market, next to Faneuil Hall, dates back to the 1820s. Today, it is always an entertaining and lively place to be

BOSTON DINING PERSPECTIVES

Both the Prudential Tower and John Hancock Tower have stunning high-level views of the city by night. But the 52nd-floor Top of the Hub restaurant in the Prudential and the Bay Tower Room on the 33rd floor at 60 State Street allow diners to enjoy superb views at their leisure. Dinner cruises on the *Odyssey* from Rowes Wharf get a low-level but equally fascinating perspective on Boston.

84

Nightlife

There's a lot going on in Boston and Cambridge at night, although it is not an all-night city in the way New York is. The liveliest areas popular with visitors are Kenmore Square and Lansdowne Street (near Boston University), Harvard Square in Cambridge (by Harvard University), Copley Square and Boylston Place, and Faneuil Hall Marketplace. The Theatre District has some comedy clubs, and Roxy, an upscale nightclub. A little farther out, Davis Square in Somerville has some lively nightspots.

Listings and tickets Full listings, covering theater, concerts, cinema, bars, and clubs, appear in the *Boston Globe* on Thursdays, the *Boston Herald* on Fridays, *The Improper Bostonian* (biweekly; also includes restaurants), and Stuff@night, a guide to Boston's nightlife. The website www.Boston.com has details of all kinds of events. For bookings and half-price tickets on the day of performance, contact Ticketmaster (tel: 617/931-2000), or visit the BosTix ticket booth in Faneuil Hall Marketplace or Copley Square.

Theater The Theatre District, just south of Boston Common, has mainstream and avant-garde offerings. The Charles Playhouse in Warrenton Street is still showing the comedy whodunnit Shear Madness, America's longest-running play, in which the audience helps solve a murder mystery.

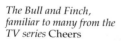

Bars and Clubs There are over 20 clubs offering billiards to slam-dancing in the Lansdowne Street/Kenmore Square area. Avalon is good for dancing, Mama Kin and Axis for rock and roll. Jillian's Boston offers pool, billiards, and virtual reality games, Bill's Bar is funky and relaxed. Gay venues abound in Kenmore Square, and in the South End. Sunday night tends to be gay night at many clubs; the Club Café (Columbus Avenue) is a club and bar open seven days a week.

The Bull and Finch, familiar to many from the TV series Cheers

The Charles Hotel's Regatta Bar provides a stylish ambience for an evening of jazz

Boylston Street has outdoor bars, such as the Cactus Club, which attract the younger set. Zanzibar is a club with a Caribbbean atmosphere, Bar 101 is small, cozy, and funky. In Somerville, Johnny D's in Davis Square has a welcoming crowd, good food, and great music. In Beacon Hill, the Bull & Finch pub, famed for its appearance in the TV series *Cheers*, is at 84 Beacon Street. Faneuil Hall Marketplace has plenty of piano bars, pubs, dance venues, and comedy clubs to choose from.

Those who enjoy comedy will find Dick Doherty's Comedy Vault, 124 Boylston Street, Nick's Comedy Stop in the Theatre District, and The Comedy Connection, at Faneuil Hall, are leading clubs of their kind.

Jazz and Blues the Regatta Bar in the Charles Hotel, 1 Bennett Street, Cambridge, is a top-class jazz venue, hosting an annual festival from January to April; don't miss the Sunday Gospel Group brunch. The House of Blues, 90 Winthrop Street, and Scullers, 400 Soldiers Field Road are favorites. Wally's, on Mass Avenue is also a major attraction. In Somerville the Willows Jazz Bar, Ball Square on Broadway, with its smoky intimate environment, is for serious jazz aficianados.

Classical and Light Music The BSO (Boston Symphony Orchestra) performs at Symphony Hall from the beginning of October to the end of April (tel: 617/266 2378). The New England Conservatory gives a series of free concerts from January to March, many in the glittering Jordan Hall, 290 Huntington Avenue (tel: 617/536 2412). The Boston Pops Orchestra performs light classics and popular favorites at Symphony Hall from May to July (see page 25), and in early July there is a series of free Boston Pops outdoor concerts at the Hatch Shell on the Esplanade (tel: 617/266 1492). From June to September, the "big name" Harborlights Festival is held in a 4,000-seat "tent" on the Waterfront.

Boston Lyric Opera, New England's leading opera company, stages productions at 114 State Street (tel: 617/ 248 8811). Ballet is performed at the Wang Center for the Performing Arts (tel: 617/695 6950), at 270 Tremont Street, and by Boston Ballet, at 19 Clarendon Street.

BOSTON: FIRST BUILDINGS IN U.S.A.
- First public school (Boston Latin School, 1636).
- U.S. post office (1639).
- Lighthouse (1765).
- Chocolate factory (1765).
- Branch Library (1871).
- Telephone Exchange (1877).

OTHER BOSTON U.S. FIRSTS
- Military training field (1631).
- First fire law (banning wooden chimneys, 1632).
- Law against smoking (1633).
- Football game (Boston Common, 1862).
- Computer (Differential Analyzer at MIT, 1928)

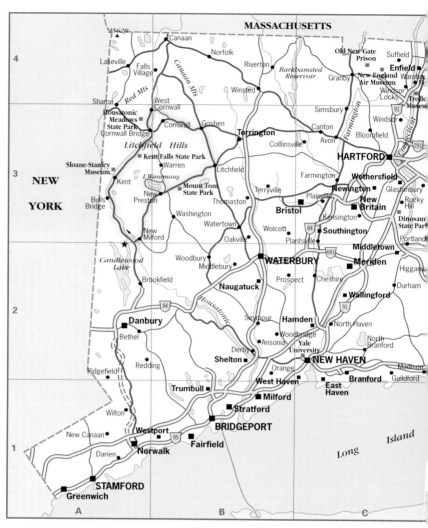

MASSACHUSETTS

NEW YORK

2562ft

Canaan
Norfolk
Lakeville
Falls Village
Riverton
Old New-Gate Prison
Suffield
Enfield
New England Air Museum
Wareho
Granby
Windsor Locks
Troll Museu
Canaan Mts
Winsted
Barkhamsted Reservoir
Red Mts
Sharon
West Cornwall
Simsbury
Housatonic Meadows State Park
Cornwall
Goshen
Canton
Avon
Bloomfield
Windsor
Cornwall Bridge
Torrington
Colllinsville
HARTFORD
Litchfield Hills
Kent Falls State Park
Warren
Litchfield
Farmington
Wethersfield
Sloane-Stanley Museum
L Waramaug
Terryville
Newington
Glastonbury
Kent
New Preston
Mount Tom State Park
Thomaston
Plainville
New Britain
Rocky Hill
Bulls Bridge
Washington
Watertown
Bristol
Kensington
Dinosaur State Par
New Milford
Oakville
Wolcott
Southington
Portland
Plantsville
Middletown
Candlewood Lake
Woodbury
WATERBURY
Meriden
Middlebury
Higganu
Brookfield
Prospect
Cheshire
Durham
Housatonic
Naugatuck
Wallingford
Danbury
Seymour
Hamden
North Haven
Bethel
Woodbridge
Ansonia
North Branford
Derby
Yale University
Redding
Ridgefield
Shelton
Orange
NEW HAVEN
Madison
Trumbull
West Haven
Branford
Guildford
Wilton
Milford
East Haven
New Canaan
Westport
Stratford
Norwalk
Fairfield
BRIDGEPORT
Darien
Long
Island
STAMFORD
Greenwich

A   B   C

4

3

2

1

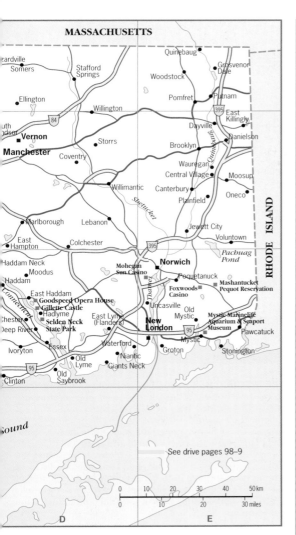

See drive pages 98–9

| 0 | 10 | 20 | 30 | 40 | 50 km |

| 0 | 10 | 20 | 30 miles |

CONNECTICUT Named after New England's longest river, Connecticut extends some 90 miles west–east and 55 miles north–south. The state's rolling terrain is bisected by the Connecticut River, which flows south along a fertile valley into Long Island Sound. The shoreline has sandy beaches and quiet coastal towns, as well as more urbanized parts close to New York City. The coastal hinterland is a gentle plain, which rises farther inland into forested uplands near the New York and Massachusetts borders. Connecticut is America's third smallest state (after Rhode Island and Delaware) and is densely populated. Yet the state has genuinely rural tracts that belie its proximity to the Big Apple. In all, two-thirds of Connecticut is rural, and most of that is forested.

Roseland Cottage in the quiet village of Woodstock

▶▶▶ REGION HIGHLIGHTS

Connecticut

The coastal strip looks out across Long Island Sound, where the Gulf Stream entices tropical underwater marine life

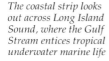

THE NUTMEG STATE
Legend has it that local traders cunningly passed off wooden nutmegs as real ones, hence Connecticut's nickname.

"Here's to the town of
  New Haven,
The home of the Truth and
  the Light,
Where God talks to Jones
  in the very same tones
That he uses with Hadley
  and Dwight."
– F.S. Jones, *On the Democracy of Yale.*

"Connecticut in her blue-laws, laying it down as a principle, that the laws of God should be the law of the land."
– Thomas Jefferson, letter to John Adams, January 24, 1814.

THE HISTORIC HERITAGE The Connecticut River brought in the first Puritan settlers in the 1630s after Boston and Massachusetts had become too religiously intolerant for their tastes. Hartford, Windsor, and Wethersfield were the original trio of towns they established, hence the three clusters of grapes on the state's coat of arms. These settlements merged to become the Hartford Colony, later named the Connecticut Colony. The Fundamental Orders of Connecticut, adopted in 1638, are widely held to have been the world's first written constitution of a democratic government—hence the state's official nickname, the Constitution State, on every vehicle license plate. Connecticut has also been named the "Nutmeg State"—its inhabitants being "Nutmeggers" (see sidebar)—and, during the Revolutionary War, the "Arsenal of the Nation." The state retains plenty of mementoes of those times.

Yankee ingenuity also made Connecticut the "Gadget State." This was the birthplace of the cylinder lock, the pay telephone, the steel fishhook, the stonecrusher, and the submarine torpedo. Samuel Colt's firearms company manufactured the famous .45 revolver and other guns in Hartford, while pioneer clockmakers Seth Thomas and Eli Terry had Thomaston and Terryville named after them. Eli Whitney devised interchangeable parts, which made him in effect the father of mass production. Charles Goodyear manufactured improved car tires, and the first American copper coins were minted here. Even today, despite a decline in industrial activity, the state leans heavily toward manufacturing, including the output of ball bearings, jet engines, nuclear submarines, and sewing machines. The state's oldest-established towns are found along the 253-mile shoreline and along the principal waterways, notably the Connecticut River. Early colonial days saw Yankee traders flourishing in shipbuilding, seafaring, and commercial ventures at Mystic, Stonington, New London, and elsewhere. The insurance industry that began in conjunction with this maritime activity gathered momentum. Today, insurance is still the state capital's *raison d'être*.

VISITOR ATTRACTIONS For the visitor, Connecticut's maritime heritage is an obvious attraction and is admirably presented in the great museums of Mystic and Norwalk. But other industrial ports bordering Long Island Sound in the state's southwestern territory have only patches of interest; one such oasis is Yale University, an architectural treasure house in New Haven. In the Hartford area, the former homes of Mark Twain, Noah Webster, and Harriet Beecher Stowe can be visited. Offbeat whimsicality can be found at Gillette Castle, in the Connecticut River Valley, while the Lockwood-Mathews Mansion in Norwalk, the most sumptuous house of its day, foreshadows the opulent "cottages" at Newport in Rhode Island. Fine art collections are found at Hartford, Yale University, New Britain, and in private houses such as the Hill-Stead Museum.

Elsewhere in the state, pristine white clapboard villages such as Litchfield, Wethersfield, Ridgefield, and Farmington await discovery, grouped around their characteristic village greens, each stubbornly refusing to concede to urbanization. By the Massachusetts border is the state's highest terrain and most scenic drive, along the fast-flowing Housatonic River in the Litchfield Hills, an area well endowed with arty crafts shops and galleries. The Connecticut and Housatonic rivers are both noted for fishing, the latter especially for trout, as well as for the more adventurous pursuits of tubing, canoeing, and kayaking. Near Litchfield, the White Memorial Foundation offers hiking, cross-country skiing, horseback riding and bird watching. Connecticut also has some gentler drives through landscapes dominated by cornfields, orchards, old barns and silos; one of the most scenic roads is Route 169 from Lisbon to Woodstock.

Several major locales exist for spectator sport. The Hartford Whalers is a major-league hockey team. The sport of jai alai can be seen inexpensively at Milford (the biggest jai alai arena in New England). Auto racing takes place at Lime Rock, and the Pilot Pen International Tennis Tournament is held at New Haven. The Canon Greater Hartford Open is an annual golf event.

89

Below: at Coventry, in the northeastern corner of the state, the Nathan Hale Homestead was built by the patriot's family in 1776, the year he was executed

Connecticut

Events

For further information, contact the state tourist office (see page 266) or chambers of commerce.

January–March
Warm Up to Winter, Farmington Valley area: history and good food at museums and period homes.

May
Dogwood Festival, Fairfield.
Lime Park Grand Prix, Lakeville.
Lobster Fest, Mystic: lobster served al fresco, on the waterfront.

June
A Taste of Hartford: food, comedy, music, and more.
Farmington Antiques Weekend.
Yale–Harvard Regatta, New London.
Canon Greater Hartford Open, Cromwell: attracting top names in golf.

June–July
Barnum Festival, Bridgeport: parade and festival to honor P.T. Barnum.

July
Antique and Classic Boat Rendezvous, Mystic Seaport.
Guilford Handicrafts Exposition, Guilford.
Historic Homes Tour, Litchfield: houses open their doors to the public.
Riverfest, Hartford/East Hartford: July 4 river festival.
Blessing of the Fleet, Stonington

August
Brooklyn Fair, agricultural fair.

Connecticut River Powwow, Durham: crafts, dancing, etc.
Great Connecticut Jazz Festival, Moodus.
Outdoor Art Festival, Mystic: the streets close to traffic as the artists take over.
Pilot Pen International Tennis Festival, New Haven: this is a major men's professional tournament at Yale University.
Quinnehtukqut Rendezvous and Native American Festival, Haddam Meadows State Park.

September
Durham Fair, Durham.
Oyster Festival, Norwalk: tall ships, arts, crafts, oysters.
Woodstock Fair, South Woodstock: agricultural show, animals, crafts.

September–October
Mum Festival, Bristol: parade, arts, crafts, drama.
Walking Weekend, guided walks; statewide.
Chowder fest, Mystic Seaport.

November
Thanksgiving Day Road Race, Manchester.

December
Christmas season, Mystic Seaport: Lantern Light Tours give a one-hour "interactive play."
First Night, Hartford: fireworks, procession, etc.

Mystic Seaport, venue for a variety of events and activities

Shelf clocks, the invention of Eli Terry, in the Clock and Watch Museum

EARLY CLOCKMAKING

Connecticut's clock-making industry, now all but defunct, originated in the late 18th century. In 1792, Eli Terry began making his name and money by mass-producing wooden cogs at his water-powered mill in Connecticut, by standard-izing gears and by intro-ducing interchangeable parts. Brass gears came in after 1800.

91

HILL-STEAD'S CREATOR

Theodate Pope (later Theodate Riddle) was pri-marily a self-trained archi-tect who gained much of her initial experience when she engaged the firm of McKim, Mead and White to build her parents Hill-Stead as a retirement home. She played a large part in influencing the vernacular New England farmstead design, which incorporated elements of Georgian and Greek Revival styles.

*Left: a carving in the Carousel Museum
Below: architecture from Bristol's 19th-century heyday*

▶ Bristol and Area 86C3

From the late 18th century until 1929, the neighboring towns of Bristol, Thomaston, Terryville, Winsted, and Waterbury played important roles as the center of America's clock industry. Aptly, Bristol is home today of the **American Clock and Watch Museum▶▶** in an elegant post-Revolutionary mansion at 100 Maple Street off Route 72 (*Open* Apr–Nov). The collection is eclectic, charting the history of American horology. In all, the museum has 1,600 watches and 1,800 clocks. Look for the re-created 1825 clockmaker's shop and an 1860 novelty clock from New York featuring a lion's eyes moving in time to the tick. At 95 Riverside Avenue (Route 72), the **New England Carousel Museum▶** has over 300 antique carved horses and carousel chariots.

On Route 6, opposite the church at **Terryville**, stands the **Lock Museum▶**, close to the former Eagle Lock mills, which opened in 1854, some 20 years after the lock industry began in Connecticut. The display features around 20,000 items, from a 1580s Spanish Armada chest to a 1920s lock-demonstrating machine used at trade shows.

East of Bristol, **Farmington▶** has numerous Federal-style houses and has become a select satellite of Hartford. It was a key point on the underground rail-road as well as the village where the freed *Amistad* slaves awaited return to Africa (see sidebar, page 105). In the village, the **Stanley-Whitman House** has been painstakingly restored to its 1720 colonial appearance and contains period furnishings. The house has diamond-pane leaded windows and an overhanging upper story. The nearby **Hill-Stead Museum▶▶**, a turn-of-the-century colonial revival home, exemplifies good taste. It belonged to industrialist Alfred Pope (see side-bar). The family adorned the interior with French Impressionist paintings, including two of Monet's *Haystack* series and *The Absinthe Drinker* and *The Guitar Player* by Manet (*Open* year round except Mon).

GENEALOGY AT MIDDLETOWN

Middletown was settled in 1650 and prospered in the late 18th century, as ship-building and trade with the West Indies made it the richest community in the colony. The town attracts genealogists on the trail of British and European ancestors, many of whom settled here. The Godfrey Library is the chief source of information and has records for the whole U.S. before the 1850s.

The eccentric exterior of Gillette Castle befits the reclusive actor for whom it was built

► **Connecticut River Valley**   *87D2*

After its 410-mile journey along the New Hampshire–Vermont border and through Massachusetts, the Connecticut River finally crosses Connecticut itself before flowing into Long Island Sound. The Connecticut scenery along New England's longest river is pleasantly mild rather than spectacular, but a scattering of good sights, mostly in the county of Middlesex (at the southern end of the river's course), makes it worth taking in. Antiques shops, art shows, country fairs, concerts, and festivals are plentiful along the entire valley.

South of Hartford At the mouth of the river is **Old Saybrook**, the earliest settlement in the valley; nearby Essex is home to the **Connecticut River Museum**, pleasantly sited by the river. Though not extensive, the museum's displays illustrate shipbuilding and maritime life in the context of the Connecticut River Valley. On show is a replica of the *American Turtle*, the first submarine, a claustrophobic-looking one-man vessel invented to sink British ships in the Revolution.

At Essex, the **Valley Railroad**▶ ▶, one of only two steam railroads in New England (the other is at North Conway, NH), operates 1½-hour round trips to Chester and Haddam. Period carriages make it a nostalgic treat: original 1920s furnishings include padded armchairs in Pullman class and cane seats in standard. An optional extra is to stop off at Deep River for a connecting boat trip upriver to East Haddam. The **Ivoryton Playhouse** provides entertainment at nearby Ivoryton, where there is a **Fife and Drum Museum**, open on summer weekends.

Gillette Castle▶ ▶, high above the river, south of East Haddam, is a fantasy re-creation of Rhenish medievalism, or something approaching that style. It was built in 1914–19 for actor William Gillette, who was famous for his Sherlock Holmes performances, but, despite public prominence, was something of a recluse. A system of mirrors was placed so that he could watch from his bedroom for unwelcome visitors and decide whether to be indisposed, and his dinner table was almost comically small. His passion for railroads led to the creation of a 3-mile railroad (no longer existing, although one carriage is preserved) on the grounds. The castle's idiosyncrasies reveal themselves inside, its 24 rooms displaying wooden light switches, Javanese matting, walls made of field stones, light fixtures made with pieces of bottle glass, and bizarre lock systems.

Horse and carriage rides are provided daily in summer at the castle and on weekends during most of the rest of the year. A scenic approach to the castle is on the **Chester–Hadlyme ferry** (Apr–Dec). There has been a ferry here since 1769, making it one of the oldest such continuous services in the country. It is feasible to leave the car on the far side, cross the river as a foot passenger, and walk up a path to the castle. **Selden Neck State Park**, devoid of facilities and accessible only by boat, is an ideal tonic for escapists who like to rough it. Canoe rental is available from below Gillette Castle.

At Middlefield, **Lyman Orchards** has been a family farm since 1741; its Apple Barrel Farm Store stocks a wide selection of local produce.

Chester▶ is a village graced with an unblemished main street. Close by is the delightful **Goodspeed Opera House** (tours available; tel: 860/873 8668), with musicals usually

Passengers on the Valley Railroad's early 20th-century steam train enjoy views of the Connecticut River and Valley

NEW ENGLAND'S LONGEST RIVER
Named by Algonquin people as the Quinnetukut ("the long river whose waters are driven by wind and tide"), the 397-mile-long Connecticut River flows from its source near the New Hampshire–Canada border through four states and is tidal from Hartford.

First charted by Dutchman Adriaen Block in 1614, the valley was, by the 19th century, an important cigar tobacco-growing area. But, as in much of New England, forest has taken over Essex, which once had six shipyards, and other communities grew as river settlements. Shipbuilding, however, never recovered from a flood in 1936 and a hurricane two years later.

CRUISES

Deep River Navigation (tel: 860/767 0103 or 860/526 4954) offers trips from Old Saybrook and Hartford, in Long Island Sound, and hour-long river voyages aboard the steamer *Becky Thatcher*. Camelot Cruises (tel: 860/345 8591) runs a sailing murder mystery cruise. *Sea Mist II* (tel: 203/488 8905), at Stony Creek, makes 45-minute trips around some of the 365 Thimble Islands; Money Island is where the pirate Captain Kidd reputedly used to draw in his boat.

AIR MUSEUM HIGHLIGHTS

Despite losing 23 vintage aircraft in a freak tornado in 1979, the New England Air Museum boasts a number of choice exhibits, including:

● 1911 Ernest Hall No. 1 Blériot: the same design of craft as that flown by pioneer aviator Louis Blériot when he made the first crossing from England to France in 1909.

● 1934 Marcoux-Bromberg Special: an R-3 racer which won a 150-mile contest in California in 1938 achieving an average speed of 265mph. It featured in the Clark Gable movie Test Pilot.

running for six or seven weeks and audience participation on Wednesdays. You can arrive for a performance by boat, picnic on the lawn, and have drinks at the intermission on a balcony overlooking the river. A tiny one-room schoolhouse at **East Haddam** was where patriot Nathan Hale taught in 1773–74 and is open on weekend afternoons for a nominal fee. Its bell was made in Spain in AD 815 and is still in working order.

At Higganum, the **Sundial Herb Garden** is a compact but prettily contrived knot garden and topiary in 17th-century style, with miniature vistas opening up through its "outdoor rooms." It was created over a period of 20 years by an Irish and German couple who offered specialty teas (with English-style scones and clotted cream) and also stocked a shop with a worldwide selection of herbs and spices.

Dinosaur State Park, on Route 91 at Rocky Hill (closed Monday), has in its exhibition hall some 500 dinosaur footprints in what was a shallow, stagnant lake 185 million years ago. Life-size models, a diorama, and a commentary flesh out the details of their history, and there is a discovery room for children. If you bring your own plaster of Paris, you can make casts of actual dinosaur prints. The impressions were uncovered in 1966 during renovations.

For Hartford, see pages 95–97.

North of Hartford On Route 140 at **East Windsor**, the **Trolley Museum** dates from 1940. Volunteers run the trolleys along a 1½-mile section of the former Hartford–Springfield Street Railroad and have rescued old trolleys from other places: one was found in a scout camp being used as a laundromat. On Route 75 situated close to Bradley Airport, the **New England Air Museum▶** exhibits over 70 military and civil airplanes, from early biplanes to experimental fighters and modern home-built machines.

Old New-Gate Prison (*Open* May–Oct, Wed–Sun), off Route 20 in East Granby, retains its castle-like walls. The

Cruising on the Connecticut River near East Haddam

overgrown sandstone ruins have atmosphere, and children will enjoy exploring the mine. The prison dates from 1773, when it was built to provide laborers to work on the copper mine. This became the first state prison in the U.S. in 1776, and British loyalists were jailed here during the Revolution. The opportunities this presented, with shafts providing convenient exits and the availability of gunpowder, proved irresistible, and a mass escape by British prisoners of war and Tories occurred in 1781. The prison was abandoned in 1827.

▶ Foxwoods   87E2

Foxwoods Casino, on the Mashantucket Pequot Indian reservation, has become very big business (see page 125)—the largest casino in the U.S. and a huge crowd-puller. It may not be everyone's idea of heaven, but the place is so bathed in commercialism as to be an experience in itself. Financed by some of the bucks cascading into the thousands of gambling machines, the **Mashantucket Pequot Museum and Research Center▶▶▶** is on an impressive scale, featuring a re-creation of a Pequot village, a diorama depicting a caribou hunt scene, a re-created 1780 Pequot farmstead and site tours of the excavation of a 17th-century fort. Other attractions on site include the **Cinedrome 360° Theater**, the **Turbo Ride and Virtual Adventures**. Nearby on Route 2A at Uncasville, **Mohegan Sun** is another casino, a vast tentlike structure based on an Indian longhouse design.

▶▶ Hartford   86C3

America's insurance industry capital stands on the Connecticut River. Downtown is dominated by high-rise office buildings (many belonging to insurance companies), the second tallest of which is the 527-foot **Travelers Tower▶▶**, offering a 37-mile view (tours by appointment, May–October; there are 72 steps; tel: 860/277 0111).

Virtually next door, at 600 Main Street, the Gothic Revival **Wadsworth Atheneum▶▶▶** (Open daily except Mon; free Sat morning and Thu) was, in 1842, the first public art museum in the U.S. (see sidebar). The original castle has been extended to form an architectural blend of five interconnecting buildings.

95

Above left: a "starburst" quilt in the Wadsworth Atheneum textile collection
Below left: local schoolmaster and patriot Nathan Hale

CARILLON CONCERTS

Trinity College, a liberal, prestigious institution in Hartford, has a fine chapel modeled on the English Perpendicular (late Gothic) style and a Romanesque crypt. Carillon concerts are sometimes given.

INSURANCE

Hartford's insurance industry began in the 18th century to cover ship owners against loss of vessels. After the decline of shipping in the area, fire insurance grew in importance in the 19th century. Today, about 40 companies, including Aetna, Travelers, and CIGNA, are based here.

Hartford's State Capitol: its exuberant design reflects Victorian pride

Bushnell Park, the nation's first landscaped public space, cuts a green expanse across the center of the city and counts exotic rarities among its fine trees as well as a preserved carousel dating from 1914; a 1925 Wurlitzer organ provides the music. A grandiose brownstone structure known as the **Soldiers and Sailors Memorial Arch** (1886) honors citizens who served in the Civil War; its terra-cotta frieze depicts war scenes. In the park rises the gold-domed **State Capitol▶**, built in 1878 to the design of Richard Upjohn and adorned externally with bas-reliefs of historic scenes. Its lavishly ornate legislative chambers, Hall of Flags, and gaudy silver and gold marble hall are grand gestures of civic pride. There are free tours (Mon–Fri, 9:15–1:15, Sep–Jun; 9:15– 2:15, Jul–Aug; also Sat, 10:15–2:15, Apr–Oct), or you can just walk around by yourself. Since 1988, the Capitol has been connected by walk-way to the new Legislative Office, an impressive addition in polished granite.

At 800 Main Street is the **Old State House▶** (*Open Mon–Sat. Admission* free), which was designed by Charles Bulfinch and served as the state capitol from 1796 to 1878, and then as the city hall up to 1915. Today, it contains exhibitions of early Connecticut and Native American life and a visitor information center. State memorabilia and a collection of Colt firearms, are displayed at the **Museum of Connecticut History** at 231 Capitol Avenue (*Open Mon–Fri. Admission* free).

West of downtown, at 351 Farmington Avenue, is the red-brick Gothic **Mark Twain House▶ ▶ ▶**(reached by bus E from the central transit station in Hartford).

Samuel Clemens, alias Mark Twain (see page 46), stipulated that his 19-room house should be unique. His personality still pervades what a local newspaper in 1874 described as "the oddest house in Connecticut if not in the whole of America." Here he wrote *Huckleberry Finn*, *Tom Sawyer*, and five other major works up to 1891. Many of the original family pieces survive, including the items ranged on a mantelpiece, about which he used to tell stories to entertain his children. Each of these items had to feature in his story, and he had to start over again if he missed anything (*Open daily, Memorial Day–Oct 15, and Dec; rest of the year daily, except Tue*).

Immediately adjacent is the **Harriet Beecher Stowe House▶**, the home of the author of *Uncle Tom's Cabin* (see pages 46–47) from 1873 to her death in 1896, though most items here are not original. Harriet Beecher moved here while the Twain house was being built; at that time the neighborhood was known as Nook Farm and comprised a small literary colony (*Open daily, except Mon in winter*).

At 950 Trout Brook Drive, **West Hartford**, is the **Science Museum of Connecticut**, which has animal and planetarium shows and hands-on exhibits. At 227 South Main Street, the **Noah Webster House▶**, the birthplace of the author of *An American Dictionary of the English Language* and *The American Speller*, has absorbing Webster memorabilia (*Open daily in summer, except Wed; other seasons, afternoons only*). On the north side of the city, at 200 Bloomfield Avenue at the University of Hartford, the **Museum of American Political Life▶** (*Open daily except Mon*) charts political campaigns, women's rights, and prohibition movements from the time of George Washington.

Off I-91 at exit 26, the town of **Wethersfield▶▶**, settled in 1634, is one of the earliest settlements in the state. Its charming historic district, the state's largest, includes several early 18th-century sea captains' homes set along Broad Street, a huge, long green with houses set back. The **Webb-Deane-Stevens Museum▶**, on Main Street (*Open May–Oct, Wed–Mon; weekends only in winter*), comprises three well-restored houses. At the Webb House, General George Washington and the Comte de Rochambeau planned the final campaign in the Revolution, leading to the British defeat at Yorktown in 1781. More period charm and a fascinating early kitchen are found in the historic **Buttolph-Williams House** built in 1692, on Broad Street (*Open Wed–Mon*). The **Keeney Memorial Cultural Center** has good information and changing exhibitions on local history. Main Street ends at **Cove Park**, where one 17th-century warehouse survives from the days when the town of Wethersfield was a port on the Connecticut, before the river changed course.

Mark Twain's house, in the Nook Farm district of Hartford

THE CHARTER OAK
A royal charter of 1662 gave a measure of independence to the Hartford colony; but in 1687 the new royal governor insisted it should be returned. At the meeting held to discuss the matter, the candles were suddenly extinguished and the charter vanished. It remained hidden (reputedly) in an oak tree for two years until the governor returned to England. In the 19th century, Hartford's famous Charter Oak, as it had come to be known, was felled. Numerous items are said to be made from it, including the chair of the lieutenant-governor in the State Capitol.

Drive

Early autumn in the Litchfield Hills

Wed–Sun) exhibits bygone country tools collected by the late Eric Sloane. He considered these objects as "symbols of American heritage, worthy of at least the same recognition as the popular current sculpture made from American junk." He himself was a landscape painter and his studio has been re-created. Remains of an iron furnace in the grounds recall a vanished local industry. **Kent Falls State Park** is a roadside picnic stopoff, with swimming pools where water tumbles down a 200-foot flight of natural steps. **Housatonic Meadow State Park** has picnic benches with a riverside setting and is popular with anglers. Just north, a sign on the west side of the road marks the start of the Pine Knob Loop Trail, leading up to a summit with a fine view. At **West Cornwall**, cross the covered bridge over the Housatonic River on the right.

Take Route 128 east to **Goshen**, then Route 63 to **Litchfield ▶ ▶**, the first National Historic District declared in the state and widely regarded as one of the finest towns in New England. In its heyday, it was an industrial center, with grist- and sawmills, iron forges, tanneries, fulling mills, carriage makers and clockmakers, and hatters' shops. During the Revolution, it became a depot for military stores on roads linking Connecticut with the Hudson River Valley. The obvious legacy of the past is the wealth of Federal-style architecture along North, West, South, and East streets, which radiate from

The Litchfield Hills

See map on pages 86–87 (yellow route).

A 64-mile tour of the highlands of Connecticut, taking in the best of the Housatonic Valley and the picture-postcard town of Litchfield. The autumn colors are superb.

Start from **New Milford**, with its attractive green. Take Route 7 north past **Bulls Bridge**, which boasts one of only two covered bridges in the state still open to motor traffic (off Route 7 to the left). The scenery becomes increasingly unspoiled and rugged along the **Housatonic Valley ▶ ▶**, although foliage restricts views. The valley is known for trout-fishing and canoeing.

At **Kent**, there are more antiques and crafts shops, and the **Sloane-Stanley Museum ▶** (*Open* May–Oct,

A good place for an overnight stop is in this inn at Torrington

the town's prominent and much-photographed Congregational Church (1829) on the spacious green.

In the middle of town is the **Litchfield Historical Society▶**, which maintains an archive library and a museum. By a genealogical fluke, the society inherited the world's largest collection of pictures by Ralph Earl, who was an eminent portrait painter in the U.S.A. in the 18th century. The collection contains examples of Litchfield County furniture from the days when the area was a major craft producing center. Close by, the **Tapping Reeve House** of 1774 (*Open*

May–Oct, Tue–Sun) belonged to Judge Tapping Reeve, who in 1784 built America's first law college—a primitive, single-room, unheated structure—in the grounds. A small exhibition commemorates its history and graduates, who included vice-presidents Aaron Burr and John C. Calhoun.

Route 202 west passes the entrance to **Mount Tom State Park▶**, where a 1-mile trail leads to a tower at the 1,325-foot summit and a pleasant local view. At the junction with Route 45, go northwest a short distance to take in **Lake Waramaug▶**, idyllically set beneath hills and offering boating, swimming, picnics, and camping; the far end of the lake has a tiny beach. Close by the lake is **Hopkins Vineyard**, which provides free tours and tastings.

Route 202 takes you back to New Milford. An optional detour is via Route 47 to the **Institute for American Indian Studies▶** at Washington. It has Algonquin arts and artifacts from up to 10,000 years ago. Highlights include a longhouse, a 17th-century Native American village, and a simulated archeological site.

99

Litchfield, a perfect New England town

If there is one image that first-time visitors to New England bring with them, it is of white clapboard houses grouped around a village green, overlooked by the tall, white spire of a wooden church and set in rolling countryside against a backdrop of flaming, autumnal trees.

A CHANGING FACE
The New England village did not always present the face that is so cherished today. What is now a neat, attractive green, with its bandstand and war memorial, was once an unsightly, scrubby piece of common land. The clapboard house was not always archetypal white; until idealization set in during the 19th century, houses were painted in a range of colors: reds, russets, and blues. Even that icon, the tall, white church spire, has not always been there—many were added in the 19th century.

FARM BUILDINGS
While houses within the village itself are nowadays most often white, old wooden farm buildings are traditionally a deep red in color. Particularly in the colder areas of New Hampshire and Maine, farm buildings are connected, so the farmer can go from barn to shed to kitchen to house protected from the weather. (This also means, however, as many have learned to their cost, that fire, too, can move swiftly from barn to shed to house.)

100

The truth is that the New England village lives up to every expectation, serene as any calendar picture. The ingredients are always much the same. Facing onto a green is the white timber church, most often Unitarian or Congregationalist. Then there is the country store, a treasure chest that every visitor must delve into, selling anything from freshly made doughnuts and gourmet local products to cans of kerosene and farmers' rubber boots.

Larger villages often have a number of other, individually owned and equally enticing stores, selling clothes, gifts, books, or crafts. Then there will be the town hall, seat of local government. And filling in the gaps around the green, and lining the roads leading to it are the timber-built houses that typify New England, usually painted white but occasionally traditional dusky shades. Some may fly the flag, many have a seasonal wreath of dried flowers on the door. One or two of these houses may be inns that offer accommodations and meals. Often dating back to colonial days and furnished with antiques, inns are a delightful way to enjoy the charm and hospitality of a New England village. Every village also has its burial ground, a plot of land set apart from the church or meeting house.

The village way of life Because the houses are of timber, the local fire department is often a focus of social life, organizing parades and, along with the churches, events such as barbecues and ice-cream socials. The green is a setting for regular flea markets and, during the Christmas season, for the tree that, like others, is decorated with white lights. Some villages boast a theater.

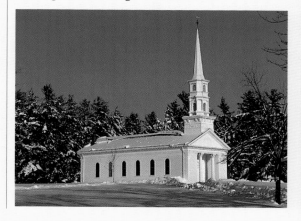

Village scenes: (top) autumn in Cohasset, MA, and (right) winter in Sudbury, MA

▶▶▶ Mystic

Mystic Seaport▶▶▶ is placed by the Mystic River, where numerous boat and ship yards flourished before decline set in during the 1880s. The museum features an admirable re-creation of life in a late 19th-century coastal community with period buildings that include a drug store, sailor's tavern and printing press. Over 400 small craft make up the largest such collection in the world, while among the larger ships that you can board are the *Charles W. Morgan* (1841), the last surviving American wooden whaler. A replica of *Amistad*, the notorious slave ship (see panel, page 105) is being built for the year 2000 using traditional techniques and authentic materials. Indoor exhibits include superb displays of scrimshaw and figureheads.

Mystic Marinelife Aquarium▶▶▶ is one of New England's largest. Much emphasis is placed on state-of-the-art viewing: in addition to the spectacular marine life displays—which include the world's largest artificial beluga whale habitat—you can take a simulated dive to the bottom of the ocean and experience the sounds as you descend. The Jason project (to open by 2000) will allow visitors to watch broadcasts of underwater journeys through kelp forests, deep water canyons and coral reefs—and even to see the resting-places of the *Titanic*, *Bismark* and other shipwrecks. There are seal, eagle and whale-watching cruises in season (tel: 860/572 5955). Ocean samples are studied in Project Oceanology at Groton (see page 107). The town of Mystic has a row of captains' houses standing by the waterfront and a drawbridge (raised hourly, Apr–Oct), and a specialty shopping area called **Olde Mistick Village**, replicated to look like the original colonial settlement. More delightful shoreside architecture awaits at **Noank**, a lobstering and oystering village, with views of Fisher's Island (N.Y.); Abbott's, something of a Connecticut institution, sells ocean-fresh lobsters straight from the boat.

The **Denison Homestead** on Pequotsepos Road has been restored in the styles of five eras, from colonial times to the 20th century (*Open* Memorial Day weekend to Columbus Day weekend, Thu–Sun 1–5).

Masted sailing vessels moored on the Mystic River

STONINGTON'S SURVIVALS
Stonington, Mystic's coastal neighbor, also has several charming 18th- and 19th-century homes recalling the maritime heyday. Settled in the mid 17th-century, it became a whaling, sealing and shipbuilding community.

MYSTIC CRUISES
Educational cruises, with a naturalist on board, can be taken on the windjammer *Argia* (tel: 860/536 0416). You can cruise on the SS *Sabino*, the last operating coal-fired steamer in the U.S., or try the *Resolute*, a 1917 motor launch. Or sail the *Breck Marshall*, a catboat (tel: 860/572 0711).

Life in a 19th-century seaport reenacted at Mystic Seaport

HISTORIC HAMBURGERS

Not many fast-food establishments get onto the National Register of Historic Places. However, family-run Louis' Hamburgers in Crown Street, New Haven, made it by dint of being the birthplace of the American hamburger in 1900. Louis' retains its original grilling equipment. This is puritanical cuisine: toast, burger, lettuce and tomato only—strictly no ketchup or mustard. The turn-of-the-century furnishings and Tiffany lamps are a far cry from McDonald's, too.

▶▶▶ New Haven   86C2

Although it would take courage to rate the relative academic standards of Yale University at New Haven and Harvard University at Cambridge, Yale by far outstrips Harvard for visual interest for the day visitor. Eye-catching imitations of the medieval universities of Oxford and Cambridge in England are Yale's architectural hallmark. However, Yale and New Haven have little of the student–town interaction found between Harvard and Cambridge.

Founded in 1638 by the Puritans as an independent colony, New Haven is today a major cargo port, with a profusion of galleries, upscale shops, and good restaurants along Chapel Street.

Museums Natural history displays make up the bulk of the **Peabody Museum**▶▶ (*Open* daily). Most popular is the dinosaur collection, including the first discovered specimens of *Brontosaurus* and *Stegosaurus*. The *Deinonychus*, or "Terrible Claw," inspired the vicious Raptor in the movie *Jurassic Park*. In the Hall of Mammals, an 11,000-year-old ground sloth (found in a tar pit in New Mexico) is remarkable for still having part of its skin and hair attached. Elsewhere, the museum displays Egyptian and Polynesian artifacts, geology exhibits, natural history dioramas, and birds, and has a discovery room for children.

At 1080 Chapel Street, the **Yale Center for British Art**▶ ▶ (*Open* Tue–Sun. *Admission* free) has a magnificent collection of works by Turner, Hogarth, Constable, Reynolds, and others, and puts on special exhibitions, talks, and films (for details, tel: 203/432 2800). Less well known is the **Yale Collection of Musical Instruments**▶, at 15 Hillhouse Avenue, where 800 instruments include antique keyboards and entertaining oddities such as a 19th-century Italian-made Russian horn with a representation of a snake's head whose tongue vibrates when it is played (*Open* Tue, Wed, and Thu 1–4; closed Jul and Aug). The Yale University Art Gallery▶ ▶ at 1,111 Chapel Street (*Open* daily except Mon, Sep to Jul), founded in 1832, has especially fine sections devoted to European paintings, a reconstructed Mithraic shrine, and a representative collection of American paintings and decorative arts.

*Above left and below:
Yale University is an
architectural showpiece,
with buildings by leading
20th-century architects
rubbing shoulders with
Gothic Revival and
Georgian creations*

The University Tours of *Yale University*▶ ▶ ▶ from 149 Elm Street are provided free by students at 10:30 AM and 2 PM on weekdays; 1:30 PM on weekends.

The university was founded at Branford in 1701, moved to Old Saybrook the same year, and then to New Haven in 1716. Yale is the only collegiate university in the U.S.A., with students attached to the 12 colleges that belong to the university; the system is modeled on Oxford and Cambridge universities in England. Some 300 students live in each college, plus 100 freshmen on Old Campus.

In the present century, the architect James Gamble Rogers gave Yale an "Oxbridge" look with his Georgian and Gothic-style buildings. To age the buildings, tiles were buried under different soils so that they would discolor and their edges become chipped. Acid was poured on the stonework, and glass was deliberately broken and releaded. Niches were left empty, as at Oxford and Cambridge, where so many statues have been stolen or otherwise destroyed through the ages.

The Green dates from colonial days when Puritan settlers laid out the town in neat squares, including this grazing ground. On one side, Phelps Gate leads into the **Old Campus**, where **Connecticut Hall**, built in the 1750s, is the oldest university building. The patriot Nathan Hale, industrialist Eli Whitney, and lexicographer Noah Webster were students here. Hale's statue was made in 1914 by a sculptor who had no idea of his subject's appearance, so a handsome Yale student was used as a model. The Theodore Dwight Woolsey statue is the only true likeness in the courtyard; his right foot is polished by students who rub it for good luck.

WHERE THE SHOWS BEGAN
From 1938 to 1976, New Haven's Shubert Theater was the favorite spot to première new productions before transferring to Broadway. Début shows and plays have included *Oklahoma!*, *My Fair Lady*, *Blithe Spirit*, *The Sound of Music*, *A Streetcar Named Desire*, *Long Day's Journey into Night*, and *Annie Get Your Gun*. W.C. Fields, the Marx Brothers, Sarah Bernhardt, and Marlon Brando have all graced its stage. The theater reopened in 1983 and gives performances between October and May. Tours are given Sep–Jun, Mon–Fri (tel: 203/624 1825).

Above: home of the Yale Repertory Company
Right: Harkness Tower, a High Street landmark

SPORTING SPECTACULARS

Football in autumn at the Yale Bowl has been a major feature of New Haven life since 1913. Once every two years, Yale and Harvard, the two old Ivy League rivals, battle it out in "The Game." Tennis superstars compete each August at the Pilot Pen International Tennis Tournament. At Milford, jai alai, a Basque sport similar to squash, takes place daily (matinees Sat–Mon; evenings Mon, Wed–Sat) from June to December. Although it is watched mainly for gambling, it is exciting, and the entrance fee is nominal.

Beyond the Old Campus is the neo-Gothic **Harkness Tower** (1920), the country's tallest free-standing tower when built (221 feet) and modeled on Boston Stump in Lincolnshire, England. Around its clock are sculptures of the eight great men of Yale: Nathan Hale, Eli Yale, Jonathan Edwards, Samuel F.B. Morse, Noah Webster, Eli Whitney, James Fenimore Cooper, and John C. Calhoun. **Wrexham Tower** was modeled on St. Giles Church, Wrexham, Wales (where Eli Yale is buried), while **Pierson College**'s tower is based upon the design of Philadelphia's Independence Hall. **Davenport**, ex-President Bush's college, displays the ubiquitous Gothic treatment on the street façade, but its courtyard is in a very different Georgian style.

The art-deco **Hall of Graduate Studies** (1932) resembles a miniature New York skyscraper with its checkered motif and flat relief. President and Hillary Clinton attended the **Law School**, opposite, whose stonework displays carvings of cops and robbers. Part of the building was inspired by King's College, Cambridge, England. The **Sterling Memorial Library**, known as the "Cathedral of Knowledge," looks intentionally like a medieval European cathedral, with cloisters decorated with stone carvings (one showing a student with a book of nude pictures and a glass of ale) and telephones masquerading as confessionals; the "altar" is the main desk. There is also a mural depicting a Mary Magdalene-like figure of Mother Yale holding the Book of Truth, with an orb of light. To the right are three men representing Art, Literature, and Philosophy (then, as now, these are the principal subjects studied at the university).

Woolsey Hall, a large circular building, holds regular concerts by student and visiting musicians. In the courtyard beyond is the **Beinecke Rare Book and Manuscript Library**, perhaps the most memorable of the university's modern buildings. The library's ingenuity

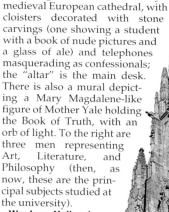

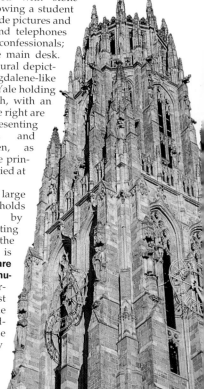

is revealed inside: the outer shell of Vermont marble shields a skyscraper-like stack of priceless books and manuscripts from the sun's ultra-violet rays, while halon gas is used to protect the contents from fire. The library is best seen on a sunny day when the translucence of the marble is apparent. There is no admittance to the stacks

themselves, but a complete Gutenberg Bible of 1455, one of only 22 known, is displayed in the public area. Outside, you look down into the **Sculpture Garden**, a compact landscape of geometrical shapes formed in white marble by Isamu Noguchi (the library desk has a leaflet outlining the artist's ideas).

A windowless building close by is home to secret university societies, such as George Bush's Skull and Bones Society. Note how the **President's Office** is purposefully smaller than the other buildings: administration is seen as less important than academic life. In **Berkeley College**, Cross Campus Lawn is reputed to be the birthplace of the game of frisbee, first played here by students using pie plates, which evidently had aerodynamic qualities.

Out of town At Ansonia is **General David Humphreys House**, home of the aide to General Washington and the first U.S. ambassador (*Open* Mon–Fri. *Admission* free). It is a museum with a difference, presented as a hands-on, late 18th-century experience, in which visitors dress up, spin wool, cook, and make bread and chowder in the manner of the period.

The **Eli Whitney Museum** at 915 Whitney Avenue (*Open* Wed–Sun), Hamden, pays tribute to the inventor of mass production and charts 200 years of industrial development in the New Haven area. Over 100 restored trolleys can be found at the **Shore Line Trolley Museum** at 17 River Street, East Haven, from where you can take a 3-mile trolley ride.

Northwest on Route 69 is **Shepherd's Farm**, a dairy farm whose Jersey herd provides the raw material for a celebrated ice cream made on the premises. Farther on, a sign on the left leads to the **Whitlock Book Barn** (*Open* Tue–Sun), which has countless used and antiquarian tomes, maps, and prints crammed into two old turkey-brooder houses.

105

Take a trolley ride at the Shore Line Trolley Museum, East Haven

NEW HAVEN'S STRONGHOLD
On July 5, 1779, 3,000 British and German Hessian troops were sighted in Long Island Sound. They succeeded in capturing the important port town of New Haven, but only after astonishing resistance from just 19 patriots ensconced at Black Rock Fort on the east side of the harbor. This fortification was rebuilt as Fort Nathan Hale and served in the War of 1812. It has since been restored and is open from Memorial Day weekend to Labor Day, free of charge.

Connecticut

A DRAMATIC TRAINING CENTER

The Eugene O'Neill Theater Center at Waterford has been the training ground for hundreds of American actors; Meryl Streep and Al Pacino have been among them. Here, during the Playwright's Conference in July (drama) and August (musicals), you can watch new works in various stages of production. Performances are inexpensive, and the producer may substantially vary the presentation from one day to the next. You can listen in on rehearsals for free. (*Open* daily except Sundays; at other times of the year, you can see students rehearse and perform.)

▶ **New London**   *87E2*

The seafaring town of New London has a mixture of gracious houses with lawns sloping to the water's edge and a brick-built port area. A number of the houses are survivors from the town's whaling days. Also of note is the Maritime Museum inside the **Custom House**. The door timbers of this building were taken from the USS Constitution, the historic fighting ship of the War of 1812 (see page 67).

Captains of industry lived in Greek Revival mansions in Whale Oil Row (1832), which, together with the imposing railway station, echo former prosperity. Starr Street (1835) is strikingly uniform, its houses recently revamped. The **Joshua Hempsted House** (1678) and **Nathaniel Hempsted House** (1759) are typical of their period and are open to the public. Other notable attractions are the Burial Ground (1653), the New London County Courthouse (1784), and Union Station (1888). Incongruous beneath the huge I–95 viaduct is **Ye Olde Towne Mill** (free), which originally dates from 1650 and retains its waterwheel and some historic documents.

On the harbor, a statue of the young Eugene O'Neill pays a belated tribute to the playwright, who was once held in popular esteem as no more than a drunken reprobate. His father bought **Monte Cristo Cottage▶**, close by the water, in 1880 and the summers spent here made a great impression on Eugene. The house (open to the public) was the setting of his autobiographical drama, *Long Day's Journey into Night*.

The **U.S. Coast Guard Academy**, situated opposite Connecticut College, trains aspiring coastguards from the age of 18. Below the visitors' center on the grounds, the famous tall ship *Eagle*, where sea skills are taught, can be boarded free of charge on Sunday afternoons when in port. The vessel was built by the Germans in 1936, captured, and brought back after World War II.

The U.S. Coast Guard cutter Eagle, *a square-rigger used by the Coast Guard Academy as a training ship*

Ocean Beach Park,
Waterford, a few miles
south of New London

BATTLESITE MARKER
A granite obelisk of 1830 above the east bank of the Thames by Fort Griswold marks the site of the Battle of Groton in 1781, the only British victory in Connecticut. Climb the 160 steps for views of Long Island.

Across the Thames River is the naval base of **Groton**, no great beauty in itself but offering a free tour of the **USS Nautilus**▶ (*Open* Wed–Mon 9–5, Tue 1–5), the world's first nuclear submarine, and film shows about life on board. At Niantic, the **Children's Museum of South Eastern Connecticut** has plenty to keep youngsters occupied. At Waterford, miniature golf, a 1-mile boardwalk, and a water slide are found at **Ocean Beach Park**. **Rocky Neck State Park**, 3 miles west of Niantic, has a crescent beach and is good for swimming, fishing, and scuba diving. There are also picnicking and camping facilities.

SEA ADVENTURE CRUISES
Project Oceanology, based at Mystic Marinelife Aquarium (tel: 860/572 5955), operates 2½-hour trips from Groton to Ledge Light in summer. Participants set lobster pots, examine fish life and mud samples, and learn about marine pollution. Captain John's (tel: 860/443 7259) runs whale-watching and deep-sea fishing excursions from Waterford. At South Norwalk, cruises depart for Sheffield Island Lighthouse (tel: 203/838 9444), which guarded Norwalk Harbor from 1868; its 10 rooms are open to the public.

▶ ▶ ▶ Norwalk   86A1
This oystering town is home to the **Maritime Museum**▶ ▶ ▶, one of New England's most ambitious maritime museums. Housed in an old brick foundry, the museum features everything about the human and natural life of Long Island Sound, where even tropical fish can live because of the presence of the Gulf Stream. Its aquarium leads visitors through the inshore world of salt marsh habitats and out to sea, with curved glass tanks and video selections explaining aspects of the ocean. Sharks and striped bass feature in the largest tank. Other displays include oyster boats, Long Island boats, diving equipment, and boat building. Hands-on activities make the atmosphere distinctly lively, with opportunities to design your own boat and to work out how sail and wind interact. Children can try out water flows and more in the "Wet Lab." Call ahead for details about lectures, events, cruises, and demonstrations (tel: 203/852 0700); reservations are recommended for the IMAX movie theater, with its screen as tall as a six-story building.

Close by, at 295 West Avenue, the astonishing **Lockwood-Mathews Mansion**▶ ▶ was the ostentatious 1860s precursor to the mansions of Newport (see pages 216–18), with cavernous frescoed rooms, inlaid doors, and magnificent staircase. Its semi-restored state (see sidebar) lends it an atmosphere of faded grandeur verging on the theatrical. Upper rooms give a good idea of the mansion's former glory and contain a wide-ranging collection of 19th-century music boxes.

REBIRTH OF A MANSION
The Lockwood-Mathews Mansion was built for LeGrand Lockwood, who lost his fortune in a Wall Street crash in 1869. The house was sold to the Mathews family, then taken over by the city in 1938. The contents were sold, the floors covered with linoleum, and the rooms used to store voting machines. The mansion, which narrowly avoided a threat of demolition in 1959, has been reunited with some of its former contents. Restoration began in 1966 but will take many years to complete.

▶ ▶ ▶ Yale University   86C2
See New Haven, pages 102–5.

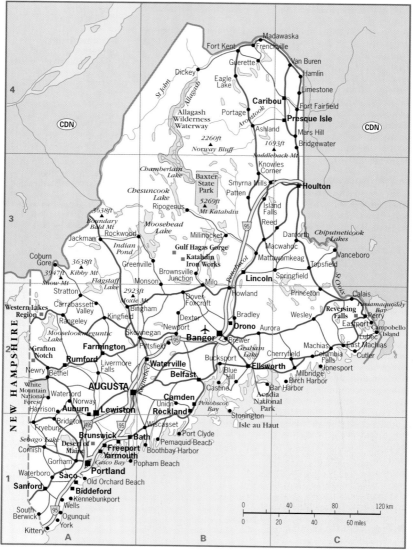

MAINE The summer vacationland of Maine is slightly larger than all the other New England states put together and has the lowest population density. Even with a massive influx of summer visitors to the coast, there are still places where you can find isolation. Easily the most crowded part is from Camden to the New Hampshire border; even here, there are areas of quiet charm if you are prepared to seek them out, but development along and around Route 1 is dense and often disappointingly drab. Farther up the coast and including most of Mount Desert Island is **Acadia National Park**, the jewel in the crown and the coast's only appreciable hilly area. Beyond that, the crowds thin out substantially. Even then, the intricate coast is elusive, except from a boat: drivers won't see much of it, and access on foot is limited.

Augusta is the state capital, but **Portland** is the cultural epicenter, and the only place that feels like a big city. Freeport and Kittery are factory outlet shopping towns.

TREES AND MORE TREES With forests covering 17 million acres, Maine is nicknamed the Pine Tree State. About 90 percent of the land is forested, and Maine has long lived off its appreciable timber supplies. The state is also referred to as Downeast, as the prevailing wind pushes sailboats eastward "down" the coast. The term "Downeaster" refers to any Maine-built ship.

Many Maine villages are now gentrified, but pockets of Downeast atmosphere remain at numerous fishing villages and coastal settlements. Distances between towns increase as you head north or east, and the towns get smaller and roads emptier. Inland, paper companies own vast tracts of Maine's forests; many of the roads are private. Today, paper-making accounts for nearly 35 percent of the state's total value of manufactured products.

On the few public roads in the big forests, you will encounter huge and somewhat terrifying lumber trucks every few minutes or so, which have the right of way (and should be given a very wide berth).

Rocky shores and dark coniferous trees typify the coast of Acadia National Park

109

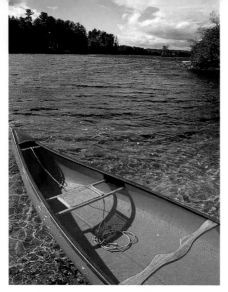

EARLY DAYS The state was settled by European explorers from early times. In the early 1600s, French and English settlers established themselves on the St. Croix and Kennebec rivers respectively. Charles I then gave the territory to Sir Ferdinando Gorges and made him Lord of New England in 1635. The Massachusetts Colony purchased Maine, which remained part of Massachusetts until it became an independent state in 1820.

From colonial times up until the latter part of the 19th century, Maine supported a flourishing shipbuilding industry. America's first sawmill was built in 1634 at South Berwick, and by 1840 this number had increased to 1,400. Maine has produced more wooden sailing ships than any other state in the Union.

Sebago Lake offers boating, swimming, and fishing

Maine salt-of-the earth

MAINE TRAITS Inhabitants of Maine have a reputation for being frank and down-to-earth. They keep their cool and don't always smile at strangers (an unpleasant attitude to some).

Maine is among the nation's poorest states. While that may seem hard to believe as you scan the antiques and crafts shops in the classy resorts of Penobscot Bay, Kennebunkport, Ogunquit, and elsewhere, the remoter areas see younger people drifting out of the state, and there are high unemployment rates (particularly on the Native American reservations). Much employment is seasonal. Tourism is the biggest earner—hence the "Vacationland" on license plates. Crowds flock to the coast in summer and, in the fall, foliage and winter sports draw visitors inland.

LUMBER FACTS

● From the 1630s to 1850s, sawmills made use of the "sash saw," an up-down moving frame. A later invention was the circular-saw blade.
● Winter is the best season for felling, when the sap is down.
● In former times, logs were placed on ice-covered lakes or rolled down to streams or rivers to be carried toward the sea each spring. As sawn logs could not be floated, sawmills were located close to shipping ports.

BLUEBERRY BOUNTIES

Blueberries are harvested by a special rake, boxed on three sides. Cherryfield, the "blueberry capital of the world," and Machias are the main processing centers.

Native Americans used to dry the berries for winter rations and used them in healing potions.

MAINE AT WORK Agricultural laborers spend August and September working on the wild blueberry harvest. Maine produces 90 percent of the nation's output of this fruit, which grows mostly in Washington County in the state's eastern corner. Potatoes are the largest crop in the state, with over 1 million tons harvested each year. From late October to early November, the Christmas wreath industry is in full swing. Maine has just the right type of balsam fir brush for this purpose, and the finished product graces the doors of many American homes.

Because of the harsh winters, the fishing and packing industries operate at maximum capacity when the weather allows it. Some three-quarters of the nation's lobsters come from Maine. Lobster is a ubiquitous menu item; even McDonald's restaurants offer lobster sandwiches in their Maine branches in summer. Meanwhile, Rockland, Prospect Harbor, and Lubec are major centers for sardine canning.

Events

For further information, contact the state tourist office (see page 266) or chambers of commerce.

January
Sugarloaf U.S.A./Carrabassett: Children's Festival Week: fireworks, torchlight parade, pool parties.

February
Western Mountain Winter Wonderland Week, Bethel: balloon and sleigh rides, dog-sledding.
Annual National Toboggan Championship, Camden: races, chowder challenge, numerous events.
International Snowmobiles Festival, Caribou.

March
Ice-fishing Tournament, Rockwood, Moosehead Lake.
New England Sled Dog Races, Rangeley.
Log Drivers Bean Hole Bean Cookout, Island Falls: torchlight parade, bonfire, and other events.

April
Fishermen's Festival, Boothbay Harbor.
Kenduskeag Stream Canoe Races, Bangor: whitewater open canoe races.
Maine Maple Sunday, statewide: sugar houses demonstrate the production of "liquid gold" maple syrup.

May
MooseMania, Rockwood: month-long moose-related activities and events.

June
Rodeo and Country Weekend, Farmington.
Windjammer Days, Boothbay Harbor: schooner races.
Acadian Festival, Madawaska: dance, food, music, heritage.

July
Bar Harbor Music Festival: classical and popular music (summer series).
Camden Garden House Tour: houses and gardens open to the public.
Clam Festival, Yarmouth: the biggest festival in Maine, with carnival, seafood, crafts, fireworks, children's parade, and other events.
Great Schooner Race, Blue Hill.

August
Blueberry Festival, Machias: harvest celebration.
Indian Day Celebration, Perry: Pasmaquoddy crafts, dancing, meals, traditional games.
Retired Skippers' Race, Castine.
Maine Lobster Festival, Rockland: a feast of Maine's most succulent crustacean in its busiest fishing port.

September
Blue Hill Fair, Blue Hill: on Labor Day weekend.
Bluegrass Festival, Brunswick.

October
Living History Days, Leonard Mills, Bradley: waterwheel and sawmill demonstrations, horse and buggy rides, antique costumes.
Harvestfest, York: colonial celebration.
Fryeburg Fair: Maine's largest agricultural fair.

November
Lighting of Nubble Lighthouse, Long Sands Beach, York.
Christmas United Maine Craftsman Show, Bangor.

December
Christmas Prelude, Kennebunkport.

A maple sugaring demonstration at the big agricultural fair held annually in Fryeburg

112

ACADIA TRIPS

Horse-and-carriage tours can be taken from Wildwood Riding Stables from Memorial Day to October (tel: 207/276 3622). Sailing trips on *Blackjack* run four times daily from Northeast Harbor (tel: 207/288 3056), while two-person glider rides leave from Bar Harbor Airport on Route 31 (tel: 207/667 SOAR). For mountain tours: Acadia National Park Tours (tel: 207/288 3327), and Oli's Trolley (tel: 207/288-9899). Biking on the traffic-free carriage roads and on the Loop Road is possible; for rentals, Acadia Bike & Canoe, 48 Cottage Street, Bar Harbor (tel: 207/288 9605).

►►► Acadia National Park   *108B2*

This scenic national park is dominated by the 1,530-foot granite form of **Cadillac Mountain►►►**, the highest point on the U.S. Atlantic coast. While no one can expect solitude in high summer, Acadia is undeniably the most rewarding place for hiking on the entire New England seaboard. It gives outstanding opportunities for observing wildlife, both flora (boreal northern and temperate southern species) and fauna.

In 1919, Acadia became the first national park east of the Mississippi. Mount Desert Island (the major part of the national park, connected to the mainland by bridge) was endowed a 57-mile system of scenic carriage roads by John D. Rockefeller, Jr. He considered Mount Desert Island "one of the great views of the world" and donated more than 10,000 acres to the national park. Meanwhile, Bar Harbor became the summer society rival of Newport, Rhode Island, as the Astors, Rockefellers, Vanderbilts, Fords, and others ensconced themselves here for the season. In 1947, a fire destroyed more than 60 of the millionaires' "summer cottages." Today, everything is very much visitor-oriented.

Visiting Acadia In July and August, **Bar Harbor** (outside the park boundary) becomes one of the busiest points on the Maine coast. It is the most practical place for

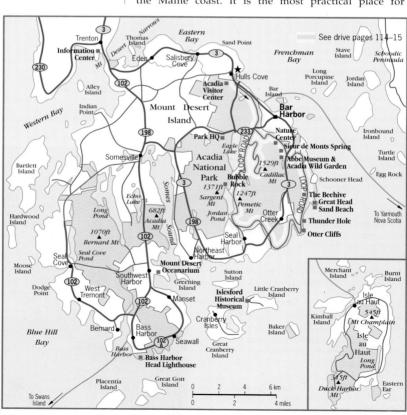

accommodations, eating, and shopping, as well as a starting point for whale-watching cruises, bike rentals, kayaking tours, and sailing trips. Ferries sail from here for Nova Scotia. In the town are the Natural History Museum, the Oceanarium, the Wendell Tiley Museum of Bird Carving, and the Bar Harbor Historical Museum.

Route 3 makes a drab entrance to Acadia, a virtually unbroken strip of motels, malls, and amusement parks, but things soon get better. Most visitors concentrate on the east side of Mount Desert Island by following the **Park Loop Road▶▶▶** (see pages 114–115).

The west side is much quieter and less dramatic, but tempting as an escape from the crowds, with few views from the wooded summits. Bass Harbor, Bernard, Southwest Harbor, and Northeast Harbor are typical Maine fishing villages, and not particularly touristy. **Echo Lake** is good for swimming by virtue of being warmer than the waters on the coast. **Northeast Harbor** is a starting point for cruises into the Sound and out to the Cranberry Isles. From the village, the **Sargent Drive** (cars and bicycles only) skirts the east side of **Somes Sound▶▶**, the East Coast's only fjord, carved by glaciers then flooded by the sea. An undemanding 2½-mile walk from Route 102 up Acadia Mountain on the sound's western side offers an outstanding view. **Bass Harbor Head Lighthouse** (1858) ranks among Maine's most photogenic lighthouses and can be reached by car.

Route 186 leads to **Birch Harbor**, where you can follow the one-way coastal loop road to **Schoodic Point▶**, which gives views of Mount Cadillac.

Acadia's farthest-flung outpost, **Isle au Haut▶**, lies in Penobscot Bay and is reached by ferry from Stonington (no cars taken; tel: 207/367 5193). Quiet trails wind through the island's spruce forests and along its rugged shores; there is a small campsite. Ranger-led excursions are offered to **Great Cranberry Island**. **Little Cranberry Island** has a free museum covering maritime and local history. Ranger-led walks, often with a natural history content, are given free of charge in the park. Trailheads are mostly well marked from the road.

With temperate and sub-Arctic species, such as this wild iris, Acadia is a rich hunting ground for naturalists

INFORMATION SOURCES
Thompson Island Information Center can help with accommodations and campsites, while the national park Visitor Center provides information and hiking maps.

For information and reservations, contact Acadia National Park, Bar Harbor, ME 04609 (tel: 207/288 3338); for camping reservations, call 800/365 2267. Between June and October, the park publishes Acadia Beaver Log, a free newspaper listing ranger-led tours, cruises, and walks.

113

Bar Harbor

From the loop road views extend across tiny bays backed by cliffs

Drive

Acadia's Park Loop Road

See map on page 112.

This scenic (mostly one-way) 27-mile road skirts Cadillac Mountain and provides a series of views that encapsulate the stunning beauty of Acadia. Although the loop can easily be driven in two hours or so, it merits a full day so that some of its trails can be experienced to the full. It may also be undertaken as a bicycle tour (there are several bike-rental shops in Bar Harbor), although some may find the traffic at peak times mars enjoyment. Parking is rarely a problem as you can stop anywhere on the right-hand side of the two-lane road along its one-way section. Week-long or seasonal passes must be bought on entering the park; entrance is free for U.S. citizens over 62 or registered as having disabilities.

ACADIA NATIONAL PARK
UNITED STATES DEPARTMENT OF THE INTERIOR
NATIONAL PARK SERVICE

Some of Mount Desert's early summer residents (in 1913) presented the U.S. government with lands which, in 1919, were declared a national park

The **Hulls Cove Visitor Center▶** marks the start of the Loop Road and has a diorama of the park and a film show about Acadia's natural history. The **Acadia Wild Garden▶**, created by the Bar Harbor Garden Club in co-operation with the national park, demonstrates the range of wild flowers and vegetation that can be found in contrasting sites such as beach, bog, mountain heath, and mixed woodlands. Immediately adjacent are the Nature Center, the **Sieur de Monts Spring**, and the **Abbe Museum▶** of Indian artifacts, which tells the story of the local Native American inhabitants before the Frenchman Samuel de Champlain discovered Mount Desert Island in 1604.

One of the toughest walks, definitely not for vertigo-sufferers, is the **Precipice Trail▶**, which ascends lofty crags by means of rungs and ladders. In recent years, peregrine falcons have been nesting here and consequently the trail has been closed in the summer months. **Sand Beach▶**, the only sandy beach in the park, has great beauty, but the water stays decidedly cool on even the hottest August day. If you turn right out of Sand Beach parking lot along the road, the trailhead for the **Beehive Trail▶** is almost

Silver birch trees growing behind the sandy shore of Sand Beach

immediately on the left. The short but strenuous path makes a spectacular ascent. There is an easier (less interesting) route that may be taken as a safe descent. Go right at the first path junction, and from the summit go forward, following signs for the Loop Road.

Exquisite views can be enjoyed from the **Ocean Trail▶** (3.6 miles there and back), one of the most scenic easy walks in the national park. It runs closely parallel to the road, along the cliffs between Sand Beach and Otter Point. **Thunder Hole**, beside the road, needs bad weather, when the waves are tossed into the rock niche and the spray slants across its entrance, to look its best. Otherwise, it is little more than a minor chink in the coastline with pleasant rocks on which to sit.

The **Gorham Mountain Trail▶** offers further spectacular high-level views that are similar to those on the Beehive Trail (you can make a longer walk along the ridge to take in the Beehive), but the trail itself is less demanding. Just below the trail is Cadillac Cliff, an overhanging rock with a small cave.

Where the one-way traffic ends, you can detour south past **Seal Harbor**, a sandy beach, to **Northeast Harbor**, from where you can take a cruise (see sidebar on page 112). Alternatively, continue north to

115

Jordan Pond▶, which has nature trails through the woods and along the lakeside. A longer scenic trail encircles the entire lake. The half-mile trail to South Bubble Summit, a 768-foot protuberance with a fine panorama, passes **Bubble Rock▶**, a classic glacial "erratic" (deposited boulder), balanced on its side.

The scenic summit road to **Mount Cadillac▶ ▶ ▶** needs careful timing to catch the best of the light and the view, both of which can change in quality for better or worse within only a few minutes. When conditions are right you can see as far as Mount Katahdin (5,267 feet), Maine's highest point, located inland in distant Baxter State Park. Hikers who want the satisfaction of reaching a similar viewpoint without the crowds should follow the Dorr Mountain Trail, a short distance east of Sieur de Monts Spring.

So prolific was the lobster in colonial days that colonists would catch it with hooks or spears in shallow waters and feed it to chickens and prisoners. Today, lobstering is one of New England's proudest traditions, and the king of seafood is dispatched to top restaurants across the world.

LOBSTERING LORE
Each harbor has its own close-knit society, one that guards its trade fiercely. Fishing territories are strictly defined, by tradition, and each fisherman's buoys are painted in his own colors. Trespass and you may find, as one Portland fisherman did in 1993, a bomb in your trap. The scalloper who drags his nets and scoops along the ocean floor and falls foul of a lobster pot or two won't find a warm reception either.

FOR A CLOSER LOOK
Several ports operate trips on lobstering boats in summer months, including Bar Harbor, Boothbay Harbor, and Ogunquit in Maine, and Gloucester in Massachusetts. Remember to take warm clothes.

Lobster pounds are the best place to enjoy the day's catch—straight from the sea

The tradition The American lobster, *Homarus americanus*, lives along the Atlantic coast between Labrador and North Carolina and is particularly plentiful off the coast of New England. Trapping on a commercial basis began in southern New England by 1800. By the mid-1800s, the hoop net had been introduced, which meant lobster could be caught without damage, and Maine, by now heading the trade, was transporting live lobsters in sailing "smacks" to New York and Boston, where they were boiled and sold on the streets. The Maine fishery also supplied no fewer than 23 canning factories with smaller, less salable lobster. Canning ceased at the turn of the present century, but lobstering is still a vital part of the coastal economy, not only attracting tourists but also providing work for local industry producing the boats and the slatted trap that, with modifications, has been used for decades.

The catch Harbors bobbing with boats and wharves stacked high with traps and buoys reveal little of the tough life the "trapper" leads. In all weathers he (and occasionally she) heads out to his line of buoys at daybreak and winches up the strings of pots. Many trappers have up to 50 traps per string and 1,000 traps in all. Each lobster is measured to ensure it is of legal size; "keepers" are typically 10 inches long overall, 1–1½ pounds in weight, and about five years old. The bait (dead fish) is renewed, the lobster pots are returned to the ocean floor, and then the catch is turned in to the dealer. It's no easy way to make a living.

116

► Augusta
108A2

Maine's state capital is not a place that routinely attracts visitors, but it has a handful of good sights justifying a brief detour. The town lies on the Kennebec River at the site of an early Pilgrim colony. Along the river extends the green expanse of 34-acre Capitol Park. Above stands the prominent **State House►**, dating from 1832 but extended twice since Charles Bulfinch designed it. The façade is original, although the dome replaced a cupola in the early 1900s. The building is open during normal office hours (*Open* Mon–Fri). Wall panels provide a self-guided tour to its function and history. Next door, the **Maine State Museum►** presents attractive displays covering various aspects of the state's industry and life from the Ice Age to the present. Lumbering and ice harvesting, two of the city's former mainstays, feature in the "Made in Maine" displays, together with exhibits of the state's shipbuilding, sardine canning, and farming industries.

Fort Western►, the oldest wooden fort in the U.S.A. (1754), occupies the site of a Pilgrim trading post established near the river in the 1620s (*Open* daily, Memorial Day–July 4, 1–4; July 4–Labor Day, weekdays 10–4 and weekends 1–4; Labor Day–Columbus Day, weekends 1–4). The need for the fort arose from the colonists' fear of the French and Native Americans. It was never besieged, and it became a trading post during its 12-year history as a fort. Its design was that of a typical New England fort, with a 100-foot-long main house. William Harvard, the commander, made the fort his home from 1766 to 1810, which is why it has survived; today it is presented as a house rather than a barracks. Reconstructions of the stockade blockhouses, with replica cannons and guns, date from 1921. Cannon firing takes place on weekends, and guides in period costume show visitors around.

Out of town, the **Matthews Museum** at Union comprises a collection of the past, including a schoolroom, a horse-drawn hearse, a cooper's shop, a colonial kitchen, spinning and weaving items, and farm tools.

The Federal-style Blaine House (1833) in Augusta is the official residence of the state's governor

117

THE BIRTH OF MOXIE
The locally popular soft drink known as Moxie began life at Union, near Augusta, in 1885. Its inventor, Dr. Augustin Thompson, originally sold it as Moxie Nerve Food. The Matthews Museum in the village has an interesting collection of memorabilia.

Maine

Above and below right: ships' figureheads and marine art feature among the indoor displays at Bath's maritime museum

KING OF BANGOR
Author Stephen King lives on West Broadway, Bangor, and his fans frequently track him down. Many of his novels and films have a local setting. Betts Bookstore in Main Street specializes in Stephen King books and memorabilia.

LUMBER CAPITAL
In the 19th century, Bangor was the world's largest lumber exporting center. The industry peaked in 1872, when 2,200 ships entered Bangor via the Penobscot River in a year, but the timber supply waned and shipbuilding declined as paper making assumed an important role in the state. At Bradley, off Route 178, the Maine Logging Museum at Orono stands on the site of Leonard's Mills (1790). It features a working water-powered sawmill, a sawing demonstration, a trapper's cabin, and more. For opening times tel: 207/581 2871.

► Bangor
108B2

Bangor is more a commercial center than a visitor destination. Although victim of a fire in 1911 and much redeveloped in the 1960s, the city retains some fine buildings, notably along Broadway, High Street, and the streets leading off them. The **Thomas Hill Standpipe** in Summit Park is a unique contribution to Bangor's skyline. Built in 1897, this water tower observation point is floodlit at night. The **Historical Society** operates a museum in a Greek Revival house at 159 Union Street (*Open* Mar–mid Dec, Tue–Fri 12–4; Jul–Sep, also Sun) and runs bus tours round the city (Jul–Sep, Thu, and first Sat of the month).

Bangor's heyday is chronicled in the **Old Town** Museum on North 4th Street (*Open* Wed–Sun. Admission free). At the I–95 and I–395 intersection, the **Cole Land Transportation Museum** boasts over 200 vehicles, including snowplows and logging trucks from old Maine (*Open* May–Nov).

►► Bath
108A1

Bath's **Maine Maritime Museum and Shipyard►►**, at 243 Washington Street, is the most ambitious museum of its kind in the state. It occupies the last surviving wooden ship-building yard in the nation, used by Percy & Small from 1897 to 1920. The *Wyoming*, the largest sail vessel used in the country, was built here. Inside the Maritime History Building, a museum display tells the story of Maine's seafaring past from the days of the early explorers to 20th-century tourism and fishing. The museum possesses over 200 paintings and drawings, 250 models, and 100 boats.

In the Percy & Small shipyard, you can see apprentices at work restoring and building wooden boats on weekdays. Five of the original buildings survive; displays include small craft and the story of lobstering. Tours of the shipyard, available at no extra cost, are highly recommended.

Special cruises usually take place on Tuesdays, in addition to a regular program of 50-minute narrated boat trips on *Hardy II*. The latter pass the Bath Iron Works, the state's largest industrial employer, and a major shipyard. It is usually possible to board vessels by the museum piers, including the *Sherman Zwicker*, where you can get an idea of the tough life endured by the Great Banks cod fishermen.

►►► Baxter State Park   108B3

The park is one of the more accessible parts of Maine's unpopulated mountains and forests. Wild flowers, hiking, geology, whitewater rafting, cross-country skiing, moose-spotting, hunting, canoeing, and fishing are among its attractions.

Baxter Peak (5,267 feet) is the summit of **Mount Katahdin►►►** and marks the northern end of the 2,035-mile Appalachian Trail to Georgia. It is the highest point in Maine and probably the only mountain in the state to have remained bare of trees since glaciation. Several trails lead to the top, including the famous **Knife Edge Trail**, which edges its way along a sharp glacial ridge, or arête. Two cirques (glacial hollows) flank the Knife Edge, which is just 3 feet wide in places and has dizzy drops on either side of up to 2,000 feet. The trail is strictly for experienced walkers in calm weather conditions.

Great Basin is the finest of seven cirques on the mountain; the Chimney Pond Trail from Roaring Brook campsite gives access. Outstanding for its arctic wild flowers, the Tableland has abundant evidence of freeze-thaw weathering processes on the rocks scattered over it.

Other notable trails include **Doubletop Mountain**, **South Turner**, the **Owl**, and **The Brothers**. Moose can often be seen at **Big** and **Little Niagara Falls**.

Southwest of Baxter State Park, the West Branch of the Penobscot River has its moment of glory as it gushes though **Ripogenus Gorge►►** (access by unpaved road). Over a mile long, the gorge has almost vertical sides up to 200 feet high, with the rock strata exposed like a school textbook diagram. It can be seen on foot or by whitewater rafting or canoeing.

Farther south, near Brownville Junction, is **Gulf Hagas►►**, another magnificent canyon best reached from Lloyd Pond. Here, the West Branch of the Pleasant River tumbles over five waterfalls, a memorable sight when in full spate in spring. Allow six hours for the hike.

The Lumberman's Museum (*Open* Memorial Day to September), at **Patten**, has 10 buildings that tell the story of the state's lumber industry. There is also a museum of bygones at the paper-producing town of **Millinocket**.

AN INDUSTRIAL GHOST TOWN
Gulf Hagas canyon can be included in a visit to the site of the Katahdin Iron Works—look for signs off Route 11 south of Millinocket. Now a state memorial park, it retains kilns and a stone furnace as reminders of a mining town that, in the 19th century, produced almost 2,000 tons of raw iron per year and employed nearly 200 men.

CAMPING AT BAXTER
For information about camping in Baxter State Park, contact Baxter State Park Authority, 64 Balsam Drive, Millinocket, ME 04462 (tel: 207/723 5140). Reservations are advisable in summer, as the numbers of campsites and lean-tos (simple shelters) are deliberately restricted.

Baxter State Park is remote, but one of the best places in Maine for moose-spotting

SUNRISE CANOEING

A memorable way to enjoy the wildlife and scenery of the Western Lakes area is to take a dawn canoe trip. Look for advertisements in Rangeley, for instance, for a guided trip that offers the chance to watch beavers and moose, and be serenaded by birdsong as the mists rise.

MOSS GARDEN

A few minutes' walk from Moose Cave in Grafton Notch State Park (look for signs at the rest area on Route 26) is this little fairy-tale clearing. A silvery carpet of reindeer moss (*Cladonia rangifera*), an exquisite erect ferny lichen, is interspersed with other mosses, some cool green and smooth, others darker and upright. With the tiny pine seedlings, it looks like a miniature forest.

New England cameo: rocking chairs and a pumpkin on a porch of a house in Bethel

▶▶ Bethel and the Western Lakes   108A2

The Western Lakes Region, stretching north from Sebago Lake up to the lakes and mountains around Rangeley, includes some of New England's most beautiful countryside, with forested hills rolling down to crystal lakes and rivers. The farther north you go, the more remote and wild it all becomes. It offers excellent opportunities for walking, camping, fishing, golfing, sketching, and moose-spotting. In summer, there is boating of all sorts on the lakes and rivers, in winter every type of snow sport, and in autumn, of course, the brilliant foliage.

At the heart of the region is **Bethel▶**, a classic New England small town with a handful of crafts shops, inns, and restaurants. Nearby is the burgeoning Sunday River ski resort (see page 229). Alongside the road that passes the resort from Newry is one of Maine's most photographed covered bridges, **Sunday River Bridg**e, built in 1870. Northwest of Newry is **Grafton Notch State Park▶▶**, an area of gorges, waterfalls, and mountains, where walks range from short hikes such as Screw Augur Falls Gorge to challenging trails up Table Rock. Northeast of the papermill town of Rumford, **Kingfield** has an absorbing rainy-day option in the Stanley Museum (*Open* Tue–Sun 1–4; closed Apr and Nov), with items relating to the versatile Stanley family, whose early 20th-century work encompassed steam-powered cars, violin-making and photography. Nearby, **Sugarloaf Mountain▶▶**, Maine's second highest peak (4,237 feet) and a winter sports resort, merits taking the chairlift even outside the skiing season for the far-ranging views from its treeless summit.

Rangeley▶ is the hub of the Rangeley Lakes region, which offers canoeing, sailing, swimming, fishing, and walking. The town has hotels, restaurants, campsites, and sports shops. The Rangeley State Park has chalets, picnicking, and boat-launching areas.

South of Bethel is **Fryeburg**, a canoeing center (with rentals available) famed for its agricultural fair in October. **Harrison**, set between Long Lake and Crystal Lake, is a another good center for the outdoor enthusiast. Famous for its trout and landlocked salmon fishing, **Sebago Lake▶▶** is ringed with small towns offering plenty for the watersports enthusiast.

Boothbay Harbor is a busy boating resort as well as an active fishing port

VISITING MONHEGAN ISLAND
In 1614, Captain John Smith landed here, and settlers followed 11 years later.
  Trips are offered from Boothbay Harbor by Balmy Days Cruises (tel: 800/298 2284), and from New Harbor by Hardy Boat Cruises (tel: 800/278 8346)

RAFTING
New England Whitewater Center operates raft trips on the Kennebec, Dead, and Penobscot rivers between April and October: Box 669, Millinocket, ME 04462 (tel: 800/766 7238).

Lobster fishing has been a vital economy in Maine since the 19th century

▶ **Boothbay Harbor**   *108B1*
Settled in the 17th century and developed for tourism from the 1870s, Boothbay Harbor is the largest boating harbor northeast of Boston, as well as a busy resort town packed with boutiques and galleries. The self-proclaimed "boating capital of New England" offers over 50 daily cruises, the best choice in Maine—including seal-, whale- and puffin-watching trips, deep-sea fishing expeditions, and tours of the coast and islands. By the Lobsterman's Co-op, the Sea Pier Aquarium is stocked by local fishermen and contains a good variety of species from the Gulf of Maine.
  On the east side of Route 27, near its intersection with Route 1, is **Boothbay Railway Village**, a village theme park encompassed by a railroad, where an original train hauls you through woods inhabited by garden gnomes. There is a collection of re-erected buildings to explore (a black-smith's shop, an old fire station, a village school, and more). For the most part, you can only look inside the buildings from the entrances.
  Some 10 miles offshore is **Monhegan Island▶ ▶**, only 1½ miles across at its widest, but with surprising variety, including some 400 species of wild flowers. The Cliff Trail runs the length of the island, and, there are fine walks in the balsam-scented Cathedral Woods, as well as 160-foot cliffs on the east side. The island is partly developed for visitors, with shops and restaurants. Monhegan's impressive ocean panoramas made the island a popular artists' haunt: Rockwell Kent and Edward Hopper are among those who have come and painted the scene.
  Across the inlet east of Boothbay Harbor is one of the loveliest parts of Maine's seaboard, **Pemaquid Point▶ ▶**, which is graced by wave-sculpted rocks and wind-battered ledges. Pemaquid Point Light (1827) presides over the scene, while the former lighthouse keeper's cottage functions as a museum of commercial fishing and a small art gallery, open in summer. At nearby **Pemaquid Beach▶**, a sand beach (rare for these parts), is the Colonial Pemaquid Restoration, the excavated site of an early 17th-century mariners' settlement, with an adjacent museum. Fort William Henry is a replica of a 1692 fort.

Massachusetts Hall, Bowdoin's oldest building, dates from 1799

RECORDED FOR POSTERITY
The substantial film and video heritage of New England is being preserved by Northeast Historic Film, which operates from a restored 1916 cinema building in Bucksport, within sight of the massive form of Fort Knox. The exhibition "Going to the Movies" looks at the movie-watching tradition from the early days (*Open* weekdays 9–4, plus Jun–Labor Day, also Sat. *Admission* free). For information about showings, tel: 207/469 0924, or E-mail oldfilm@acadia.net; there is a website at www.acadia.net/oldfilm/.

FOREIGN VISITORS
Visitors to Campobello Island must bring their passports. Citizens of Australia, United Kingdom, New Zealand, and Ireland need no visa, but should be sure not to surrender their visa waiver forms. Tell the passport control officer that you intend to return the same day. Drive over International Bridge or take a ferry from Eastport via Deer Isle.

► **Brunswick**   *108A1*

Bowdoin College►, in the center of Brunswick, was founded in 1794 and counts among its former students the writers Henry Wadsworth Longfellow and Nathaniel Hawthorne, and President Franklin Pierce. Two fine museums (both free) flank the attractive campus green. Hubbard Hall, a tall and prominent tower, houses the Peary-MacMillan Arctic Museum, which tells the story of these two former students who made the first successful expedition to the North Pole in 1909. Displays feature three rooms of sleighs, guns, equipment, and writings. To the right of Hubbard Hall, the Art Museum has American colonial and federal portraits (among them Gilbert Stuart's painting of Thomas Jefferson), paintings by Winslow Homer, and classical antiquities.

In town, the Pejepscot Historical Society maintains three museum properties. The Italianate **Skolfield-Whittier House** at 161 Park Row (*Open* summer, Tue–Fri 10–3, Sat 1–4) was closed up and forgotten about from 1925 until 1982, and inhabited by a sea captain. It contains exotic items he brought back from his voyages and family possessions spanning three generations. Its north side houses the free **Pejepscot Museum** (local history and genealogy). The **Joshua L. Chamberlain Museum** (*Open* summer, Tue–Sat 10–4) commemorates the college professor who achieved fame as the hero of Little Round Top in the Civil War Battle of Gettysburg.

► **Bucksport**   *108B2*

This small port on the Penobscot River is busy with tankers unloading petroleum products and picking up coated paper manufactured locally. Route 1 crosses the Penobscot by Waldo-Hancock Bridge, affording a spectacular view of the formidable **Fort Knox►►**. Not to be confused with its more famous namesake in Kentucky, the fort was built between 1844 and 1869, originally because of the British threat from Canada. It was never completed but saw activity in the Civil War and Spanish American War of 1898. An annual Civil War encampment, with costumed actors and cannon firing, enlivens the fort on two weekends in July and August. Take a flashlight for exploring the inside of the structure (in restoration).

▶▶ Campobello Island
(New Brunswick, Canada)
108C2

Franklin D. Roosevelt's "beloved island," where he found rest and freedom from care, is just over the Canadian border, but his family summer house is jointly maintained as an International Park by the U.S.A. and Canada. The park comprises 2,800 acres of deep forest, bogs, stone and sand beaches, oceanside trails, and outlooks in addition to the house. Maps are available from the visitors' center near International Bridge. (See also sidebar, page 122.)

The Roosevelt Cottage▶▶ is in Dutch colonial style and retains the original furniture. The atmosphere is comfortable and personal rather than grand, with the president's umbrellas and books put out as if the great man had just stepped outside. The adjacent **visitor center** shows a film on Campobello and the Roosevelts (*Open* cottage and visitor center, daily, May–Oct. *Admission* free). Next door is the opulent **Hubbard Cottage**, which was home to Gorham and Sara Hubbard, an insurance businessman and a concert pianist, who became friends of the Roosevelts. The cottage is open to the public.

Roosevelt spent his boyhood summers at an adjacent cottage, which his father built in 1885 (it was demolished in 1951). His family later made the existing building the summer home.

123

Roosevelt's house on Campobello Island

One of New England's most familiar lighthouses, West Quoddy Light

Many roads on the 9-mile-long island are unpaved but are passable in dry conditions. The northern tip offers a fine view, and whales can often be seen. **Friar's Head Outlook▶▶** (look for signs between International Bridge and the Roosevelt Cottage) commands an impressive view of Passamaquoddy Bay.

On the way to Campobello is **Lubec**, the last village in Maine, noted for sardines and smoked herring. Aptly, it is home to the Old Sardine Village Museum, with displays including canning equipment, boats, a sheet-metal shop, and a company store (*Open* Jul and Aug, Wed–Sun PM; Jun–Sep, weekends only).

To the south, **Quoddy Head▶** marks the - easternmost point of the U.S. mainland. **West Quoddy Light**, built in 1858, sends out a 20-mile beam. A 4-mile trail along high cliffs provides opportunities for spotting whales.

"In 1492 Native Americans discovered Columbus lost at sea!" reads the T-shirt slogan. And not long afterward these so-called "American Indians" met the first European colonists on the shores of New England. This was a meeting of two cultures, which to this day are as different as night and day.

A PROUD TRADITION

Keeping the tradition of basket-making alive is seen as important to the preservation of Native American culture. The Maine Arts Commission has developed a program through which basket-makers pass on their skills to apprentices. These works of fine craftsmanship may be bought at crafts festivals and through cooperatives or shops.

124

A Passamaquoddy native of Maine

Windsong, a Massachusetts Wampanoag who does not live on an Indian reservation, is a deeply spiritual man. For his traditional, sacred rituals he needs eagle feathers. But the eagle is a protected bird and only Native Americans living on registered land are entitled to their feathers. This lack of awareness of the spiritual needs of another culture is, he says, typical of a white man's society brought up on images of peace-pipe-smoking "Indians" who raise one hand and call out "How!," images that have more to do with Hollywood than real life.

Cultural and social issues For hundreds of years, the Native People of the eastern United States have mixed with other elements in society—with blacks and, in more recent decades, with whites. Yet, although there is a degree of integration that may not exist in the western states of the U.S., where reservations are often enclaves of poverty and social disintegration, there is considerable resentment—on both sides.

In the workplace, for instance, Native Americans once felt a bitter sense of discrimination as they were overlooked for promotion. Now, however, antidiscriminatory regulations mean that this can no longer happen legally, and the pendulum has swung so far that the playing field is somewhat more even. Nevertheless, the clash of cultures remains, and a common stereotype suggests that the archetypal conscientious and diligent Yankee may find the Native American frustratingly casual.

Today there is far less social distinction between Native Americans and other Americans. Yet the Native American culture is still widely celebrated, notably with the opening in 1998 of the Mashantucket Pequot Museum and Research Center at Foxwoods, Connecticut (see page 95), built

at the cost of $135 million. Staking a claim So regulations are bringing Native Americans closer to full integration into New England society. At the same time, the tribes are actively reasserting their own rights. In Maine, the Penob-scots and Pass-amaquoddy have long fought for legal control of fishing, mineral, and forest rights

Top: spinning the wheel at Foxwoods
Left: a Connecticut Algonquin

on their lands. In Vermont, the Abe-naki threaten legal claims on much of the land. But the hottest issue concerns the Mashantucket Pequots in Connecticut.

In 1992, the Pequots, a tribe that had all but died out, opened Foxwoods High Stakes Bingo and Casino (see sidebar). It currently brings in more than $1 million daily on slot machines alone. It is the largest casino in the Western Hemisphere, a vast operation through whose ever-open doors pass 40,000 Americans a day, some bused in for two hours from New York and Boston. Awaiting them are the 1,500 clattering slot machines, bingo rooms, and blackjack, craps, baccarat, roulette, acey-deucey, money wheel, pai gow poker, and chuck-a-luck, to name but a few of the table games. In an area of dire unemployment, Foxwoods is now one of the biggest employers. Moreover, Connecticut's coffers are fatter by well over $100 million per year as a result of a deal with the governor whereby 25 percent of slot machines tak-ings are handed over in exchange for a monopoly control of all gaming machines in the state. Foxwoods looks after its employees well, but along with jobs it brings traffic, noise and, potentially at least, some of the less desirable members of society to the neighborhood. Now its owners plan to buy more land, annexing it into sovereign Indian land and thereby removing it from local control and, signif-icantly, state and federal tax rolls. This is cause for deep concern in the nearby villages and for bitter resentment among some of New England's taxpayers.

SOVEREIGNTY OF LAND
A tribe that is federally recognized can assume responsibility for its own internal control. The Pequots, for instance, have established their own police force, housing authority, ambulance and fire service, as well as their own court system. They also have their own water supply and sewage system. No federally rec-ognized tribe pays state or federal taxes. This means that cigarettes and alco-hol can be sold more cheaply on a reservation than elsewhere.

PLAYING THE GAME
Federal law allows recog-nized Indian tribes to con-duct gambling if the state in which they live allows gambling. Connecticut allows fundraising, non-profit "casino nights" (for example, church bingo evenings), and the Pequots took advantage of this, opening Foxwoods Bingo in 1986. It began to make a profit, and the state of Connecticut sued them. The case went to the Supreme Court, where the state lost. The Pequots obtained invest-ment capital from Malaysia and opened the casino. In 1993, Rhode Island, not liking the possibility of a similar temple to gambling, repealed its law allowing fund-raising bingo.

Almost extinct 100 years ago, the puffin has recently been making a comeback in the Gulf of Maine

WILDLIFE SANCTUARY
Moosehorn National Wildlife Refuge, 5 miles north of Calais (pronounced "Callous"), itself north of Eastport on Route 1 on the Charlotte Road, consists of 23,000 acres of bogs, woods, and marshes, inhabited by 216 species of birds, plus moose, deer, bear, beaver, mink, and woodchuck. Some 50 miles of roads and trails are open to hikers.

Revolutionary memorabilia is displayed in the Burnham Tavern, Machias

► **Eastport** 108C2

This is small-town Maine at its most seductively peaceful, far removed from the crafts designer stores and tourist crowds of the more frequented parts of the coast. Eastport's population numbers under 2,000 but is rated important enough to have its own city hall. High, Ray, Washington, and Water streets contain an attractive mixture of architectural styles, from colonial to Victorian.

In the town itself, seek out Raye's Mustard, the last stone-ground mustard mill in the U.S.A., a legacy of the days when mustard was used as a preservative. In the summer months (afternoons only) you can visit the local history museum, which is housed within the old Sullivan Barracks (1809). The garrison surrendered to the British in the War of 1812 without a shot being fired.

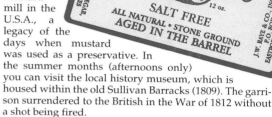

The town, sited on Moose Island and linked by causeway to the mainland, is a sardine, granite, timber, and processed-paper port. It lies on **Passamaquoddy Bay► ►**, site of the world's largest lobster pond, and notorious for treacherous waters that include fast incoming tides and great changes in water levels. Old Sow, the world's second-largest whirlpool, can be seen from the car ferry to Deer Island. The curious tidal phenomenon of **Reversing Falls**, where the current goes in the contrary direction to the tide at certain times of day, occurs near Pembroke (for directions, see sidebar opposite). Two dams near Lubec are all that remain of an abandoned project begun in 1919 to harness tidal energy from the bay.

A little farther south, **Cobscook Bay State Park** has two trails, one leading to the coast, the other along the creek.

There are ferry connections to **Deer Island**, connecting with another ferry for **Campobello Island► ►** (see page 123). At the far end of Deer Island, a free ferry crosses to L'Etete on the Canadian mainland.

In the former lumber town of **Machias**, the **Burnham Tavern►** on High Street (dating from 1770) is eastern Maine's oldest building. Here patriots planned the capture of the British schooner *Margaretta* on June 12, 1775, after the British captain had ordered locals to take down their liberty pole. This was the first naval battle of the Revolution, the "Lexington of the Sea." Now a museum, the tavern has Revolutionary-era furnishings and items from the British vessel.

On Route 92, half a mile from town, the Maine Wild Blueberry Company produces around 20 million pounds of berries a year; free tours (weekdays in summer, best by appointment; tel: 207/255 8364) show the processes of cleaning, freezing, and grading the berries. Route 191 leads through the town of Cutler, where the lobster hatchery is open to the public in summer. Route 187 reaches Jonesport, a typical Downeast fishing village, linked by bridge to Beal Island, where clams are raised. A causeway gives access to the Mud Hole Trail (from Black Duck Cove), with good views across to the islands.

▶ **Ellsworth**   *108B2*

An unassuming small town on the way to Bar Harbor, Ellsworth has a fine First Congregational Church (1846), thought to be Maine's best example of a Greek Revival church. The steeple is a faithful fiberglass replica. The Old Hancock County Buildings, on Cross Street, are in similar style. The Big Chicken Barn, on Route 3 in town, is Maine's largest antiquarian bookstore and antiques shop.

Just out of town is the **Colonel Black Museum▶** (*Open* Jun–mid-Oct), built in 1824–1828 by land agent Colonel John Black. This charming Georgian home has original furnishings, a fine circular staircase, and delightful formal gardens. The carriage house on the grounds contains old sleighs and carriages.

Out on Route 3, the **Birdsacre Sanctuary** covers 100 acres, with trails leading past ponds and nesting areas. The Stanwood Homestead Museum here is dedicated to pioneer ornithologist Cordelia Stanwood.

Lamoine State Park▶, on Route 184, has excellent views of Mount Desert Island and a safe beach. At Columbia Falls, just off Route 1, is **Ruggles House▶** (*Open* Jun–Oct), which dates from 1818 and was inhabited until 1920. The house is noted for its "flying" staircase (supported only at the top and bottom); the woodcarving on the staircase was executed with a jackknife over a three-year period.

GRANITE MEMENTOES
On Route 1 between Calais and Robbinston are 12 granite milestones erected by James Shepherd Pike in 1870. Pike, a lumberman, abolitionist, ambassador and writer, had a summer residence in Robbinston. By measuring the circumference of his cartwheels, he placed the stones to check the speed of his horses.

REVERSING FALLS
The "Falls" take some effort to find. Turn off Route 1 at Pembroke, taking the road to the right of the post office. Very soon turn right and then left (follow signs to the shore), then, after 3.2 miles, turn right past a cemetery. Bear left at a fork with a dirt road. Continue for 1.4 miles, then fork left beyond a covered picnic bench up on the left: the parking lot is just beyond.

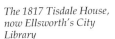
127

The 1817 Tisdale House, now Ellsworth's City Library

L.L. BEAN

This famous store started as a humble one-man mail-order operation and has since boomed. In 1912, Leonwood Bean marketed his invention, the Maine Hunting Shoe: "designed by a hunter who has tramped the Maine Woods for the past 18 years. They are as light as a pair of moccasins with the protection of a heavy hunting boot." Today, the store sells over 6,000 products. It is still largely mail-order, but there are factory outlets at Ellsworth, ME, and North Conway, NH.

128

▶▶ Freeport   108A1

Freeport, Maine's biggest visitor attraction along with Acadia National Park, consists of a main street lined wall-to-wall with factory shopping outlets. There are over 100, and most of the time sale prices are offered somewhere. Serious shoppers journey up here from New York and even farther to make Christmas purchases.

It is a matter of dispute whether Freeport is really such good value (compared to North Conway, for instance), but the selection (candles, kids' clothes, maps and guides, crafts, sports equipment, soap, and so on) is impressive. Although village-sized, Freeport is crammed with shoppers transporting bulging shopping bags, and the traffic and parking lots are on an urban scale. Maps showing locations of the stores are given away at Bean's and other shops. Freeport has inns, motels, and B&Bs as well as a beach, and it is the starting point for ocean cruises.

Outside Freeport is the **Desert of Maine▶**, a curiosity. This really is a small desert, an eye-opening example of 18th-century bad farming practice, where the soil was depleted and massive erosion followed. Entire farm buildings and trees were engulfed in the dunes, and telltale treetops still protrude like small bushes. From May to Columbus Day, a tour is provided of this odd tribute to human failure. Also south of town, live osprey and seals may be spotted from **Wolf Neck Woods State Park▶**, which has trails and wooded shores as well as some unusual rock formations. At **Bradbury Mountain State Park▶** a 20-minute trail to the summit leads to views over Casco Bay, while other paths head along the bay and Harraseeket River.

▶▶ Penobscot Bay   108B2

The biggest indentation in Maine's coast, Penobscot Bay and its islands offer some of the loveliest panoramas along New England's seaboard. Boating has been big here for centuries. The Penobscot River once supplied over 20 towns with timber for shipbuilding, and today the ports are busy with pleasure and commercial craft. Rockland and Camden are the busiest boating areas; Camden is much prettier and more of a resort. Be warned, though: the sprawl along Route 1 is unsightly, and in summer driving along it is no pleasure.

Above: Freeport is home to the popular mail-order clothing company L.L. Bean

Penobscot Bay has long been busy with boats, both large and small

The West side Port Clyde, on the west side of the bay, is the departure point for ferries making crossings to **Monhegan Island▶▶** (see page 121). On the way to the town you pass through Tenants Harbor, a typical and picturesque fishing village complete with lobster boats moored in the harbor.

Farther north, **Owls Head Transportation Museum▶▶** opens year-round and displays New England's largest collection of pioneer vehicles from the early 20th century. They include vintage bikes, early horseless carriages and gas-powered cars. A schedule of events features airshows and motorcycle and tractor meets.

Nearby **Rockland**, New England's biggest distribution center for the lobster industry and a major sardine port, has a workaday atmosphere. The local processing of sea-weed gives the place a wholesome aroma.

The **Old Conway Homestead and Museum**, Route 1 and Conway Road (*Open* Jul and Aug, Tue–Fri 10–4), is an atmospheric 1770s farmhouse and barn with farm tools, a blacksmith shop, and a maple-sugar house (with sugaring demonstrations in spring).

On the move at Owls Head Transportation Museum

THE BEANS OF EGYPT, MAINE
No relation to the Beans of Freeport, the Bean family of Egypt was a fictitious invention of novelist Carolyn Chute. Her book *The Beans of Egypt, Maine* (1985) is the saga of a violent and primitive family, prisoners of rural poverty in the woods of Maine. Despite its bleak setting, the novel has moments of black humor.

129

BAY ISLANDS
Penobscot Bay's main islands make attractive hiking or bicycling country. Vinalhaven, the largest at 14 miles long, and Islesboro (12 miles long) have accommodations, but no camping is allowed. North Haven and Matinicus both have accommodations and camping by permission. Isle au Haut is part of Acadia National Park (see pages 112–13). For Monhegan Island, see page 121. Islesboro is reached by ferry from Lincolnville Beach; North Haven, Vinalhaven, and Matinicus from a car ferry at Rockland. For details, call the Maine State Ferry Service (tel: 800/529 3939).

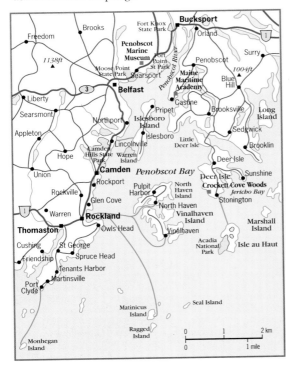

CASTINE'S MILITARY PAST

Castine had a strategic importance and was fought over by the French, Dutch, British, and Americans for nearly two centuries. Above the Maine Maritime Academy are the grassy ramparts of Fort George, built by the British in 1779 to protect Canadian interests and the last fort they abandoned at the end of the Revolutionary War. It retains its moat and earthworks.

Crammed into the **Shore Village Museum▶▶**, at 104 Limerock Street, Rockland, is the largest collection of lighthouse lenses and paraphernalia in the U.S.A., plus coastguard buoys, bells, ship models, navigational instruments, Civil War memorabilia, and 19th-century costume dolls (*Open* daily, Jun 1–Oct 15, 10–4. *Admission* donation). Also in Rockland is an outstanding art collection at the **Farnsworth Art Museum and Homestead▶▶** (*Open* Nov–May, Tue–Sat 9–5, Sun 12–5). The display is rotated and features Maine and New England art and artists. Winslow Homer's *Girl in a Punt* is one of the best-known works. The 19th-century Greek Revival homestead of William A. Farnsworth, the lime baron who endowed the museum, has period décor in its 12 small rooms. Andrew Wyeth had a studio at the **Olson House** on Hathorn Point Road, Cushing (*Open* daily, Jun–Oct). He depicted the owner in front of the house in *Christina's World*, one of the most evocative of all American paintings.

The bold and bright Romance of Autumn *by George Bellows (1882–1925), on display at the Farnsworth Art Museum in Rockland*

Rockport▶ has a charming village center, little changed from the 19th century, that overlooks a marina, old lime kiln, and oceanside park. The best of **Camden▶** lies off busy Route 1: Chestnut and Bayview streets are conspicuously attractive. Crafts shops and traffic jams are the norm in summer, with window-shoppers spilling off the sidewalks. The village keeps going all year, with events, a community theater, an opera house, and a winter carnival. In summer the village becomes the home port for a number of boat races, including the Camden–Castine Race.

Mount Battie is the crowning glory of **Camden Hills State Park▶▶** (*Open* Nov 1–May 1), where a toll road winds up to the top for a glorious view of the bay and over the strikingly empty countryside. Hikers can walk 25 miles of park trails; it takes 1–1½ hours to ascend the mountain on foot.

Searsport is Maine's "antiques capital," well endowed with shops and flea markets. **Penobscot Marine Museum►►** in town (*Open* Memorial Day weekend to Oct 15) chronicles the maritime history of Penobscot Bay. Searsport once specialized in building trading ships, and several captains' houses (including the Fowler-True-Ross House) survive from those times. The museum is on several neighboring sites; one ticket covers them all. The main building has a notable collection of maritime art, a remarkable film of a 1929 voyage around Cape Horn in a hurricane, and a quaint assemblage of 200 butter dishes collected by a captain's wife. Other buildings display small craft, whaling and scrimshaw, and shipbuilding.

The East side By complete contrast, this side of Penobscot Bay has few attractions but has a quiet charm of its own by virtue of its inaccessibility. A causeway links Deer Isle to the mainland, with the sleepy fishing village of Stonington at its southern tip, where ferries leave for Isle au Haut in Acadia National Park (see pages 112–13). **Blue Hill►►** rises to 934 feet just north of the village of the same name: from the village take Route 15 north, then turn right into Mountain Road; the trail starts on the left-hand side and ascends for a view over Acadia and Penobscot Bay. Easier to reach is the Caterpillar Hill picnic area, a mile south of the junction of Routes 15 and 175.

Castine►►, one of the most attractive villages in the state, has some gracious early 19th-century homes, with plaques recording their history, in Main and Perkins streets. By the common is the First Parish Church, begun in 1790 and eastern Maine's oldest church. At shore level, lawns slope to the water's edge, and there are two museums. The entire village has been designated a National Historic Site (see sidebar opposite). Berthed here is the *State of Maine*, a former troopship used by the adjacent Maine Maritime Academy for training merchant midshipmen. Regular tours are given round the ship; for hours, call 207/326 4311.

Crockett Cove Woods Preserve is a 100-acre site maintained by the Nature Conservancy and comprising coastal spruce woods and a miniature bog. A self-guided trail leads visitors around the preserve, and brochures are available from the entrance registration booth.

A NOSTALGIC SIDE TRIP
At Belfast, the Belfast & Moosehead Lake Railroad (tel: 800/392 5500) runs narrated two-hour trips to Brook in 1920s Pullman cars. This is a 25-mile round trip (it is extended to 33 miles in the autumn), and you get "ambushed" by comic bandits on the way. A critically acclaimed theater shares the train station, located near the water's edge. The railroad operates on weekends in spring, daily except Monday in summer; there are autumn foliage specials on Friday and on weekends.

131

WINDJAMMER VACATIONS
Companies in Penobscot Bay offer vacations on schooners known as windjammers (see picture below). Participants stay for the week and can enjoy sailing trips lasting from two hours to several days on tall-masted wooden sailing ships (some are magnificent 19th-century restorations). You can hoist the sails, take a turn at the wheel, and help navigate. Anyone sailing alone in the Boothbay or Penobscot Bay areas should have plenty of experience and be able to read a nautical chart.

Camden has the largest fleet of windjammers

For lovers of the great outdoors, New England has something for everyone, whether lone fishermen or families, adventurous young or "active seniors." From spring to autumn there is first-rate hiking, biking, fishing, and golfing. There are watersports from sailing and windsurfing to canoeing and whitewater rafting.

132

CANOEING

The Appalachian Mountain Club (AMC) publishes *Quiet Water Canoe Guide, New Hampshire/Vermont* and *River Guide, Central/ Southern New England.* Contact AMC, P.O. Box 298, Gorham, NH 03581 (tel: 603/466 2721).

Canoes can be rented and trips operate from dozens of locations, including the Rangeley Lakes area, Maine; the Lamoille and Batten Kill rivers, Vermont; the Saco River at Conway, and the Connecticut River at Hanover and Balloch's Crossing (all in NH).

Hiking and biking Hiking, popular throughout New England, is on marked trails (see page 257). All state parks have clearly signed trails, and bulletin boards often indicate length and difficulty. Trails range from easy to extremely challenging, but with vast areas of New England covered in forest, the terrain is not always particularly varied.

New Hampshire's White Mountains make superb hiking territory (see page 208). The lakes and forests of Maine's Kennebec Valley and the Western Lakes and Mountains are popular for both hiking and biking. Bicycles can be rented in many places. Naturalists will enjoy the trails in the wilds of Baxter State Park. As with several other ski areas in Maine, Vermont and New Hampshire, Sunday River in Maine has a network of mountain-bike trails using the ski lifts. The Cape Cod National Seashore has 40 miles of hiking and cycling trails; the Berkshires is another favorite area. Nantucket, Massachusetts, and Block Island, Rhode Island, have miles of attractive biking paths.

Fishing and golfing There are excellent fishing opportunities throughout New England. Lake Champlain, 100 miles long, has dozens of public access points for fishing for lake trout, landlocked salmon, bass, walleye, and the brightly colored, tasty pumpkinseed. The lake is also superb for ice-fishing, an increasingly popular winter sport.

From mid-April to the end of October, there is excellent fishing for landlocked salmon and trout in the lakes and ponds of New Hampshire and areas of Maine such as Bethel and Rangeley, the Winthrop Lakes, and around The Forks and Jackman in the north. Vermont's Northeast Kingdom region is especially popular. You'll need a map to reach the numerous "backwoods" ponds, remote and lovely beaver ponds teeming with brown trout. The Connecticut River is scenic, and peaceful—a delight for anglers.

New England's spectacular natural scenery makes a glorious backdrop for hundreds of public golf courses. Some of the most magnificent courses are offered by grand resort hotels such as The

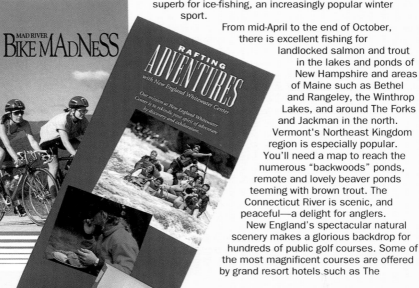

Anywhere in New England, fishing provides beautiful scenery: above, near the Mohawk Trail

Balsams at Dixville Notch, New Hampshire, the Mount Washington in the White Mountains, or Tory Pines, set in the Monadnock region. Outstanding courses in Vermont include the Woodstock Inn Resort as well as clubs in Stratton and Manchester Village (The Equinox). In Connecticut try Lyman Orchards in Middlefield and the Richter Park or the Hilton in Danbury. There is a fine course near Rangeley in northern Maine, and in the Berkshires Cranwell is an old country hotel with a splendid course.

Watersports There is good sailing from many places around the coast. Newport, Rhode Island, former home of the America's Cup, and the Penobscot Bay section of the Maine coast are the best-known areas (but much of the Maine coast has odd currents and is not for the novice— see sidebar page 131). Inland, Lake Champlain and the bigger lakes in New Hampshire and Maine are popular for sailing, sailboarding, canoeing, and windsurfing, and most have boats for rent. The Connecticut River and the Housatonic provide easy canoeing. Canoeing is a peaceful way to explore the remoter areas of northern New England, offering intimate encounters with beaver, moose and other wildlife.

Whitewater rafters await the spring runoff, when the rivers start to swirl and swell. Mecca is The Forks, in Maine, where several companies organize trips down the Kennebec, Dead, and Penobscot rivers. In the far north, experts relish the challenges of the Allagash Wilderness Waterway. In Vermont, whitewater rafting trips operate on West River. There is rafting on seven rivers from Conway, New Hampshire, and in western Massachusetts there are rafting centers on the Deerfield River.

FISHING
Licenses may be obtained from town clerk offices, local sporting shops, or the state Fish and Wildlife Office (see below).
Vermont Fish and Wildlife Department, 103 South Main Street, Waterbury, VT 05676, publishes a *Guide to Fishing* leaflet.
Other useful addresses for further information on fishing:
● Connecticut Department of Environmental Protection, 79 Elm Street, Hartford, CT 06106.
● Maine Department of Inland Fisheries and Wildlife, 284 State Street, Augusta, ME 04333.
● Massachusetts Division of Marine Fisheries, 100 Cambridge Street, Boston MA 02202.
● New Hampshire Fish and Game Department, 2 Hazen Drive, Concord, NH 03301.
● Rhode Island Division of Fish and Wildlife, Government Center, Tower Hill Road, Wakefield, RI 02879.

THE APPALACHIAN TRAIL
The Appalachian Trail (2,035 miles) stretches from Maine, through New Hampshire, Vermont, Massachusetts, and Connecticut, continuing south to Georgia. Road access makes it easy to cover short stretches. The Appalachian Mountain Club estimates that of some 2,000 to 3,000 who attempt the trail each year, only 10 percent complete it.

133

Maine

CASCO BAY

Casco Bay is the largest deepwater haven on the Atlantic coast; the islands that protect the bay are said to number 365. The first secret war conference between Churchill and Roosevelt took place on a battleship off Long Island in the bay, when the Atlantic Pact was signed. Several fortifications can be spotted on the islands, including forts Scammel, McKinley, and Gorges. South Portland is the water terminal for the Portland–Montreal pipeline. Crude oil supertankers from South America and the Middle East are common sights.

Brewed in Portland

CRUISES FROM PORTLAND

Casco Bay Lines' mailboat run is the longest such operating service in the U.S., stopping at the islands of Cliff, Chebeague, Long, Little, and Great Diamond. The company also provides cruises to Bailey Island (tel: 207/774 7871). Eagle Tours (tel: 207/774 6498) offers seal-watching and fishing trips, as well as cruises to Eagle Island.

▶▶ Portland   108A1

Maine's largest city prospered as a port on the basis of its accessibility to Europe. Its decline after World War II was reversed by a revival in fortunes, spearheaded by the revitalization of the Old Port Exchange district, with its uniform grid of red-brick streets rebuilt in the 1860s after a disastrous fire. This part of the city is pleasant for walking and has restaurants, boutiques and specialty shops. Portland's face is unmistakably urban, but the city has good cultural attractions. Commercial Street runs along the harbor, where you can join cruises (see sidebar).

The **Portland Museum of Art▶▶**, in Congress Square, houses one of New England's finest art collections. The American collection includes Maine scenes by Winslow Homer, Andrew Wyeth, Marsden Hartley, and Rockwell Kent. European art features sculpture by Henry Moore and Rodin and Impressionist and Cubist works. The museum is closed Monday, with late nights on Thursday and Friday; gallery tours are at 11 and 2 daily (for current opening hours, tel: 800/639 4067).

Next door is the **Children's Museum of Maine▶**, 142 Free Street (*Open* daily; until 8 PM on Fri; free admission Fri 5–7), which ranks among the best of its kind in New England. At 485–489 Congress Street is the **Wadsworth-Longfellow House▶**, the childhood home of Henry Wadsworth Longfellow, America's most popular 19th-century poet. His family was comfortably well-off but not wealthy, and in the house are numerous family possessions and portraits (*Open* June–Columbus Day, Tue–Sat 10–4). Longfellow was inspired to write several poems about Portland, including *The Lighthouse*, *My Lost Youth* and *The Ropewalk*. He penned *The Rainy Day* in the house.

Portland Observatory, at 138 Congress Street, was built in 1807 and is a rare example of a signal tower on which signal flags would be flown to identify incoming vessels.

Victoria Mansion▶▶, on the corner of Danforth and Park streets, is an ornate Italianate brownstone house, built 1858–60 and reflecting northern European taste. The interior is a lavish showpiece, with plasterwork made to resemble wood, an eye-catching chandelier, painted walls and ceilings, and a Moorish-style smoking room (*Open* Memorial–Labor Day, then weekends only to Columbus Day; closed Mon.)

Tate House, 1270 Westbrook Street (*Open* May–Oct, Tue–Sat 10–4, Sun 1–5) is a fine colonial period house with a riverside setting and 18th-century herb garden. A worthwhile free visit is the **Neal Dow Memorial**, at 714 Congress Street, a Federal mansion of 1829 that belonged to a leading figure in the temperance cause (*Open* Mon–Fri 11–4).

Fort Williams Park▶ occupies a fine section of rocky coast south of the city. Adjacent to the fort, Portland Head Light (1791) is the oldest lighthouse in Maine and inspired Longfellow. A museum in the lighthouse keeper's quarters tells its story (*Open* Jun–Oct; weekends only in Nov, Dec, Apr, and May). Lighthouse devotees may also like to visit nearby **Two Lights State Park**. Not far away, artist Winslow Homer made his home at Prout's Neck (also open).

▶ Wiscasset   108B1

On the Sheepscot River at Wiscasset is one of the most evocative sights on Route 1: the two huge wrecks of the *Hesper* and *Luther Little*, the world's last four-masted schooners, here since the 1930s. Every July 4 they are set alight, and their eventual demise seems inevitable.

Fort Edgecomb▶ (*Open* in daylight hours, May–Labor Day), reached by turning off Route 1 on the east side of the river bridge, is a well-preserved octagonal wooden blockhouse of 1808–1809. It was one of four defensive forts on the Lincoln County coast. Although there is nothing to see inside, the riverside setting is superb.

In town, at Lee and High streets, is **Castle Tucker** (*Open* Jul–Aug, Tue–Sat 11–4), a grand house built in 1807 by Judge Silas Lee, later modified, and now displaying 19th-century furnishings. In Federal Street, the **Old Lincoln County Jail** (*Open* daily, except Mon in summer) was built in 1811 and in use until 1953. Visitors can see the cells and jailer's house.

Rail and sail excursions run from Wiscasset (see sidebar below)

135

RAIL AND SAIL
Combined rail and sail excursions from Wiscasset from May to October are offered by Maine Coast Railroad (tel: 800/795 5404). The excursion train features restored 1920s and 1930s cars, and the cruise explores the Sheepscot River and passes Fort Edgecomb.

LONGFELLOW'S TRAGEDY
On Longfellow's marriage to his cousin, Fanny Appleton, in 1843, her father presented the house in Cambridge, Massachusetts (see page 75) to the couple as a wedding present. She died 18 years later when her hoop skirt caught fire while she was melting sealing wax to preserve locks of her children's hair. Henry grew a beard to cover the physical scars incurred while trying to save her, but remained emotionally scarred.

The hulks of two schooners, built around the end of World War I, dominate the scene at Wiscasset

Hancock Warehouse, York, dates from the mid-1700s and is still used as a boathouse today

BLOWING CAVE

Located between Walker Point and Cape Arundel, just east of Kennebunkport, this sea cave is a curious phenomenon. As waves enter it, air is trapped and compressed; as the water recedes, the trapped air is released, sometimes sending out a spray of seawater. Unfortunately, it is difficult to see this happen as the cave is only really accessible at low tide, but it is fun to explore just the same.

IN LOVE WITH THE PAST

Elizabeth Perkins and her mother fell in love with their house in York and spent their summers there. Proud of their New England heritage and ancestors, the Perkins crammed the house with antiques and furniture, creating a comfortable rather than historically accurate house for entertaining and vacationing. Elizabeth took an interest in preserving York and was responsible for saving the schoolhouse and wooden bridge. She loved collecting antiques and installed old-fashioned beams and paneling for effect in the dining room. Both women's ashes are in the garden.

Elizabeth Perkins House, transformed into an idyllic weekend retreat by a wealthy New York family

►► York and Kennebunkport   108A1

York is a composite place: just off Route 1 lies historic York Village, alone worth at least half a day to explore. Along the shoreline are Long Sands Beach (popular for surfing) and the famous Nubble Lighthouse (also known as Cape Neddick Lighthouse), built in 1789 on York Beach, which itself retains a graceful 19th-century air. York Harbor is a small area between the old village and the beaches.

The Old York Historical Society sites These include a number of buildings, some with tours conducted by interpreters, others self-guided. Tours start on the hour; the last are at 4 PM. Jefferds Tavern (1754), where you buy your ticket, features displays about York and is often filled with the aroma of hearthside cooking. Next door is the **Old Schoolhouse** (1745), which has a small exhibit on schooling and apprenticeship in Maine.

Made from two colonial houses put together, rooms in the **Emerson Wilcox House**► illustrate a variety of periods, from the 1765 parlor to the 1930s dining room. The bedroom possesses the oldest known complete set of American bed-hangings, done in crewel work in 1746 and in pristine condition (notice the original spelling mistakes in the words of a hymn that have been worked into the design).

The **Old Gaol**►, in use from 1719 to 1860, took in about 14 prisoners per year; interpreters fill in the facts and legends. Jail quarters and the jailer's chambers are on show.

The **Hancock Warehouse**►, once owned by John Hancock, occupies a charming spot on an unspoiled creek, near a wooden bridge. A replica of an 1880s gundalow (a flat-bottomed boat) is often on the river here. The warehouse is the last commercial colonial building in town and is still used as a working boathouse. It houses a small exhibition on shipbuilding, timber, shipping, farming, and lobstering.

By the York River is the **Elizabeth Perkins House▶ ▶**, a fascinating example of the Colonial Revival style—a colonial house furnished during the 1920s to 1940s in an idealized conception of the colonial style itself. Its transformation began in 1898 when the Perkins bought the (then four-roomed) 18th-century farmhouse (see sidebar on page 136).

Elsewhere along the coast The yachting and fishing village of **Kennebunkport** is the home and former Summer White House of ex-President George Bush, who used to jog along the beach (often with scores of red-faced reporters and photographers in tow). His house at Walker's Point can be seen from the seafront, otherwise memorable for its drawbridge. On Route 9A/35 is the Wedding Cake House, a particularly fetching yellow and white confection.

The **Brick Store Museum▶**, at 117 Main Street, Kennebunk (*Open* Tue–Sat; closed Sat in winter), is a fine local history museum with rotating exhibits on both maritime and social history and on the decorative arts. Three miles north of Kennebunkport, the **Seashore Trolley Museum▶** (*Open* May –Nov) has the world's largest collection of trolleys and offers an opportunity to take a nostalgic ride.

Route 1 in this area is packaged-fun country. At York itself is York's **Wild Kingdom** (with zoo and amusement park). The **Wells Auto Museum** has more than 130 vintage automobiles as well as an entertaining assembly of antique arcade games, nickelodeons and other items; it is open in summer. Saco is home to **Funtown**, the **Maine Aquarium**, and **Aquaboggan Water Park**. **Old Orchard Beach**, on the coast, has a sandy shoreline and is densely developed with fast-food outlets and amusements; **Palace Playland** is a major attraction whose seaside rides are reminiscent of New York's Coney Island.

Ogunquit is an upscale resort village and was once an artists' colony. Cove views are available from a pretty drawbridge leading to Perkins Cove and from a mile-long coastal path known as Rustic Way. Ogunquit's Museum of Art is open in the summer months, and there is a summer theater season.

Kittery▶ has similar factory shopping outlets to Freeport (see page 128); there are over 100 such discount stores along Kittery's "miracle mile" offering savings of up to 70 percent.

WEBHANNET RIVER MARSH
The marsh, off Route 1, is an important bird habitat. Species include the scarce piping plover, a small buff and white bird with a black band around its neck. Ducks, grebes, loons, gulls, and herons may also be seen at the marsh.

BEACHES
Beaches in this area are safe for swimming, and the water is clean. The main ones are Long Sands Beach at York; Ogunquit, one of the best in Maine, stretching 3 miles; Goose Rocks at Kennebunkport, a favorite with families; and Kennebunk Beach.

137

Travel through time at the Trolley Museum near Kennebunkport

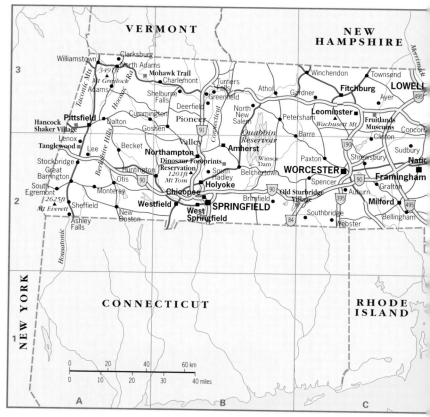

VERMONT

NEW HAMPSHIRE

Williamstown • Clarksburg
North Adams
3490ft • Mohawk Trail
Mt Greylock • Charlemont
Adams
Taconic Mts
Hoosac
Shelburne Falls
Deerfield
Cummington
Goshen
Pittsfield • Dalton
Hancock Shaker Village
Lenox
Tanglewood • Lee
Becket
Berkshire Hills
Stockbridge
Great Barrington
Huntington
Otis
Monterey
South Egremont
2625ft
Mt Everett • Sheffield
Ashley Falls
New Boston
Housatonic

Pioneer
Valley
Connecticut
Northampton
Dinosaur Footprints
Reservation
1201ft
Mt Tom
Chicopee
Holyoke
Westfield
West Springfield
SPRINGFIELD

Turners Falls
Greenfield
North New Salem
Quabbin Reservoir
Winsor Dam
Amherst
South Hadley
Belchertown
Brimfield
91
90
84
90

Winchendon • Townsend
Athol
Gardner
Petersham
Leominster
Wachusett Mt
Barre
WORCESTER
Paxton
Spencer
Old Sturbridge Village
Southbridge
Webster
395

Fitchburg • Ayer
LOWELL
495
Fruitlands Museums
Clinton
Concord
190
Shrewsbury
Sudbury
Natick
Framingham
Grafton
Auburn
Milford
Bellingham
495

NEW YORK

CONNECTICUT

RHODE ISLAND

0   20   40   60 km
0 10 20 30 40 miles

A   B   C

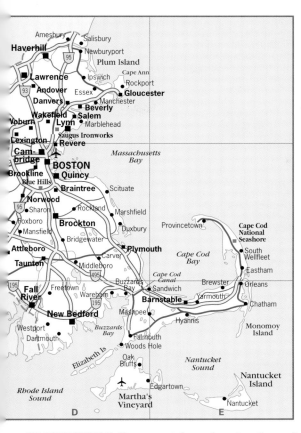

MASSACHUSETTS Even apart from the attractions of Boston and Cambridge (see pages 48–85), there is plenty in the rest of Massachusetts to excite the curious traveler. The state is the cradle of modern America and as such is packed with history. In 1620, the Pilgrim Fathers landed at Provincetown, some 600 miles farther north than they had intended (they were bound for Jamestown in Virginia), before finally establishing themselves at Plymouth. In 1775, the first shots of the American Revolution sounded at Lexington and Concord. In the 19th century, the first large-scale textile mills appeared in Lowell, heralding the birth of industrial America. Massachusetts is seen as a center of political and intellectual thought: great names associated with the state include Ralph Waldo Emerson (1803–82), Henry David Thoreau (1817–62), Herman Melville (1819–91), Emily Dickinson (1830–86), Louisa May Alcott (1832–88), Edith Wharton (1862–1937), and John F. Kennedy (1917–63).

ALONG THE COAST Early settlers ensconced themselves along the coast, often referred to as the North Shore and the South Shore, with Boston at the pivot. Today, the coast is a place for summer relaxation, though the sheer

Autumn color on the Mohawk Trail

numbers of visitors trying to get away from it all can be self-defeating. North Shore towns are select and picturesque, notably Salem, Marblehead, Rockport (on Cape Ann), and Newburyport. Each makes a feasible day trip from Boston, with good public transportation links. Of these, Salem has the most to see, with its gruesome episode of the witches' persecution told in a variety of styles.

On the South Shore is Plymouth, a pleasant town with several mementoes of the pioneer days, most notably the re-created Pilgrim village at Plimoth Plantation and the *Mayflower II*. Cape Cod needs time to appreciate fully, although quirky Provincetown is an entertaining day out by ferry from Boston. Ideally, Cape Cod should be seen "out of season," and the trip should include visits to the islands of Martha's Vineyard and Nantucket, both haunts of the rich but remarkably different in character; in particular, the towns of Oak Bluffs and Nantucket have their very own, inimitable period atmospheres. New Bedford, the whaling port that succeeded Nantucket, looks unappetizing as you speed through its industrial outskirts on I–195, but its old center has atmosphere and a good whaling museum.

The huge granite blocks of a pier at Rockport on Cape Ann, mementoes of a former local granite industry

"Listen to the surf, really lend it your ears, and you will hear in it a world of sound: hollow boomings and heavy roarings, great watery tumblings and tramplings, long hissing seethes, sharp rifle-shot reports, splashes, whispers, the grinding undertone of stones, and sometimes vocal sounds that might be the half-heard talk of people in the sea."
– Henry Beston, *The Outermost House* (1927), written in a coastal shack on Cape Cod.

HEADING INLAND Concord and Lexington lie just beyond the western suburbs of Boston; in addition to the Revolutionary battle sites, there is a rich literary heritage to explore at Concord. Worcester, a large industrial city, deserves a look for its Armory and art museum.

Of much more mainstream appeal is the evocation of 1830s New England at Old Sturbridge Village—sheer pastiche, but convincingly done and atmospheric when not too crowded. Even the farm animals resemble authentic early 19th-century breeds.

Up to the late 18th century, New England extended only as far west as the Connecticut River (known here as Pioneer Valley), where you will find an academic center, the so-called Five Colleges Area, plus the industrial centers of Holyoke and Springfield. There are some good walks along the river, with abrupt cliff edges in places. Historic Deerfield is the best sight in the valley. Here the

140

*Spectacular autumn
views at Shelburne Falls
in western
Massachusetts*

141

mile-long village street has none of the period-clad actors found in Old Sturbridge, but some will find the uncommercialized and slow-paced atmosphere appealing.

THE FAR WEST Massachusetts now extends west of the Connecticut River into Berkshire County, which borders New York State. This hilly and predominantly rural region has much to offer in the arts: Tanglewood hosts the premier summer musical event in Massachusetts and is the summer base of the Boston Symphony Orchestra (see page 79). Artist Norman Rockwell (see page 150) is remembered near Stockbridge by an excellent museum, and at Chesterwood the house and studio of sculptor Daniel Chester French makes an absorbing visit. Hancock Shaker Village gives a fascinating insight into the virtually vanished lifestyle of the Shaker sect.

TRUSTEES OF RESERVATIONS A useful source of information for exploring the farther-flung sights of Massachusetts is the handbook published by The Trustees of Reservations. Established in 1891, this is the world's oldest preservation society. It owns over 70 houses and areas of countryside, including woodlands, gorges, waterfalls, and wildlife refuges throughout Massachusetts. Members are admitted to most properties free of charge and to the remaining few at reduced rates. Information and membership details can be obtained from 572 Essex Street, Beverly, MA 01915 1530 (tel: 978/921 1944).

Events

The precise dates of festivals vary from year to year. Book in advance for popular events, such as the Tanglewood summer concerts. For further information, contact the state tourist office (see page 266) or chambers of commerce.

April
Daffodil Festival, Nantucket: flower show and vintage cars.
Re-enactment of the Battle of Lexington and Concord.

May
Brimfield Antique Flea Market, Brimfield: New England's prime antiques event.
Seaport Festival, Salem: crafts, walks, exhibitions, and children's activities.

June
Craft Fair, Old Deerfield.
Jacob's Pillow Dance Festival, Becket: renowned modern dance event (until August or September).
St. Peter's Fiesta, Gloucester: Blessing of the Fleet; fireworks, parade, music.

Plymouth Rock, the stone onto which the Pilgrim Fathers are supposed to have stepped when they came ashore from the Mayflower

Tanglewood Music Festival, Lenox: Boston Symphony Orchestra concerts (until August or September).

July
Barnstable County Fair, East Falmouth: major Cape Cod event.
Brimfield Antique Flea Market.
Lowell Folk Festival: music, crafts and ethnic food.

August
Annual Teddy Bear Rally, Amherst: dealers, teddies' hospital, entertainment, contests.
Fall River Celebrates America, Fall River: ships, boat races, fireworks.
Feast of Blessed Sacrament, New Bedford: the country's largest Portuguese festival, with the Blessing of the Fleet, food, dance, and parade.
Marshfield Fair, Marshfield.
Martha's Vineyard Agricultural Fair.
Marshfield Fair.
Waterfront Festival, Gloucester: pancake breakfast, Yankee lobster bake, whale watching.
Waterfront Festival, Newburyport: art, crafts and entertainment.

September
Brimfield Antique Flea Market.
Harwich Cranberry Festival, Harwich: country and western music, fireworks, and parade spread over 10 days.
The Big E, West Springfield: New England's great state fair.

October
Haunted Happenings, Salem: magic, witches, costume parade, and candlelight tours at Halloween.
Topsfield Fair, Topsfield: oldest continuous fair in the U.S.A. Includes a pumpkin weigh-in.

November
Thanksgiving Day Celebration, Plymouth: Pilgrims' procession, Thanksgiving service, and dinner.
Bright Nights at Forest Park, Springfield (until January).

December
Christmas Shoppers' Stroll, Nantucket: carol singing, theater, house tours.
First Night Celebration, Cape Cod, Lowell, Newburyport, New Bedford, Northampton, Pittsfield, Quincy, Salem, and Worcester.

▶▶▶ Berkshire Hills 138A2

The Berkshires is the hilliest and western-most part of Massachusetts and was a fashionable summer resort area for wealthy urbanites in the late 19th century. Summer nowadays is busy with arts events, with some 300,000 people attracted to Tanglewood (see page 146) for the Boston Symphony Orchestra summer concert series alone. The area's autumn foliage brings in more crowds later on in the year, and there are many opportunities for downhill and cross-country skiing enthusiasts in the winter. Compulsive antiques-shop browsers may like to head for the area around Route 7 between South Egremont and Ashley Falls. Many of the museums and houses close between mid-October and late May.

The Mohawk Trail and the Northern Berkshires The **Mohawk Trail▶**, the country's first designated Scenic Road (opened 1914), follows Route 2 for 63 miles from the Pioneer Valley to the New York State border. The trail dates back to 1663, when the Pocumtuck tribe invaded Mohawk Territory by creating this route over the mountains from Deerfield to Troy, New York. Much of it is unspoiled even today, although motels and "Indian trading posts" (with racks of plastic totem poles and the like) dot the highway in places. **French King Bridge▶** is a scenic crossing of the Connecticut River, the first point on the trail worth stopping for; the river is 140 feet below. Farther west

Shelburne Falls▶, is known for its Bridge of Flowers, an old trolley bridge graced with colorful blooms. Near the Salmon Falls dam, jagged rocks in the river attract swimmers and picnickers. The road passes the **Hail to the Sunrise Monument**, erected in 1932 by tribes and councils of the Approved Order of Red Men, showing a Mohawk with arms outstretched. Signs soon begin to announce 4 miles of steep gradients and sharp curves, culminating spectacularly at **Hairpin Turn▶▶**, a fine outlook. Go north along Route 8 toward Clarksburg for **Natural Bridge State Park**. Waters tumble through a small chasm gouged out by glacial meltwater and spanned by a natural bridge. Adjacent is an abandoned white marble quarry.

The Mohawk Trail passes through some spectacularly rugged scenery— and there are plenty of reminders of its origins Left: the "Hail to Sunrise" memorial at the entrance to the Mohawk Trail State Forest

143

INFORMATION FOR THE BERKSHIRE HILLS
For further information, contact the Berkshire Visitors' Bureau, Berkshire Common, Plaza Level, Dept MT, Pittsfield, MA 01201 (tel: 413/443 9186, or toll-free 800/BERKSHR). *Berkshires Week* is a free weekly listings magazine containing information on state parks, campgrounds, sights, children's activities, shopping, and events; it is available at all chambers of commerce.

*Aerial view of
Williamstown in the
Berkshires*

**THE HOOSAC RAILROAD
TUNNEL**
This 4.7-mile tunnel near
Adams, in the northwest
corner of the Berkshires,
was constructed in
1851–75 and was the
first project of its kind to
use nitroglycerine for
blasting out the rock. The
project was costly, both in
terms of money ($24 mil-
lion) and lives (195 workers perished). It gained
the nickname of the
"Bloody Pit" and, not
surprisingly, is alleged to
be haunted.

Mount Greylock►►►, the highest peak in Massachusetts at 3,491 feet, was named after Chief Grey Lock,
who hunted here. A road climbs to the top for a grand view
over three states. Church spires dominate **North Adams**, a
red-brick mill town. The museum at Western Gateway
Heritage State Park narrates the history of the Hoosac
Railroad Tunnel (see sidebar opposite page). Away from
the Mohawk Trail, the cotton mill town of **Adams** has legacies of the 18th century, most significantly the atmospheric
Quaker Meeting House of 1782 on Friend Street.

Founded as West Hoosac in 1750, elegant
Williamstown►► owes its name to Ephraim Williams,
who left money for the founding of an academy, stipulating
that the town must take his name; the academy opened in
1791, becoming Williams College two years later. Today, it
is among the top liberal arts institutions in America. The
superb **Sterling and Francine Clark Art Institute►►►**
(*Open* Tue–Sun. *Admission* free) is noted for French
Impressionist and American paintings, as well as British silverware. The **Williams College Museum of Art►** (*Open*
Tue–Sun. *Admission* free) possesses 11,000 works ranging
from 9th-century Assyrian stone reliefs to Andy Warhol's
last self-portrait. **The Hopkins Observatory** contains a
museum and planetarium, open during the academic year
and on occasions during the summer.

The town of **Pittsfield** has been a paper mill center since
the 19th century and is the largest town in the Berkshires
region. Art galleries exhibiting local work include
Pittsfield Arts League (2 South Street), Radius Gallery
(137 North Street), and Berkshire Artisans (28 Renne
Avenue). **Berkshire Museum►** (39 South Street) includes
art of the Hudson River school, dolls, early electric

inventions of the Stanley Electric Company and domestic relics. The Crane Paper Company's **Wahconah Mill** manufactures paper on which American currency is printed. At Dalton, east of Pittsfield, the **Crane Museum**, within the 1844 Old Stone Mill, tells the story of American paper-making (*Open* summer weekdays, 2–5. *Admission* free). On the outskirts of Pittsfield, off Holmes Road, is **Arrowhead** (*Open* Memorial Day–Labor Day; tours 10–4:30), the home of Herman Melville and family from 1850 to 1863. The furniture is not original but is contemporary. The house contains the room where Melville wrote *Moby Dick* (1851).

Renoir and Degas, part of the notable French collection in the Sterling and Francine Clark Art Institute

The region's best-preserved Shaker village, active from 1783 to 1960, **Hancock Shaker Village▶ ▶ ▶** is today a living museum, well worth a full day's visit if you want to catch the events held here (Open third week in May–third week in October, 9–5; plus guided tours Apr–May and late Oct–end Nov, 10–3; tel: 413/443 0188). Originally called the "City of Peace," the village is noted for its famous round stone barn. The museum's craftsmen and craftswomen continue to live out the Shaker lifestyle (see pages 148–149), tending historic livestock breeds, maintaining an authentic herb garden, and demonstrating Shaker cooking.

TRUE CONNOISSEURS
When Williamstown's Sterling and Francine Clark Institute opened in 1955 a unique collection came under the public gaze for the first time. The display was gathered by Robert Sterling Clark (1877–1956) thanks to a family fortune amassed by the Singer sewing machine empire. While living in Paris from 1911 to 1921 he married Francine Clary, who shared his passion for art; during this time he added many paintings by late 19th-century French artists. Artists represented include Homer, Sargent, Pissarro and Monet.

The round barn (dating at least back to 1830) at Hancock Shaker Village. People came from far and wide to study its ingenious design

MUSIC AT TANGLEWOOD

The Tanglewood Music Center, a training center for musicians, is the summer home of the Boston Symphony Orchestra (see page 79). The open-sided Music Shed is the main concert hall; it is cheapest to sit on the adjoining lawn for concerts (the sound does carry). Open rehearsals take place at 10:30 AM. on Saturdays; you can eavesdrop from the lawn at other times, since members of the public are admitted into the grounds. While there you can visit the Little Red House, a reconstruction of the house in which Nathaniel Hawthorne wrote *The House of the Seven Gables* (1851) and *Tanglewood Tales* (1852–53); inside is a free museum, open in summer.

STOCKBRIDGE WALKS

Just south of Stockbridge, off Park Street, is boulder-strewn Ice Glen, so called because of the presence of ice crystals well into summer; a trail climbs up to Laura's Tower for a three-state view.

Three miles south of Stockbridge, on Route 7, the Monument Mountain Reservation overlooks the southern Berkshires, with trails encountering rock outcrops, caves, and a hillside strewn with quartzite boulders. William Cullen Bryant waxed lyrical in a poem about the mountain: "the beauty and the majesty of the earth, spread wide beneath."

The Southern Berkshires An amiable small-town atmosphere envelopes **Lenox▶**, well located as a base for exploring the southern Berkshires. In the late 19th century, the estates formed rural summer retreats for the wealthy; one such was **Tanglewood** (see sidebar), near Lenox, originally owned by the Tappan family. Another was **The Mount▶**, in Lenox, summer residence of the writer Edith Wharton (see page 46) from 1902 to 1911. A sledding accident at Lenox was the basis of her novel *Ethan Frome* (1911). The restored **Lenox railroad station** (1902) also evokes the period; the Berkshire Scenic Railroad maintains a model railroad, a short section of track, and a shop.

Norman Rockwell (see page 150) put **Stockbridge▶ ▶** on the map with his depiction of Main Street. At the heart of the village is the Red Lion Inn, dating from 1773 and sporting the sign of George III. Even older is the **Mission House▶** (*Open* Memorial Day weekend–Columbus Day Tue–Sun, and holidays, 10–5), the only elegant house in a wilderness when built in 1739 for a Congregationalist minister; its furniture is original, and there is a display on the Native American

Chesterwood, the summer home of sculptor Daniel Chester French

Daniel Chester French's statue of the seated Abraham Lincoln

community of Stockbridge. Across the street, **Merwin House▶** (Open Tue, Thu, Sat, and Sun, 12–5, in summer; owned and operated by SPNEA—see page 68) is a Federal-style brick house built around 1825, furnished in turn-of-the-century style.

Located just outside town is the **Norman Rockwell Museum▶▶▶**, which holds the world's largest collection of original works by the hugely popular artist. About a quarter of the works are on display at any one time. The reconstructed studio has Rockwell's art books, easel, and many props familiar from his paintings.

Chesterwood▶▶ (*Open* daily, May–Oct; signposted from the west end of Main Street, Stockbridge), was the summer home of sculptor Daniel Chester French from 1898 ("I live here six months of the year—in heaven. The other six months I live, well—in New York"). Tours take in his studio and house (see sidebar).

The best opportunity to glimpse inside a fashionable summer house in the Berkshires is at **Naumkeag▶▶** (*Open* late May–Columbus Day, Tue–Sun). Built in 1885 by Stanford White for the Choates, it retains some of the family's eclectic possessions. Fletcher Steele later modified the gardens to create terraces with a stepped waterfall.

The **Berkshire Botanical Garden▶** (*Open* May–Oct; Route 102 west of the intersection with Route 183) is compact but varied, with an herbarium of dyer's and medicinal herbs, rock garden, lily pond, day lilies, shrubs, and wild flowers. July and August are the best months to visit.

Bidwell House▶, in Monterey (*Open* Memorial Day–mid-Oct, Tue–Sun and holidays, 11–4), is a Georgian house built for a minister; it has original features and is furnished according to an inventory of 1784.

At Great Barrington is the **Albert Schweitzer Center**, a museum and library dedicated to the humanitarian and winner of the 1953 Nobel Peace Prize. The town is popular with antiques hunters.

Colonel John Ashley House▶, Ashley Falls (*Open* Memorial Day–Columbus Day, Wed–Sun and holidays in summer; weekends in spring. *Admission* free), is a quintessential Colonial house of 1735 where Ashley and others drafted the petition against Britain in 1773 known as the Sheffield Declaration. In 1781, Ashley's slave, Mum Bett, was the first slave to win her freedom, doing so under the new constitution.

The pools below **Bash Bish Falls▶▶**, a fine waterfall cascading over huge rocks, are excellent for swimming. They can be reached from the lower parking lot (beyond the New York State sign). Nearby is **Mount Everett State Forest▶**, with a road leading to its summit.

DANIEL CHESTER FRENCH
America's most prolific sculptor, French produced some works of worldwide renown, including his first commission, the *Minute Man* (completed in 1875 and made from 10 army cannons melted down for the purpose) at Concord, the John Harvard statue at Harvard University, and the Lincoln statue in Washington, DC.

MORE TRAILS IN THE BERKSHIRES
October Mountain State Forest, off Route 20 near Lee, is Massachusetts's largest state forest, with 50 campsites and many trails, including the walk to Schermerhorn Gorge. To the south of Tyringham Center are good hill walks on Tyringham Cobble and the McLennan Reservation, the occasional haunts of coyotes, bobcats, black bears, and wild turkeys.

The 2,035-mile Appalachian Trail, from Georgia to Maine, crosses the length of the Berkshire Hills south to north.

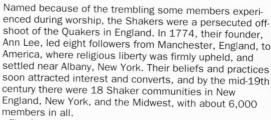

The Shaker religious sect is now almost extinct, but, in today's complex world, the purity of its followers' way of life, the simple, functional design of their architecture and furniture, and their herbal medicines and organic farming methods have an increasing appeal.

SHAKER YOUR PLATE

In the summer and autumn, visitors to Hancock Shaker Village can partake of a candle-light dinner. The Shaker practice of silence during meals is not observed, and the sexes may mix, but the dishes are taken from Shaker cookbooks. Guests should note an extract from Rules for Visitors: "At the table we wish all to be as free as at home, but we dislike the wasteful habit of leaving food on the plate." Hence the expression "shaker your plate."

The kitchen at Hancock, efficient and elegant

Named because of the trembling some members experienced during worship, the Shakers were a persecuted offshoot of the Quakers in England. In 1774, their founder, Ann Lee, led eight followers from Manchester, England, to America, where religious liberty was firmly upheld, and settled near Albany, New York. Their beliefs and practices soon attracted interest and converts, and by the mid-19th century there were 18 Shaker communities in New England, New York, and the Midwest, with about 6,000 members in all.

The Shakers were originally called the United Society of Believers in Christ's Second Appearing and believed that the millennium, a thousand years of heaven on earth, had arrived with Mother Ann. The fundamental principles laid down by Mother Ann were communal living (separate from "the world") and celibacy. In the belief that Mother Ann was the female aspect of God, her followers shared leadership and work equally between men and women. Tasks indoors and out were taken in turn so no one had to endure the unpopular jobs for too long (such as looking after the small boys sent by their parents to learn a trade in the Shaker community).

"Hands to work and hearts to God" The Shakers aimed for perfection in all they turned their hands to. Adapting the Yankee work ethic to fit their religious ideals, they became renowned for their industry and ingenuity. Their numerous inventions include the circular saw, a rotary harrow, a threshing machine, an automatic hay-seeding device, a nondrip paint can, and the flat broom.

The Shakers were also immensely practical and kept the house very clean (this was heaven on earth, and there is no dust in heaven). This explains the ubiquitous wooden peg rails for hanging clothes, kitchen utensils, mops, and their ladder-backed chairs; the built-in, floor-to-ceiling wardrobes (no need to sweep underneath or dust on top), and the beds on rollers for ease of sweeping; it also accounts for the striking efficiency of their kitchens, and the famously progressive round barn at Hancock, Massachusetts (see page 145).

In the belief that a sound soul needs a healthy body, the Shakers ate well (their recipes are famous); they also made a wide range of herbal medicines. Assiduous gardeners, they were the first to market seeds, an enterprise which developed into a most successful industry.

Villages such as Hancock (left) are preserved for posterity

SHAKER ARTIFACTS
Oval boxes, baskets, and furniture, in particular the chair, exemplify the clean, simple lines of Shaker design and their perfect craftsmanship. Everything was made purely to serve its function, without any embellishment. The chair is sturdy, but light—so it could be hung up out of the way—with a straight ladder-back. The chairs' back legs were fitted with a "button tilter," a swivel device designed to prevent wear on floors. The reproduction of Shaker artifacts is a burgeoning industry, and the Shaker villages sell beautiful examples.

THE GIFT OF SONG
Singing and dancing was, and is, an integral part of the Shaker service of worship, and 10,000 or more of their songs have been collected. Many are based on English and early American folk tunes. Aaron Copland borrowed the Shaker "Simple Gifts" melody for his *Appalachian Spring*, scored for a Martha Graham ballet in 1944:
"'Tis the gift to be simple, 'tis the gift to be free,
'Tis the gift to come down where we ought to be,
And when we find ourselves in the place just right,
'Twill be in the valley of love and delight."

Shakers and "the world" The Shaker communities adopted orphans. They also took in children indentured to the society by their parents in order to learn a trade, many of whom later joined the communities. Converts were also made from the many visitors who came to the villages, for while separation from the world was a basic principle, Shakers were happy to sell their goods— brooms, chairs, boxes, baskets, seeds, and cloaks (specially woven in bright colors for society ladies to wear to the opera)—to the "world's people."

Numbers peaked in the 1840s but, in the decades that followed, began to decline; restrictions on adoption were enforced, and the pacifism Shakerism stood for and which had attracted converts went out of favor. Celibacy began to take its toll in falling numbers, and communities could not compete with the increasing mass production of goods.

Today, only a handful of Shakers are left, living in the town of Sabbathday Lake, Maine. They generally continue to live the traditional Shaker life, worshipping devoutly, selling their goods at fairs, farming their land (though they are more likely to be seen wearing Levis for hoeing the vegetables than the long skirts or white shirts and black waistcoats still worn for services). Tours can be taken around the village, but most buildings may be seen from the outside only. At Canterbury and Lower Shaker villages in New Hampshire (see pages 192 and 195), and at Hancock village in Massachusetts (see page 145), the old buildings are preserved in recognition of the purity and ingenuity of the Shaker contribution.

"Without thinking too much about it in specific terms, I was showing the America I knew and observed to others who might not have noticed." Norman Rockwell's portrayal of scenes from everyday life touched the nation's soul and made him one of America's most popular illustrators.

150

Top: Triple Self-Portrait *(1960)*
Above: "Freedom from Want"

Born in New York in 1894, Norman Rockwell was given his first freelance commission at the age of 17 by the magazine publishers Condé Nast. In 1916, he took some paintings to the art editor of the *Saturday Evening Post*, the most widely circulated magazine in America, and thus began a partnership that was to turn Norman Rockwell into a household name, and his works into national treasures. Over the next 47 years he illustrated 317 covers for the Post, each one eagerly awaited by its readers.

The American dream In almost photographic detail, Rockwell depicted childhood, family, and small-town scenes, each tinged with affection and gentle humor: the family outing in the car, the boy who discovers his father's Santa Claus costume, a visit to the optician, the signing of a marriage license. When he moved with his wife, Mary Barstow, and their three sons to Arlington, Vermont, in 1939, the neighbors were "exactly the models I need for my purpose—the sincere, honest, homespun types that I love to paint." And it was just these people that he depicted in the famous wartime series of posters—"Freedom of Speech," "Freedom of Worship," "Freedom from Want," and "Freedom from Fear"—inspired by President Roosevelt's Four Freedoms Proclamation of 1941.

In 1953, the family moved to Stockbridge in Massachusetts, where Rockwell lived and worked right up to his death in 1978. His works include illustrations for calendars, such as the Boy Scout Calendar, covers for other magazines, advertisements, and greetings cards, as well as oil paintings and portraits.

Rockwell's work has always been a touch too sentimental for the fine art buffs, but among ordinary people, for whom he captures American life as it was always meant to be, Norman Rockwell remains as popular as ever.

WHERE TO SEE HIS WORK
The largest collection of Rockwell originals is in a museum near Stockbridge, Massachusetts (see page 147). The old carriage house he converted to a studio has been moved to this site from his Stockbridge home. In Vermont, Rockwell's hometown of Arlington has a display of prints in a 19th-century church, and in Rutland, the Norman Rockwell Museum has an exhibition covering his career (*open* all year).

BIRDSEYE'S FROZEN FOODS
Clarence "Bob" Birdseye (1886–1956) created the frozen-food business from Gloucester after observing, on an expedition to Labrador in 1914–17, that local people ate fish, meat, and vegetables that they had frozen months before. In 1925, he developed a quick-freezing system for commercial use and helped to found the General Seafoods Company in Gloucester, selling frozen foods to consumers in Springfield, Massachusetts. Birds Eye is now a household name, and the original plant in Commercial Street is still in operation.

151

▶▶ Cape Ann   *139D3*

Abutting the northern extremity of Massachusetts Bay, Cape Ann harbors many charming fishing ports, as well as idiosyncratic historic buildings and coastal views much depicted by artists. There are good bathing beaches and shops for browsing. Weekend traffic winds slowly along Routes 127 and 127A, and parking can be very difficult, particularly in Rockport. A train service from Boston's North Station and Monday to Saturday bus services provide feasible alternatives.

Manchester has an attractive harbor and clean sands at Singing Beach (the train station is a short walk away).

Gloucester▶ is a starting point for whale-watching trips and is also a working fishing port—founded in 1623, it is America's oldest. Fine beaches draw crowds on summer weekends. Artist Fitz Hugh Lane (1804–1865) lived in the three-gabled granite house on the waterfront, and the nation's largest collection of his work is exhibited with fishing industry displays at the **Cape Ann Historical Society▶**. Living artists' work can be seen in the thriving **Rocky Neck Art Colony** and at the North Shore Arts Association's exhibition center.

Hammond Castle Museum▶▶ in Gloucester (*Open* 10–6, summer and winter weekends 10–4; for details, tel: 978/283 7673) is a sham medieval folly perched just above the shore; home of the inventor John Hays Hammond, Jr., the eye-catching edifice was built around the Hammond organ in the Great Hall (see sidebar). The castle comprises a labyrinth of small rooms and passages adorned with Renaissance treasures, a library with a "whispering ceiling" that picks up the slightest sounds, and a courtyard graced by a Roman sarcophagus.

THE MIGHTY HAMMOND
The massive 8,200-pipe Hammond organ at Hammond Castle was built to play automatically because, ironically, Dr. Hammond, the inventor, was not musical enough to play the instrument himself. The immense sound of Bach's Toccata and Fugue, often played to tour groups, is astonishingly powerful. There is a program of concerts given here.

The Gloucester Fisherman *by Leonard Craske looks out to sea*

THEY THAT GO DOWN TO THE SEA IN SHIPS
1623 – 1923

Fishing floats adorn the wall of Motif No. 1 (above) at the mouth of Rockport harbor (top)

THE PAPER HOUSE
North of Rockport, off Route 127 at Pigeon Cove, is this all-paper building constructed between 1922 and 1942 by Elis F. Stenman as an experiment. He invented a special paste for the purpose and used some 100,000 newspapers: the furniture (made from hollow tubes) included a piano, a clock, a radio cabinet, chairs, and a desk. The walls are made of diamond-shaped blocks, with the headlines still legible. Stenman's wife created the bead curtains from old magazines.

A short drive south along the coast, though still in Gloucester, is the fantasy retreat of **Beauport▶** with its warren of 40 rooms, many of them devoted to historical themes (*Open* mid-May–mid-Oct, Mon–Fri, plus weekends, Sep and Oct; owned and operated by SPNEA—see page 68). The house was built, and periodically enlarged, between 1907 and 1934, by interior designer Henry Davis Sleeper. It is full of quirky visual effects, windows with colored glass, and bottles, antiquities, and curiosities—including a secret staircase. The Pine Kitchen, recalling the simple homes of the colonial era, contrasts with the Octagon Room, elegantly French in spirit, or the Belfry Bedroom, which is sheer chinoiserie. The road continues southward to **Eastern Point Lighthouse** on the east side of Gloucester Harbor.

Picturesque **Rockport▶ ▶** is the most visited place on Cape Ann. The harbor scene epitomizes coastal New England and includes the fishing shack known as "Motif No. 1," one of the most photographed and painted buildings in America. **Bearskin Neck**, the heart of the old village, is a mixture of craft shops and toytown-scale fishing huts turned into homes with tiny front gardens.

Within the 54 acres of **Halibut Point State Park▶ ▶** is a fine panorama where a dwarf forest gives way to heathland and scrub, with drops to a rocky shore.

Essex stakes a claim as "king of the clam." It has lobster shacks, seafood restaurants, fishing-tackle shops, and over 60 antiques shops. The Shipbuilding Museum expounds on 300 years of the industry in Essex. Boat trips up the Essex River give opportunities for birdwatching, while Crane's Beach at **Ipswich** ranks among the North Shore's finest.

All the way up the coast, lighthouses stand as symbols of New England's maritime history. The Coast Guard has now automated the light stations, but they remain a unique and cherished part of New England's heritage.

One of the earliest acts of Congress, signed by George Washington in 1789, provided for a program of construction and maintenance of lighthouses, beacons, buoys, and public piers. Both immigrants and traders were vital to the development of the American nation, and the safe navigation of their ships was crucial.

Unique landmarks Constructed of anything from wood or granite to concrete or iron, every lighthouse is different.

The tall New London Harbor Light was built in simple colonial style by the British, while Portland Breakwater Light (1855) is in the Greek Revival style, its height typical of the shorter lighthouses found in ports. Portland Head Light, probably the most painted and photographed on the coast of New England, stands 80 feet high above the cliffs. Owls Head and Pemaquid Point in Maine are also photogenic. The red and white stripes of West Quoddy Head will be familiar to many. At Fort Point, the wooden fog-bell house still stands, one of the last of its kind. Boston Light is America's only officially manned lighthouse and the oldest station in America. Anyone interested in lighthouses should visit the Shore Village Museum in Rockland, Maine (see page 130).

Keeping the lights shining The heroic keepers have passed into history, and today many lighthouses are in poor repair. There is, however, mounting interest in preserving them, and lighthouse cruises operate from Bath's Maritime Museum and Portsmouth, New Hampshire.

GETAWAY
For a "unique romantic adventure"—and a taste of what life was like for the keeper and his family—you can book bed and breakfast at Rose Island Lighthouse in Narragansett Bay (also available for longer spells, with record-keeping and maintenance chores). Contact Rose Island Lighthouse Foundation, P.O. Box 1419, Newport, RI 02840 (tel: 401/847 4242). Similarly, you can spend the night in the lightkeeper's quarters on the Monomoy Islands, a wildlife refuge (Cape Cod Museum of Natural History, P.O. Box 1710, Brewster, MA 02631; tel: 508/896 3867), or in Isle au Haut lighthouse, Acadia National Park (Keeper's House, P.O. Box 26, Isle au Haut, ME 04645).

153

FOR MORE INFORMATION
Contact the Lighthouse Depot, P.O. Box 1690, Wells, Maine 04090, or call 800/158 1444.

TALES OF HEROISM
Most famous of all New England's keepers was Ida Lewis (1842–1911), who took over from her father at Lime Rock Light in Newport, Rhode Island, when he was paralyzed by a stroke. She became an expert oars-woman and over half a century saved dozens of lives.

Winter comes to Nobska Light, Falmouth, Cape Cod

Massachusetts

CAMEOS OF NATURE
Cape Cod has several nesting areas for plovers and terns. Diamond-back terrapins, an endangered species, lay eggs in Sandy Neck Beach, Barnstaple. Some 90 percent of the rare Plymouth gentian, found by ponds, grows on Cape Cod. Much of the hinterland between the two coasts consists of infertile dwarf forest, characterized by pitch pine and scrub oak: coyotes have moved in since the late 1980s. Wild cranberries proliferate. Bog plants, such as bladderwort, pitcher plant, and sundew, thrive on the salt marsh.

Hyannis, for shops, ferries to the islands, and cruises around the harbor

▶▶▶ Cape Cod and the Islands   *139E1*

Cape Cod▶▶ is a busy vacation resort. Off season you may have the majestic, unspoiled beaches more or less to yourself, but in July and August traffic grinds along the roads, the beach parking lots fill up early in the day, and lodging prices are high. It's emphatically not touring territory, and there are only a few major sights. Yet it really is worth going out of your way if you are a nature lover or like a stay-put vacation with some boat trips and sights.

Physically the Cape is low-lying, covered with dwarf forest and cranberry bogs, and edged by marshes and sandy beaches. It is often likened to a bent arm: severed at the shoulder by the Cape Canal, with most of the population around the biceps portion (or Upper Cape); as it turns north (the Outer Cape), the peninsula narrows to curve around at Provincetown. The towns on the south side virtually roll into one anonymous mass. The waters on the Atlantic side are cold but are often good for surfing; the bay side (facing north and west) is calmer and warmer.

The Upper Cape: South Coast Family-style attractions (see page 245) abound on the much-developed south coast. Routes 6 and 28 cross the **Cape Cod Canal**. For a longer look at this waterway, completed in 1914 and possessing a rare vertical railroad bridge (for hoisting the tracks up to allow shipping through), look at water level from the largely reconstructed **Aptucxet Trading Post Museum** in Bourne. Also on site are reconstructed 18th-century saltworks and a train station specially built for President Grover Cleveland, who summered here.

Although much expanded, **Falmouth**▶ preserves its conspicuously pretty village center and green. The Falmouth Historical Society maintain a handsome 1790 house, subsequently home to Elijah Swift, who pioneered

The Glass Museum at Sandwich displays items from the town's 19th-century factory

the local whaling industry. A museum in the grounds honors local lady Catherine Lee Bates, author of *America the Beautiful* (1893).

Visitors may join an oceanographic cruise from Woods Hole

Like Falmouth, **Woods Hole▶** is a ferry port for Martha's Vineyard and Nantucket (see pages 160–163). The National Marine Fisheries Aquarium is stocked with local species, while Woods Hole Oceanographic Institution museum has displays on the wrecks of the *Titanic* and *Bismarck*.

At the Old Town Hall in Main Street, Hyannis, the **J.F. Kennedy Museum** has displays on J.F.K.'s vacation days on the Cape with family and friends at Hyannis Port.

The Upper Cape: North Coast The north shore is more genteel and historic; Route 6A is the Cape's "antiques road." **Pairpoint Glass Works** on Sandwich Road, Sagamore Bridge, is the oldest glass manufacturer in America, with glassblowing demonstrations on weekdays.

Sandwich▶ has a charming, tiny attractive center, with a church and pond. Dexter Grist Mill (1640) still produces cornmeal for sale, and Hoxie House is a 1675 saltbox; both are open and stand by Shawme Pond, a haunt of waterfowl. The 1641 Wing Fort House has heirlooms and period pieces and is the oldest house in America continuously lived in and owned by the same family. The **Glass Museum▶** has items made by the defunct Boston Sandwich Glass Company. **Yesteryears Doll Museum** is one of the largest collections of its kind in New England. **Thornton W. Burgess Museum** commemorates the creator of the children's stories *Peter Cottontail* and *Old Mother Westwind*.

The Heritage Plantation▶ ▶ (*Open* daily, mid-May–late Oct) is a delightful museum of Americana, displaying custom-made cars, model soldiers, Currier-and-Ives pictures, toys, and old tools. The setting is enchanting: the extensive grounds are planted with over 125 varieties of rhododendron, which bloom in May.

At **Brewster▶**, the Cape Cod **Museum of Natural History** has hands-on exhibits for children and runs outings, including trips to the Monomoy Islands (tel: 800/479 3867). Close by, the Fire and History Museum has a gleaming array of over 30 vintage firefighting devices.

Continued on page 158.

155

MARINE RESEARCH
Since the 1870s, the pleasant shoreside village of Woods Hole has been home to three important marine research establishments: the National Marine Fisheries Science Center and Aquarium, the Marine Biological Laboratories, and the Woods Hole Oceanographic Institution (WHOI). The latter exists to study rivers, coasts, seabeds, marine life, currents, pollutants, and other aspects of the oceans. In season, daily oceanographic cruises are run from here on the *Oceanquest* (tel: 800/37 OCEAN). This is an excellent introduction to the study of the sea, enabling participants to use plankton nets and microscopes under the guidance of a scientist.

Pembroke

Bryantville

Duxbury

Kingston

Gurnet Point

Plymouth Bay

Halifax

Plympton

Plymouth

Manomet

Carver

Cape Cod

Middleboro

South Carver

Lakeville

495

Cedarville

Great Herring Pond

Long Pond

West Wareham

Cape Cod Canal

Sagamore

Sandwich

Sandy Nec

Wareham

25

Buzzards Bay

Heritage Plantation

West Barnstab

Onset

Bourne

6

Rochester

Aptucxet Trading Post Museum

Monument Beach

Forestdale

Mashpee Pond

Marion

140

Pocasset

Centerville

Cragville

Acushnet

195

North Falmouth

Hatchville

Mashpee

28

Osterville

Mattapoisett

Cotuit

Fairhaven

Buzzards

West Falmouth

28

Ashumet Holly Res & Wildlife Sanctuary

New Seabury

NEW BEDFORD

West Island

Bay

Teaticket

East Falmouth

Wilbur Point

Falmouth

Great Neck

Round Hill Point

Falmouth Heights

Woods Hole

Nantucket

Nonamesset Island

Penikese Island

Elizabeth Islands

Naushon Island

Vineyard Haven

Oak Bluffs

State Lobster Hatchery

Joseph Sylvia State Beach

Pasque Island

Vineyard

Lagoon Pond

Cedar Tree Neck Sanctuary

Felix Neck Sanctuary

Cape Poge

Nashawena Island

Sound

North Tisbury

Edgartown

Chappaquiddick Island

Cuttyhunk Island

West Tisbury

Tisbury Great Pond

Edgartown Great Pond

Katama

Muskeget

Menemsha

Long Point Wildlife Refuge

Wasque Point

Channel

Gay Head

Chilmark

Squibnocket

Martha's Vineyard

Squibnocket Pond

No Mans Land

0		5		10		15		20 km
0			5			10 miles		

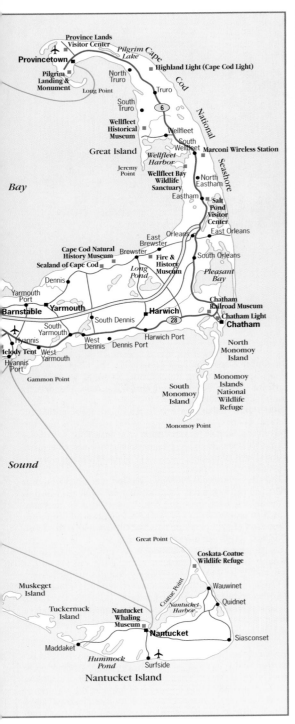

Province Lands
Visitor Center
Provincetown
Pilgrim
Landing &
Monument
Long Point
Pilgrim Cape
Lake
North
Truro
Truro
South
Truro
6
Highland Light (Cape Cod Light)

Cod

National

Seashore

Bay

Wellfleet
Historical
Museum
Wellfleet
South
Wellfleet
Marconi Wireless Station

Great Island

*Wellfleet
Harbor*

Jeremy
Point
Wellfleet Bay
Wildlife
Sanctuary
North
Eastham
Eastham
Salt
Pond
Visitor
Center
East Orleans

East
Brewster
Orleans
Cape Cod Natural
History Museum
Brewster
Sealand of Cape Cod
Fire &
History
Museum
South Orleans
*Long
Pond*
*Pleasant
Bay*

Dennis
Yarmouth
Port
Barnstable   **Yarmouth**
South Dennis
Harwich
Chatham
Railroad Museum
Chatham Light
Chatham
South
Yarmouth
Hyannis
Melody Tent   West
Hyannis   Yarmouth
Port
West
Dennis
Dennis Port
Harwich Port
28
North
Monomoy
Island
Gammon Point
South
Monomoy
Island
Monomoy
Islands
National
Wildlife
Refuge
Monomoy Point

Sound

Great Point
Coskata-Coatue
Wildlife Refuge

Muskeget
Island
Tuckernuck
Island
Nantucket
Whaling
Museum
Nantucket
Coatue Point
*Nantucket
Harbor*
Wauwinet
Quidnet
Siasconset
Maddaket
*Hummock
Pond*
Surfside
Nantucket Island

*Cape Cod National
Seashore*

Provincetown, overlooked by the belfry of the 1861 Center Methodist Church

BEACHES
The National Seashore beaches are all suitable for families; a pass covers admission to all six of them (free out of season or after 5pm). To reach Coast Guard Beach, it is best to take the free shuttle bus from the parking lot marked for that beach; lots are often full in July and August. There are numerous town beaches (fee payable). Le Count Hollow and White Crest are known for surfing, Cahoon Hollow for surfing and partying. Newcomb Hollow and Longnook are quiet family beaches. First Encounter Beach at Eastham is where the *Mayflower* landed, to be greeted by friendly Native Americans.

THE MONOMOY ISLANDS
Nature lovers should not miss a visit to the Monomoy Islands, formed of a barrier beach south of the elbow of Cape Cod. North Monomoy has dunes, beach grass, migrating birds, and a large summer population of eastern shore birds, while South Monomoy is much larger and has a wide range of flora and fauna, including deer and seals. Other sites for observing nature include Falmouth Ponds, Ashumet Holly and Wildlife Sanctuary (Falmouth), Sandy Neck (Barnstable), the beech forest at Provincetown, and West Harwich Conservation Area.

Continued from page 155.

The Outer Cape The best scenery on the Cape is found here, especially along the 40-mile National Seashore▶▶, with its superb beaches and clifflike dunes. The area is famous for its plant and bird life.

Salt Pond Visitor Center▶ is useful for information on natural history, trails, and ranger-led walks; it is also the start of the **Nauset Marsh Trail▶**. The **Rail Trail**, an inland course of some 20 miles, passes ponds, salt marshes, pine woods, and cranberry bogs; it is open to cyclists, horseback riders, and hikers.

The site of **Marconi Wireless Station** was abandoned in 1920 and only concrete foundations now remain, though a model explains how the first overseas radio message was transmitted from here in 1901 to Cornwall, England. **Cape Cod Light**, the Cape's oldest lighthouse, dates from 1857 and sends out a 20-mile beam.

On the west coast, **Wellfleet▶** is prettily sited overlooking an intricate pattern of marshy creeks and a marina. To its west, the trail along the sandy spit known as Great Island (4 miles each way) has remote beauty.

At **Province Lands Visitor Center▶** (tel: 508/487 1256), an observation platform gives a panorama of the invasive dunes resulting from the removal of trees, overgrazing, and the subsequent loss of topsoil.

Provincetown Sand spills onto the road and is whipped up by the wind as you approach **Provincetown▶▶**. On November 11, the Pilgrim Fathers first touched American soil here in 1620. The Pilgrims' arrival, and the signing of the Mayflower Compact, are commemorated by the **Pilgrim Monument▶▶** (modeled on the belltower of the town hall

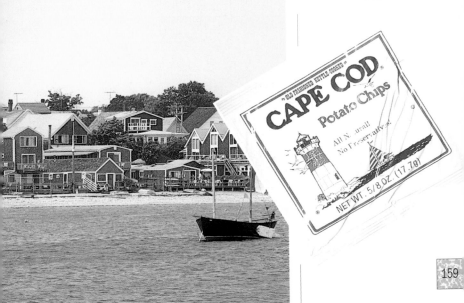

in Siena, Italy), 252 feet high and the nation's tallest granite structure. From the top, the Cape seems spread out like a map, and Boston's towers can be seen on a clear day. The adjacent museum (entry covers both sites) exhibits scrimshaw, toys, a fire engine, and items relating to the Arctic explorer Admiral Donald MacMillan.

Provincetown itself (known as "P-town") is commercialized and touristy but great fun, with shops ranging from the tastefully arty to the outrageous. The subtle lighting effects of sun and water have drawn innumerable artists, including Edward Hopper, Jackson Pollock, Robert Motherwell, and Mark Rothko. The town's galleries include the Provincetown Art Association Museum, the Fine Arts Work Center, and the Provincetown Gallery Guild. Provincetown also has a strong theatrical heritage: Eugene O'Neill had his first plays performed here, and Richard Gere, Marlon Brando, and Al Pacino have all acted in P-town. The artistic and theatrical ethos has gone hand in hand with the establishment of one of the East Coast's largest gay communities.

Accommodations are plentiful, and the town is easy to walk around. Trolleys tour the sights, and horse-and-buggy tours leave from the town hall.

CRUISES AND TRIPS
Whales can be seen around Steelwagen Bank—boats from all over the Cape, and from Boston, Plymouth, and the North Shore, head over here. Passenger-only ferries connect Provincetown with Plymouth (tel: 800/242 2469) and Boston (tel: 617/457 1428). Scenic flights can be made on a classic 1930 Stinson Detroiter plane (tel: 508/487 0240). Fishing and sightseeing cruises leave from Hyannis, Provincetown, Falmouth, and elsewhere. Cape Cod Canal Cruises depart from Onset (tel: 508/778 2688), while Water Safaris at West Dennis offer the only river cruise on the Cape (tel: 508/362 5557).

Stained-glass shop in Provincetown

Extending 2 miles north from Edgartown, Joseph Silvia State Beach flanks calm, mild waters

GETTING AROUND
Bike rental is available at ferry ports; the cycle paths are safer than the roads. A public bus network connects most places, and tour buses meet the ferries. Gas is expensive: fill up on the mainland.

WILDLIFE SANCTUARIES
● Cape Poge Reservation—salt marsh, ponds, and red cedar uplands with a range of wildlife.
● Felix Neck Wildlife Sanctuary—trails, wildfowl ponds, salt marshes, and an interpretation center.
● Cedar Tree Neck Sanctuary—good for wildlife spotting from trails and has coastal views.
● Long Point Wildlife Refuge—butterflies and moths, spring and fall bird migrations; birds of prey.

Martha's Vineyard The English explorers John Brereton and Bartholomew Gosnold landed on **Martha's Vineyard▶▶** in 1602, and Gosnold named the island after his daughter, Martha. Brereton remarked on the "incredible store of vines and the beautie and delicacie of this sweet soil."

The East Coast's largest warm-water resort island is about three times the size of neighboring Nantucket (see page 162). The rich and famous have summered here for many years: President Clinton has repeatedly taken his vacations here, and singers Carly Simon and James Taylor are among those owning houses on the Vineyard.

Variety is a key feature in the island's places, architecture, people, weather, and scenery. The north shore is craggy, the south shore sandy with a heathy hinterland speckled with ponds. Inland, a dwarf forest of scrub oak blankets much of the scene. Weather is remarkably localized; often one part of the island can be basking in bright sunshine while another is cloaked in a hot, humid mist (a "smoky sou'wester").

Most of the island's beaches are privately owned. The main public beaches are Joseph Sylvia State Beach, between Edgartown and Vineyard Haven (no surf, ideal for families); Katama (facing the Atlantic, good surf, strong swimmers only); Moshpu (by Gay Head cliffs, with surf); Oak Bluffs Town Beach (convenient, though often crowded, family beach); and Menemsha (small and quiet).

Around the Vineyard At the western extremity of the island, the village of **Gay Head** has a sizable Wampanoag community (hence the Native American crafts shops). **Gay Head cliffs▶▶** are a tumbled mass of multicolored clay, a natural landform of great geological interest with an excellent beach at the base accessible by road. The fishing village of **Menemsha►** has retained a weatherbeaten character, with little hint of gentrification. An excellent fishmarket is found among the tiny shacks in the harbor. You can take the ferry from here to Cuttyhunk in the Elizabeth Islands, where a monolith commemorates the first European settlement in America.

Immaculately preserved **Edgartown► ►**, haunt of millionaires, gained its prosperous look when sea captains from the whaling days built handsome Federal-style homes. The Old Whaling Church of 1843, an outstanding example of Greek Revival architecture, has been converted into a performing arts center; walking tours begin from here (for details, tel: 508/627 8619). Vincent House (open to the public) dates from 1672 and is the oldest building on the island. The town center is usually busy with window-shoppers admiring the jewelry stores and upscale boutiques.

Endowed with the longest beach on the Vineyard (scenes from the movie *Jaws* were filmed here), **Oak Bluffs► ► ►** is a period-piece resort where the Methodists held their first summer camp in 1835. By 1850, some 12,000 people were attending the Sabbath meetings at the open-sided tabernacle. Tents were replaced by charming "carpenter Gothic" gingerbread houses, each adorned with ornate filigree work. There are now more than 300, with no two quite alike. One house is open as a museum.

Vineyard Haven (Tisbury)► is a big yachting and boat-building center and possesses a state lobster hatchery. A fire destroyed much of the town in 1883, but Greek Revival houses survived along William Street. Ritter House Museum expounds upon times past. Crafts such as scrimshaw are exhibited in the Old School House Museum. The Seaman's Bethel (1892) was the place of refuge for seamen; gifts from those who survived storms and shipwrecks are displayed.

GETTING TO THE ISLANDS

● The Steamship Authority (tel: 508/477 8600) runs ferries from Woods Hole to Vineyard Haven and Hyannis to Nantucket plus interisland services.

I Hy-Line Cruises run from Hyannis to Oak Bluffs (tel: 508/778 0404).

● Cape Island Express Lines operate from New Bedford to Vineyard Haven and Nantucket (tel: 508/997 1688).

● Island Commuter Corporation runs a summer service from Hyannis and Provincetown to Oak Bluffs, taking about 35 minutes to the Vineyard and 2 hours 15 minutes to Nantucket from Hyannis.

● Cape Air (tel: 800/352 0714) is among several airlines serving the islands.

161

Victorian gingerbread cottages at Oak Bluffs

Lighthouse guarding the entrance to Nantucket town's harbor

NANTUCKET The island of **Nantucket▶▶▶**, 30 miles off the Massachusetts mainland, deserves the accolade "a step back in time." The town (also called Nantucket) is preserved down to the last cobblestone, and the handsome houses evoke the prosperity of the whaling days. Like Martha's Vineyard, this is a millionaires' vacationland, but while the larger island is considered the territory of the newly rich, Nantucket is more the haunt of rich Yankees who choose not to flaunt their wealth and is certainly less developed.

Nantucket▶▶▶ town preserves an air of genteel perfection. On cobbled Main Street, the oldest houses include the Three Bricks, built in 1836–1838 by Captain Joseph Starbuck for his sons. The tower of the Congregational Church offers a good view of the island. Shops tend toward artiness and good taste (although at a price), antiques shops abound, and there are weekend antiques auctions. Center Street's shops have traditionally been run by women (dating back to the time when captains' wives had time on their hands). A local specialty is the Nantucket Lightship, a woven basket into which is inserted a scrimshaw disk.

One ticket gets you into all Nantucket's museums, though apart from the Whaling Museum these are modest in scale. Housed in a former whale oil refinery, the **Whaling Museum▶▶** displays artifacts related to past whaling days, including the ship's logs of the *Essex* (the vessel immortalized in *Moby Dick*), sailors' souvenirs, a finback whale skeleton, and scrimshaw.

Local history collections forms the basis of the **P. Foulger Museum. The Museum of Nantucket History▶** covers the complete timescale from the distant geological past to the present day; a model shows how the island's coastline is changing. **Hadwen House▶**, built in imposing Greek Revival style in 1845, belonged to the same man who owned the refinery that is now the Whale Museum; it has Federal, Empire, and Victorian furnishings. A four-vane **windmill** (1746) still grinds corn today.

The little **Life Saving Museum** covers the work of the United States Life Saving Service. Both the **Old Firecart House** (vintage firefighting equipment) and the Old Gaol are open free of charge. The **Quaker Meeting House** was built in 1838, though Quaker worship on the island goes back to 1690. Simply furnished, the **Jethro Coffin House** of

TOURING NANTUCKET
Ferry boats (see sidebar on page 160) bring you directly into Nantucket town, where there are plenty of taxis. In addition to public bus services, Gail's Tour runs bus tours (1 hour 45 minutes) from Federal Street Visitor Center at 10, 1, and 3 (tel: 508/257 6557). Bicycles can be rented; bicycling the island's quiet roads and bike paths is a pleasure. Numerous boat trips depart from the wharves in Nantucket town. Walking tours (tel: 508/228 5585) start from the Atheneum Library Garden in India Street at 11 and 4.

1686 is the oldest on the island and gives a good idea of an early settler's home.

Beaches At its maximum dimensions, Nantucket is 14½ miles long by 3½ miles wide. The northern beaches are sheltered and the waves usually gentle, while the south-facing ones have plenty of surf and are strictly for strong swimmers.

Nantucket's southern beaches take the full force of the Atlantic surf

Smaller beaches in and around Nantucket town have shallow waters and are suitable for children. Jetties Beach, good for watching boats and migrating birds, is an easy walk from the town (or take a shuttle bus), past the lighthouse on Brant Point; sailboards can be rented at the beach. Farther west, Dionis is a family beach.

On the south side are Surfside (public bus service) and Nobadeer beaches (the latter popular with teenagers). Madaket Beach, at the western tip, has stunning sunsets. Siasconset Beach, served by bus, has some surf.

Farther afield The former fishing village of **Siasconset▶** (pronounced "Sconset") has tiny shacks with names such as Doll's House and La Petite Cottage, though house prices are astronomical. In the 1930s, Hollywood stars, such as Clark Gable and Carole Lombard, summered here. Nearby, Sankety Head Golf Course has a 15-year waiting list for membership! The **Coskata-Coatue Wildlife Refuge▶**, at the northeastern end of the island, is shaped like a fish-hook and formed of a huge barrier beach. Wind and sea have sculpted a remote and wild place; the refuge includes around 10 miles of shoreline, as well as ponds, forest, salt marshes, and tidal creeks.

THE INLAND SCENE
Nantucket's terrain is mostly scrub oak, with patches of heath and cranberry bogs. Altar Rock (111 feet) is the island's highest point. The lack of mammalian predators makes the island suitable for ground-nesting birds such as northern harriers, short-eared owls, least terns, and piping plovers.

A WHALING TRADITION
Settled by the English in 1659, Nantucket rapidly took off as the New World's premier whaling center, and by 1775, the export of whale oil, amber-gris, and whalebone meant that Nantucketers accounted for over a third of the hard currency earned in New England. The demise in Nantucket's whaling industry after 1842 was hastened by the emergence of the whaling port of New Bedford (see page 172) and by the collapse of the British market for whale oil with the advent of gas lighting.

Waterfront scene, Nantucket town

From the rocky inlets and myriad islands of the north through sandy beaches and salt marshes southward to the dunes of Cape Cod, the coast of New England supports an exceptionally rich and diverse plant and animal life. Opportunities abound for visitors to observe it all at close hand.

Top: dolphins may well join in a whale-watch cruise

WHALE-WATCHING CRUISES

In the 19th century, the hunting of whales was a principal source of revenue for New England; nowadays, whale-watching cruises have taken over as a burgeoning industry. In summer, boats leave from many ports, including Barnstable Harbor and Provincetown (Cape Cod); Boston, Plymouth, Gloucester, Newburyport (MA); Portsmouth (NH); Kennebunkport and Bar Harbor (ME). Qualified naturalists give commentaries while furthering research. Trips usually take half a day and go well out to sea. You may need warm clothes—and pills for seasickness.

MARINE STUDIES

A number of excellent aquariums are listed on pages 244–246, where visitors can get a close-up view of many of the creatures of the deep. For more serious naturalists, the Oceanographic Institute at Woods Hole, Cape Cod, is an international center for marine research offering study cruises. Similar cruises also run from Mystic, CT. The Shoals Marine Laboratory on Appledore Island in the Isles of Shoals, NH, offers courses for naturalists (details from Shoals Marine Laboratory, G-14Y Stimson Hall, Cornell University, Ithaca, NY).

Whales and dolphins In the Gulf of Maine is a chain of rocky ledges and underwater sandbanks. Tidal currents around their edges are constantly churning up the plentiful nutrient-rich algae. The tiny crustaceans that feed on this green-algae soup are in turn the diet of the slim, silvery, 6-inch sand eel (or sand lance), the primary food source for several species of whale. Every summer hundreds of humpbacks come up from the Caribbean to feast in these rich feeding grounds. And every summer thousands of people go out to sea for a close-up look at these captivating creatures.

There is a good chance of seeing the massive but sleek and speedy fin (or finback) whale (they grow to over 65 feet) and the smaller (less than 30 feet) minke whale. The most commonly seen, and the most fascinating in its behavior, however, is the humpback. Anywhere up to 50 feet in length and over 40 tons in weight, humpbacks will be seen raising their flukes, or tails, out of the water and then lobbing them down with a splash. They will roll onto their sides for a bit of flipper-slapping and, most exciting of all, will "breach" or jump vertically out of the water. Each humpback has a distinctive black-and-white pattern on its fluke, enabling researchers to identify and name individuals.

Just as engaging as the antics of the whales is the sight of a school of white-sided (and occasionally white-beaked) dolphins surfing the waves alongside the boat. Porpoises, too, are sometimes spotted, while the harbor seal is fairly common near port. Seabirds to watch for during the May to September whale-watching season include Wilson's petrel, great shearwater, gannet, herring gull, and cormorant.

The American lobster *Homarus americanus*, the New England variety, is known for the fearsome size of its claws. The cutter claw is used to grab and cut food (some lobsters are right-handed, some left-handed), while the broader, crusher claw is used to crush it. A nocturnal creature, of mottled green, yellow, and black (it turns red only when cooked), the lobster lives on the floor of the ocean and feeds on clams, sea urchins, and fish. Several times a year, it outgrows and sheds its shell.

Bog and marsh life The New England coast has several areas of salt marsh. Hampton Harbor and marshes are New Hampshire's largest salt marsh, rich in birdlife. Look for piping plover, whimbrel, short-billed dowitcher, black skimmer, least sandpiper, sanderling, snowy egret, osprey, and great blue heron. In Maine, the Wells

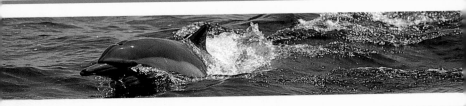

National Estuarine Sanctuary at Laudholm Farm has marked nature trails along the marsh, while Scarborough Marsh Nature Center, just outside Portland, runs guided nature walks and canoe tours (summer only). From Essex, Massachusetts, you can glide up the Essex River saltwater estuary in a glass-bottomed boat. Two-thirds of the fish caught off this coast have fed on the insects, larvae, and other rich pickings of the salt marsh "pantry."

Plants thriving in salt marsh habitats include sea lavender, sea aster, seaside and grass-leaved golden rod, cockleburr, beach grass (or "compass grass," because it sways in the wind) and "salt marsh hay," used by early colonists for cattle food, and the protected salt reed grass (Spartina cynosuroides).

Another plant that thrives on a combination of peat and sand is the cranberry. In September/October, the exten-sive cranberry bogs of Cape Cod, Nantucket, and the Plymouth area are flooded and the berries are shaken loose to float to the surface in a most spectacular sea of red. One of the trails from the Cape Cod Natural History Museum at Brewster winds through a cranberry bog.

BLOWING BUBBLES

One humpback whale eats up to 2 tons of food per day (about 250,000 sand eels). Uniquely among whales, humpbacks blow a "bubble net" below and around a shoal of fish, then rise to the surface with mouth open wide to swallow hundreds of fish in one gulp.

165

Left: a great blue heron keeps a beady lookout

A LOOK AT PUFFINS

Hunted for their meat, eggs, and feathers for over 300 years, puffins were virtually extinct in Maine by the late 1800s. Since the 1970s, the National Audubon Society has successfully encouraged the reestablishment of colonies in the Gulf of Maine. Boat trips may be taken from Rockland, Boothbay Harbor, and other Maine ports to nesting colonies on Eastern Egg Rock, Matinicus Rock, and Machias Seal Island, in the Gulf of Maine. The best time is during June and July or the beginning of August.

Salt reed grass, found in Cape Cod's salt marshes, is now a protected species

Massachusetts

The sun goes down on Columbia Street, Fall River

166

▶ Fall River
139D1

In its heyday, Fall River was one of the great textile producing centers of the world. Today, many mills survive, some empty, some as sewing-machine sweatshops, and some as factory shopping outlets. Though not picturesque, the town is set dramatically beneath the I–95 viaduct over the Taunton River.

The town's waterfront attractions begin with the **Fall River Heritage State Park** (*Open* daily, except Mon in winter. *Admission free*), which charts the checkered mill history of the town, its labor disputes, and its demise, and includes a film on Fall River's social history. The tower gives a view over the harbor and its ships.

Close by, **Battleship Cove**▶▶ features historic battleships which you can board and explore at will. The mightiest of all the vessels on display is the Massachusetts, known as "Big Mamie"; she served in 35 battles and carried a crew of 2,300. USS *Joseph P. Kennedy Jr.* was built in Quincy, Massachusetts; everything has been left out as if the ship is sailing. Meanwhile 1950s music throbs and Morse signals beep in the submarine USS *Lionfish*, which evokes the cramped lifestyle for the 76 crew members. Walk under the I–95 viaduct for the **Marine Museum**, which presents a history of steamers and steam power as well as a model of the ill-fated *Titanic*, used by Twentieth Century Fox for the 1953 movie.

The Fall River Historical Society▶ (*Open* Tue–Fri, 9–3; plus summer weekends, 1–4; closed winter) maintains a Greek Revival granite mansion at 451 Rock Street, moved in 1869 to its present location and redecorated in French Empire style. Exhibits include art, toys, china, glassware, and material on the mysterious and much publicized murder of Andrew Jackson Borden and his wife Abby in 1892 (see sidebar).

▶▶ Fruitlands Museums
138C3

Fruitlands (in the town of Harvard, northwest of Boston) owes its present form to Clara Endicott Sears, who lived in a house (now gone) by the road and who created the museums between 1914 and 1947. The site comprises four buildings. The **Fruitlands Farmhouse** was used by the Con-Sociate Family, a utopian transcendentalist community which existed for seven months in 1843 (see sidebars). The rural retreat was chosen for its contemplative setting overlooking mounts Monadnock and Wachusetts. Thoreau manuscripts are on display.

Shaker House (1794), used as an office by Harvard Shakers (extant 1791–1919), is now furnished with Shaker items. The **American Indian Museum** displays headdresses, pottery, painted leather, baskets, and clothing. The **Picture Gallery** features Hudson River School artists and portraiture (*Open* Tue–Sun, and Mon during holidays).

►►► Lexington and Concord   *138–9C3/D3*

The names of Lexington and Concord are inextricably linked with the events that sparked the American Revolution in 1775 (see pages 32–33 and 55). The historic sites where these events took place are all marked along the 4-mile road that links the two towns (see below).

In the 19th century, Thoreau, Emerson, Hawthorne, and Louisa May and Bronson Alcott all lived at Concord, and their homes give a fascinating insight into a remarkable circle of intellectual and literary talent (see also page 46).

The Battle Road At **Lexington**, a flagpole stands on the triangular Green near the statue of Captain Parker. Guides sporting hats in Minuteman style give tours on the Green (tips appreciated). On Patriots Day (the Monday nearest to April 19), you can witness battle reenactments, both here and at Concord's North Bridge. Behind the church, the Burying Ground contains 17th-century gravestones.

The Lexington Historical Society (*Open* daily, 10–5; Sun, 1–5; Munroe Tavern open Fri–Mon) maintains three historic buildings. At **Buckman Tavern►**, the American militia gathered before dawn prior to the battle on the Common. A bullet hole is visible in the front door. The **Hancock-Clarke House►** was in the parsonage of the Reverend Jonas Clarke in 1775. Patriots John Hancock (Clarke's cousin) and Samuel Adams were staying here on the eve of the battle, when Revere and Dawes alerted them of the British approach. The house contains the drum that William Diamond sounded to rally men to assemble in two lines on the Green prior to the firing of the first shot. The **Munroe Tavern►**, a mile from the center of town, was used by the British as a field hospital on their retreat.

THE FIRST SHOT
On April 19, 1775, the British marched into Lexington on their way to Concord, where they planned to seize a store of arms and ammunition. Revere and Dawes rode to Lexington to alert the colonial militia. By the time the 700 British—under Lieutenant-Colonel Francis Smith and Major John Pitcairn—had arrived, Captain John Parker and 77 American militia were waiting in two lines on Lexington Common. It will never be known who fired the first shot in the confusion, but the British ignored orders not to return fire and they shot at the fleeing Americans, killing eight.

167

Fruitlands Farm, an early, short-lived commune, is now a museum complex dedicated to the idealists who set it up

THE ADVANCE TO CONCORD

After the skirmish at Lexington, the British advanced to Concord, where they started to burn military supplies. The American militia saw the smoke and hastened to save their town. The opposing ranks met at North Bridge, and the British fired. With Major Buttrick's words "Fire, fellow soldiers, for God's sake, fire!" the Americans returned a volley and forced the British to retreat. At Lexington, Lord Percy met the British with reinforcements and the fighting intensified.

168

"When [the British] got about a mile and a half to a road that comes from Bedford and Bilrica they was waylaid and a great many killed. When I got there there was a great many lay dead and the road was bloody."
– Amos Barrat (1752–1829), recalling in 1825 the Battle of Old North Bridge.

Orchard House, home to novelist Louisa May Alcott

On the way out of Lexington is the **Museum of Our National Heritage▶** on Route 2A (*Open* daily. *Admission* free), with permanent and changing exhibits on American history; Lexington is featured in the display entitled "Let it Begin Here."

A self-guided historical trail begins from the **Fiske House** site, explaining how the silence was shattered at Ebenezer Fiske's farm that fateful day. Part of the original Lexington–Concord road here is an unpaved path, giving an idea of its appearance in 1775. Virtually adjacent, the **Battle Road Visitor Center▶▶** has guided walks and talks and an excellent movie dramatization recreating the events leading up to the battle. The **Paul Revere Capture Site** is marked by a memorial. The **Captain William Smith House** was the residence of the captain of the Lincoln Minutemen. **Hartwell Tavern** has been restored to its appearance in 1775, when it played the role of the community meeting place; here volunteers now recreate colonial life (*Open* Wed–Sun).

At **Concord**, an obelisk marks the spot where the first British soldier fell on April 19, 1775, at the **Old North Bridge Battle Site▶▶**. Adjacent is the famous Minuteman statue sculpted by Daniel Chester French (see page 147). Ranger talks and activities are scheduled in summer through the nearby National Historical Park Visitor Center (*Open* all year. *Admission* free), which has historical displays, a video, and a diorama of the Lexington–Concord road.

CONCORD Founded in 1635, Concord has numerous 17th- and 18th-century houses, many with date plaques. In the 1850s, Concord was a stop on the underground railroad for escaping slaves. One-hour walking tours on weekends and holidays begin at 12:45 from the information booth. Canoeing on the Concord River is also popular.

At the **Concord Museum▶▶**, Revolutionary exhibits include the lantern from Old North Church and a diorama of the battle at Old North Bridge. Ralph Waldo Emerson's study has been installed here, complete with

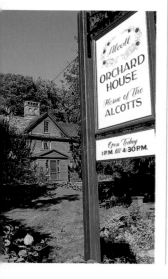

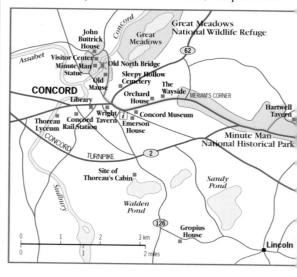

his books and rocking chair, and there is a Henry Thoreau collection. Archeological finds, communion silver, samplers, and costumes are also displayed.

Literary Concord The Ralph Waldo Emerson House▶ (*Open* Thu–Sat, 10–4:30; Sun 2–4:30) has been restored and is furnished very much as it was in the time when the author lived here, from 1835 to 1882.

Orchard House▶ ▶ (*Open* daily, except in winter) was the home of the Alcotts; the six members of the family feature in Louisa May Alcott's novel *Little Women* (1868), written and set here. The Alcotts used to host an "at home" every week, with music, singing, and acting. They were then a poor family, and the present comfortable appearance of the house owes much to Louisa's writing income. Mary's room contains several of her sketches, some drawn on the walls. Next door, the former Concord Summer School of Philosophy, extant 1880–88, was established by Louisa's father, the transcendentalist Bronson Alcott.

Nathaniel Hawthorne lived for a period near Orchard House at **The Wayside▶** (*Open* Apr–Oct, Tue–Sat), which he purchased from the Alcotts.

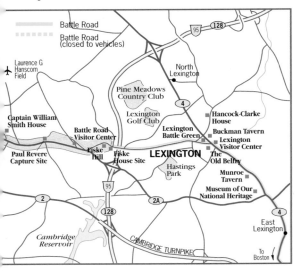

Minute Men relive the Revolution at North Bridge, Concord

"By the rude bridge that arched the flood
Their flag to April's breeze unfurled,
Here once the embattled farmers stood
And fired the shote heard around the world."
– Written for the dedication of the 1836 monument at Concord by Ralph Waldo Emerson.

"To outsiders, the five energetic women seemed to rule the house, and so they did in many things; but the quiet scholar, sitting among his books, was still the head of the family, the household conscience, anchor, and comforter, for to him the busy, anxious women always turned in troublous times, finding him, in the truest sense of those sacred words, husband and father."
– Louisa May Alcott, *Little Women* (1868).

The Old Manse, Concord, where writers Ralph Waldo Emerson and, later, Nathaniel Hawthorne lived and worked

"I went to the woods because I wished to live deliberately, to front only the essential facts of life, and see if I could not learn what it had to teach and not, when I came to die, discover that I had not lived."
– Henry David Thoreau, Walden (1854)

The **Thoreau Lyceum**, headquarters of the Thoreau Society, gives lectures and classes. A furnished replica of his famous cabin at Walden stands on the grounds.

The Old Manse▶▶, next to North Bridge (*Open* daily, 10–4:30; Sun, 1–4:30; closed Tue and winter), was built by William Emerson in 1769 or 1770. His grandson, Ralph Waldo Emerson, wrote *Nature* (1836) while living here. The house was also rented out to Nathaniel Hawthorne and his wife Sophia for three years. All the possessions are original, including Hawthorne's tiny desk and nearly 3,000 books. Sophia loved to paint in the dining room, and she etched the writing and the dates on the windows.

Sleepy Hollow Cemetery lies off Route 62 (Bedford Street). At Author's Ridge are buried Emerson, Thoreau, Hawthorne, Louisa May Alcott, and Daniel Chester French.

Thoreau made regular visits to **Great Meadows**, now a designated National Wildlife Refuge with headquarters at Weir Hill. This wetland is an important wildlife habitat, with well over 200 migratory and nesting bird species recorded.

At **Walden Pond Reservation▶**, Thoreau observed nature and faithfully recorded "the progress of the seasons" in a journal he kept while living in a cabin. Pieces of the cabin have long since been turned into letter-openers and other souvenir items for devoted admirers. Visitors in the 19th century used to sign stones and leave them in a heap on the site of the structure. There is a trail around the edge of the lake.

Further afield, the **Gropius House▶▶** (68 Baker Bridge Road, Lincoln; *Open* Jun 1–Oct 15, Fri–Sun, plus first full weekend of each month Nov–May; tours: 12, 1, 3, and 4 PM; owned and operated by SPNEA—see page 68) was designed by the architect Walter Gropius (1883–1969), founder of the Bauhaus School of Design. Built in 1938, this house is a remarkable synthesis of tradition and innovation, ahead of its time in the use of acoustical plaster, chrome, welded steel, glass blocks, and other modern materials.

At Framingham, south of Concord, **The Garden in the Woods** (*Open* Apr 15–Oct 31, Tue–Sat; last admission 4 PM, May 7 PM) is the botanical garden of the New England Wildflower Society. It covers 45 acres and is planted with a mixture of wild native flowers, shrubs, ferns, and trees.

▶▶ Lowell 138C3

When they were first built in the 19th century, Lowell's textile mills were the wonder of the age and a landmark in the early industrialization of America (see pages 36–37). Today, after a long decline, Lowell has cleaned up its 6 miles of canal and its mills to become a much-cited example of successful urban regeneration.

The **Lowell National Historical Park Visitor Center▶** (free) explains Lowell's social and industrial history through audiovisuals and exhibits. The park itself offers free ranger-led tours lasting 90 minutes and also operates a free trolley shuttle to the Boott Cotton Mills Museum (see below). An inexpensive 2½-hour **canal and trolley bus tour▶▶** (eight times daily) heads along the Pawtucket Canal, past guard locks where the water levels were measured, to the **Pawtucket Falls**, a 32-foot drop in the Merrimack River which provided power for all the mills; now it generates hydroelectric power, supplying electricity to 120,000 homes. Those wishing to explore on foot should pick up the booklet for the Lowell Waterpower Trail. The Mack Building has a Water Power Exhibit.

The fully restored Boott Cotton Mills at Lowell offer an excellent insight into the life of a major textile manufacturing town

171

At **Boott Cotton Mills Museum▶▶** earplugs are provided to counter the deafening clatter of the 88 looms. An excellent exhibition includes a model of the mill, plus videos of the 1912 strike and the reminiscences of mill workers. The **Boott Gallery** has changing exhibits of paintings and photographs, and chronicles Lowell in the Civil War.

By Boott Mill, the **Working People Exhibit▶** (Open Wed–Sun, 10–4. *Admission* free) shows the life of the first mill girls, who were well looked after, and of the bleaker conditions of the immigrants who followed. Nearby, the mills at Lawrence were the largest in the world when built; the **Lawrence Heritage State Park** (tours May–Nov) merits a two-hour visit.

NEWBURYPORT'S ECCENTRIC

Former resident Timothy Dexter proclaimed himself "the Greatest Man in the East." He wrote a book entitled *A Pickle for the Knowing Ones*, nicknamed "the Foe of Grammar" by its detractors because it was so illiterate. One critic said it would be read "when Shakespeare and Milton are forgot... but not until." Dexter arranged a mock funeral for himself, then caned his wife because she did not shed sufficient tears. In the early 1800s, his Newburyport garden was adorned with statues of great men, allegorical figures, and Native American chiefs. These he transformed with paint into new characters when the old ones fell from fashion.

Once a busy whaling center, New Bedford is now home to the East Coast's largest fishing fleet

▶ New Bedford   *139D1*

The fishing and manufacturing town of New Bedford retains an attractive old town at its heart, recalling its heyday as America's greatest whaling port. The whaling industry began in 1765, and by the 1840s there were some 10,000 seamen working here, pushing rival Nantucket into second place in the whaling league. Herman Melville enthused about the town, and some of the patrician houses he referred to in his whaling epic, *Moby Dick* (1851), can still be seen along County Street (for example the Rotch-Jones-Duff House and Garden Museum). The decline in whaling was sparked by the loss of numerous whaling ships at sea and by the discovery of petroleum, which gradually superseded whale oil as a fuel for use in oil lamps. The town remains the nation's busiest fishing port.

The **Seamen's Bethel**, with its boat-shaped pulpit, was frequently visited by mariners before they set out on a perilous voyage; it was also the setting for a chapter in *Moby Dick*.

Close by, the **Whaling Museum ▶▶** (*Open* daily) occupies an 1821 mansion. Among a fine array of model ships is the world's largest: an 89-foot-long, half-size replica of the New Bedford whaling bark Lagoda. Scrimshaw, fishing gear, figureheads, harpoons, and paintings are exhibited; William Bradford's huge 19th-century canvas, *Sealers Crushed by Icebergs*, was the first to depict the harsh reality of the life of seal hunters. Toys, samplers, dolls, and glassware are also displayed.

The **Fire Museum** (Bedford and South Sixth streets) has antique firefighting equipment. Two vessels on the water

front are the retired Lightship on State Pier (*Open* Jul and Aug) and the schooner *Ernestina*, an 1894 fishing vessel once used for Arctic expeditions (State Pier) and now available for sailings.

The village shoe-maker at work in Old Sturbridge

▶ Newburyport   *139D3*

Newburyport, pleasantly situated on the Merrimack estuary, is one of the most popular day-trip destinations on the North Shore. It is a center for fishing and whale-watching trips as well as for excursions along the Merrimack itself. It also has a seductive selection of antique shops and boutiques. The **Custom House Maritime Museum▶** (*Open* Apr–Dec), located within the granite Custom House, has displays covering 300 years of nautical history. Much of the town was rebuilt in brick after a fire. **High Street** has the finest architectural survivors, including the **Cushing House Museum▶** (*Open* Tue–Sat; tours 10–3; closed winter), a three-story brick house of 1808 with reminders of the town's maritime heyday.

Out of town, **Plum Island Beach▶▶** has 10 miles of sands and incorporates Parker River Wildlife Refuge, prolific in birdlife; in high season, this peninsula often fills to capacity quite early in the day.

▶▶▶ Old Sturbridge Village   *138B2*

Old Sturbridge Village opened in 1946 and is arguably New England's most memorable re-creation of yesteryear. Actors in period dress play the part of the villagers and craftsmen who would have inhabited a typical New England settlement of the 1830s.

The village green is flanked by several venerable buildings brought from all over New England and re-erected here. There is a bank, meeting house, shops, a saw mill, and more; a variety of ramshackle outbuildings, 19th-century cattle breeds, and roaming chickens help compound the time-warp illusion (*Open* daily, except Mon in winter; for details of special events, tel: 508/347 3362).

173

A TRIP FROM NEWBURYPORT
From the Custom House Maritime Museum you can take a boat trip to Lowell's Boatshop at Amesbury, where boat building has been carried out since 1793 and where the flat-bottomed dory was invented. Paint encrustations, hanging like stalactites from the ceiling in the paintroom, are testimony to the long history of the site, which is very prettily located and recalls the early seafaring days of New England.

► Pioneer Valley 138B3

In pioneer days, the Connecticut River in Massachusetts marked the western frontier of New England. Until westward expansion began in the 19th century, this was stock-farming country, and many trees were felled to feed the kilns making bricks to build the mills in Holyoke and South Hadley. The valley today is broad and tame, but some drama comes from the basalt ridges, where vertical splits in the rock have formed exciting cliffs and slopes. The valley's sedimentary rocks have also preserved some 200-million-year-old dinosaur footprints. These, along with fossil plants and the petrified ripple marks of a prehistoric pool, can be seen at the **Dinosaur Footprints Reservation** on the west bank of the Connecticut River near Holyoke (Route 5).

COLLEGE NUANCES
Holyoke, Northampton, and Amherst form the Five Colleges Area, the state's biggest concentration of academia west of Boston and Cambridge. Amherst College is prestigious, high-class, and preppy. The nearby University of Massachusetts (UMass) is a state university with a good academic reputation. Prestigious Smith College, Northampton, is an all-women's college; traditionally, Smith girls date Amherst boys. Hampshire College is expensive and ultraliberal. Mount Holyoke College, in South Hadley, is America's oldest women's college (founded 1837) and counts Emily Dickinson among its most distinguished alumnae.

The campus of Amherst College, founded in 1821

Holyoke itself is reached by driving north from Springfield (see page 187). Here, a modest Volleyball Hall of Fame (free) commemorates the birthplace of the sport. At **South Hadley** is the Mount Holyoke College **Art Museum►**, one of the oldest collegiate museums in the country and containing classical and Egyptian artifacts as well as American paintings. The summer festival features student theater and concerts by student and visiting artists.

Hadley Farm Museum (*Open* May–Oct, Tue–Sun. Admission free) houses historical exhibits, including the first broom-making machine, and offers teas on the porch on Saturday afternoons.

The main entrance for **Holyoke Range Park▶▶** and **Skinner State Park▶▶** is off Route 47 at Hadley. From here the park road winds up to a famous view over a loop in the river, painted by Hudson River School artist Thomas Cole as *The Oxbow* in the 1830s. Basalt columns known as Titan's Piazza add to the drama, and Mounts Monadnock and Tom are in sight. Folk, jazz, and classical concerts are given at the summit cabin in summer.

Mount Tom, south of Northampton, is equipped for year-round activity, with skiing, two water rides, a wave pool, and a chair lift to the summit. **Northampton▶** itself is a lively college town. **Smith College** has an arts museum begun in 1879 featuring European masters, the Hudson River School, and 20th-century sculpture (*Open* Tue–Sun; Wed and weekends only, Jun–Jul). **The Words and Pictures Museum▶** on Main Street pays tribute to comic-book art, including that of the the local cocreators of the Teenage Mutant Ninja Turtles (*Open* daily, except Mon and Wed; until 8 PM on Fri and Sat).

Amherst The attractive college town of **Amherst▶**, built around a sloping common, makes one of the best bases for exploring the Pioneer Valley. The **Emily Dickinson Homestead▶** at 280 Main Street (*Open* 1.30–3.45; advance booking essential, tel: 413/542 8161) was the home of the poet (see page 176). The world's largest collection of Dickinson memorabilia forms a display and archive in the Jones Library and is open free of charge when the archivist is there (tel: 413/256 4090); it also incorporates a large collection of material relating to Robert Frost. Next door is the **Strong House** (1740), with rooms in a range of styles including Colonial and Victorian (*Open* May–Oct, Wed and Sat, 2–4).

In Amherst College, the **Pratt Museum** exhibits natural history while the **Mead Art Museum▶** shows ancient art, European sculpture and paintings, and works by American masters. Just outside town is the University of Massachusetts, which has concerts during the academic year.

Continuing North The architectural highlight of the Pioneer Valley, **Historic Deerfield▶▶** is a beautifully preserved historic village displaying a variety of domestic buildings from early colonial times. First settled in 1669, the village grew rich on beef farming. Today, it is a living village-cum-museum but, thanks to its residents, it is one of the best documented places in the country. Currently 14 houses are open for 30-minute tours. Combined entry tickets are valid for a week, and opening times are staggered; guided walking tours and horse-and-carriage tours are also available.

Nearby, off Route 116, is **Mount Sugarloaf State Reservation▶**, which has a road to the top where fine views extend from a rocky cliff.

ON AND IN THE WATER
Twelve-mile cruises along the Connecticut River are offered on *Quinnetukut II* from the Riverview Picnic Area on Route 63 (tel: 413/659 3714). For canoeing, kayaking, and whitewater rafting, try the stretch from Cheapside Bridge to the Route 116 Bridge near Deerfield, or from Turners Fall Dam to Vernon Dam in Vermont. Beginners can sample the stretch from Holyoke Dam to the Northeast Utilities Power Dam in Turners Falls. The Deerfield River has mild whitewater conditions from Shelburne to Route 5 Bridge in Greenfield. Lake swimming is feasible in the Upper Highland Lake at DAR State Forest on Route 112 in Goshen.

175

Dwight House, an early 18th-century house that, like others in Deerfield that are open to the public, displays a fine collection of furniture

DWIGHT HOUSE

HISTORIC DEERFIELD

is, anu ...'
and my heart, and all l
And all the meadows wic
ure you count, should I
Some one the sum could
.... and al

id(
l f
d
ll
ve

In 1886, Emily Dickinson died in the house in which she had been born, in the village of Amherst in Massachusetts, a lyric poet unknown and unpublished. Her sister found 1,775 poems and numerous letters that revealed an original and exceptional talent. Equally extraordinary is the life led by this "New England mystic".

"There's a certain slant of
  light
On winter afternoons,
That oppresses, like the
  weight
Of cathedral tunes.

Heavenly hurt it gives us;
We can find no scar,
But internal difference
Where the meanings are.

None may teach it
  anything,
'Tis the seal, despair,
An imperial affliction
Sent us of the air.

When it comes, the
  landscape listens,
Shadows hold their
  breath;
When it goes, tis like the
  distance
On the look of death."

"It's all I have to bring to-
  day,
This, and my heart beside,
This, and my heart, and all
  the fields,
And all the meadows wide.
Be sure you count, should
  I forget,
Someone the sum could
  tell,
This, and my heart, and all
  the bees
Which in the clover dwell."

176

After her father died in 1874, Emily Dickinson left the grounds of her house only once, when her nephew next door died

The recluse Emily Dickinson was born in 1830 into a household dominated by her puritanical father, a lawyer and treasurer of Amherst College. Described by a schoolfriend as demure and shy but witty, she began to write poems when she was in her 20s, sewing them into little booklets. During her most productive year, 1862 (the height of the Civil War), she wrote 356. She tried unsuccessfully to inter-est a newpaper editor, Samuel Bowles, in her work, and in 1862 she asked a young man of letters, T.W. Higginson, for an opinion. He did not recommend publishing, although they remained correspondents, and from then on she refused to consider publication.

After the mid-1860s, Dickinson's output waned, and she began to withdraw from the world, seeing few friends. By the late 1860s, she had become known as an eccen-tric recluse, always dressed in white, who never left the grounds of her home (see page 175). From the mid-1870s, she was increasingly saddened by the deaths of many dear to her.

The poetry Emily Dickinson's themes of love, death, and nature are treated with an intensity and a sensitivity surprising for one who led such a secluded life. The poems and letters of the late 1850s and early 1860s reveal intense emotions, probably focused on a married Philadelphia clergyman, Charles Wadsworth. In her years of retreat, one person she did see was Otis Lord, an old family friend, and drafts of letters from these latter years suggest a tender and pas-sionate relation-ship. Her poems, like her letters, are composed with scrupulous artistry: words are pared down to an epigram-matic minimum, rhythms are often irregular to assist expres-sion of thought, and the rhymes themselves are some-times imperfect.

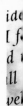

▶▶▶ Plymouth
139D2

Hallowed as the birth-place of modern America, where the Pilgrim Fathers first established themselves, Plymouth preserves the spirit of the early years. Apart from Plimoth Plantation (see page 179), the attractions are small-scale, but the town has become a place of historic pilgrimage. The **Pilgrim's Path**, a designated walking route, will lead you around the town's historic sites.

Despite a dearth of evidence that they ever landed here, **Plymouth Rock▶**, beneath its classical canopy, is, in any event, nicely symbolic of a nation that likes to think of itself as built upon a rock. *Mayflower II▶*, close by, is a faithful replica of the 104-foot-long ship in which the Pilgrims crossed the Atlantic, with period-clad actors telling the story of the 66-day voyage. The cramped conditions leave you wondering how the 102 Pilgrims dealt with frayed tempers on their long journey. The original *Mayflower* returned to England in 1621 and was scrapped a few years later.

Across the street, on Cole's Hill, a sarcophagus of 1921 contains the remains of some of the Pilgrims while a monument honors Chief Massasoit of the Wampanoag tribe, who befriended the Pilgrims. Adjacent, the **Plymouth National Wax Museum** (closed in winter) has 26 tableaus and 120 characters telling the story of Plymouth's beginnings.

North Street leads away from the sea from here and has some fine houses. Most notable is the **Mayflower Society Museum▶** (*Open* daily in summer, Fri–Sun in spring and autumn), high-ceilinged and with a magnificent flying staircase that is supported only at top and bottom. Edward Winslow, a Pilgrim descendant, built the house in 1754, and Lydia Jackson married Ralph Waldo Emerson in the east front parlor in 1835. **Spooner House** at 27 North Street has five generations of family possessions. **Hedge House▶** (1809), opposite Town Wharf, is a Federal-style home of a 19th-century merchant shipowner, one Thomas Hedge, and displays China trade porcelain, dolls, costumes, quilts, and toys.

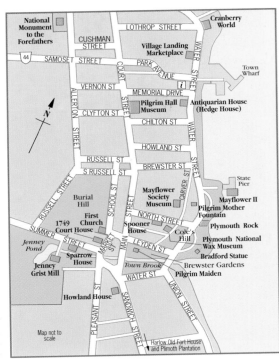

177

The Mayflower Society Museum, Plymouth

Pilgrims and Native Americans share an authenticated 17th-century meal at Plimoth Plantation

The **Pilgrim Hall Museum▶** (*Open* daily), designed by Alexander Parris (architect of Boston's Quincy Market), focuses on the Pilgrims and their voyage. Paintings show their embarkation and landing, and there are items thought to have been brought to America as part of the Mayflower's cargo, including the cradle of Peregrine White, born on the voyage. The Lower Hall contains artifacts relating to the Plymouth Colony, featuring paintings, furniture, tools, and clothes.

The 1749 **Court House and Museum** (*Open* summer. *Admission* free) is notable as America's oldest wooden courthouse. The reconstructed court room was saved from demolition during major redevelopment in the 1950s. A vintage piece of 1828 firefighting equipment is displayed. **Sparrow House** is the oldest surviving dwelling in Plymouth (*Open* Thu–Tue). The house dates from 1640 and has characteristic leaded window panes and period furnishings; pottery demonstrations are given inside.

Howland House▶ (*Open* daily, Memorial Day–Columbus Day, then weekends until Thanksgiving) is the only house where Pilgrims actually lived; *Mayflower* passengers John and Elizabeth Tilley Howland resided here and had ten children. The building was enlarged in 1750. A path along the river leads to the **Jenney Grist Mill**, America's first public utility, set up by the Pilgrims in 1636. The exterior is very picturesque, with a waterwheel still churning over the water. Along Sandwich Street is **Harlow Old Fort House** of 1677, restored to its 17th-century appearance.

The **National Monument to the Forefathers▶** is an outstanding example of 19th-century statuary, commemorating the Pilgrims. A gigantic central figure of Faith flanked by Law, Education, Liberty, and Morality stands high on elevated ground. Bas-reliefs depict the Departure from Delfthaven, the Landing of the Pilgrims, the Treaty with Massasoit, and the Signing of the Mayflower Compact. Etched in granite are the names of the 102 *Mayflower* passengers.

Ocean Spray, makers of cranberry juice (exported world-wide), shows its wares at **Cranberry World▶** (*Open* daily, May–Nov, 9:30–5, plus Jul–Aug 5–9. *Admission* free). Displays explain cranberry growing and harvesting, and there are vintage Ocean Spray TV commercials. Free samples of a range of cranberry-based juices await at the end. This is one of New England's greatest freebies, especially on a thirst-inducing summer's day!

Plimoth Plantation▶ ▶ ▶ is an impressively faithful reconstruction of the original Pilgrims' village, 3 miles south of the landing site (*Open* Apr–Nov, 9–5). The "1627 Village" has all the authentic elements: partly thatched wooden dwellings, straw on the ground, wood-smoke, cow dung, blankets hung out to dry in a yard. Dressed in period costume, interpreters answer visitors' questions as if they were Pilgrims, not tourist guides, and the authenticity extends to the carefully researched 17th-century accents. One woman talks of midwifery as she spins wool, a man tells of his voyage and another explains the schisms in the Church of England. Even the chickens resemble the breeds the settlers would have had.

Also re-created here is the homesite of a native Wampanoag who acted as counselor to the new settlers. The gentle, peace-loving Wampanoags traded with the Pilgrims, but some were later taken as slaves.

"Down to the Plymouth Rock, that had been to their feet as a doorstep Into a world unknown—the cornerstone of a nation."
– Longfellow, The Courtship of Miles Standish (1858).

"Neither do I acknowledge the right of Plymouth to the whole rock. No, the rock underlies all America: it only crops out here."
– Wendell Phillips, Speech at dinner of the Pilgrim Society at Plymouth, December 21, 1855.

179

PLYMOUTH CRANBERRIES
Plymouth County has some 12,000 acres of cranberry bogs, set within impermeable clay-lined kettleholes and dependent on supporting wetlands for their survival. In spring, the bogs look like a sea of light pink flowers. The petals fall off in mid-July, leaving a green berry which ripens spectacularly to a brilliant red and is harvested a few weeks after Labor Day. Plymouth Colony Winery, near Plymouth, claims to be New England's original cranberry winery. Cranberry juice and vodka are mixed to create the "Cape Codder" cocktail.

Visit Cranberry World to learn about cranberry growing and harvesting

Weak and weary from an uncomfortable nine-week voyage, an intrepid band of 102 English men and women arrived in Plymouth in the winter of 1620. About one-third had been driven out by their radical Puritan faith. All had hopes set high on a new life.

BLOWN OFF COURSE?...
Tradition has it that the Pilgrims, who set off heading for the James River in Virginia, were blown off course and ended up in the Cape Cod area. However, the chances of an experienced mariner such as Christopher Jones not knowing he was 120 nautical miles too far north are remote. First, he would certainly have known the latitudes of all American east coast landmarks; secondly, the astrolabe, a forerunner of the sextant, enabled navigators at that time to calculate all north and south distances with precision.

...OR A CHANGE OF MIND?
Descendants of David Thomson have claimed that when the *Speedwell* needed repair work and she and the *Mayflower* unexpectedly called at Plymouth, England, the Pilgrim leaders spoke with David Thomson about New England. The indications are that Thomson, who had been there more than once but never farther south than Cape Cod, might have recommended the Plymouth area, where his friend Squanto lived. Did the Pilgrims then change their minds about Virginia?

Puritans and Separatists At a time when the English monarch was also head of the Church in more than just name, dissenting from the Anglican Church was a treasonable offense. While some Puritans attempted to reform the Church of England, one group decided in 1608 to flee to Leiden in Holland, a center of Protestantism, to escape persecution. These Protestant Separatists lived rather discontentedly in Holland for some 12 years before deciding to start a new life in America. They managed to secure finance from a group of London investors for a pilgrimage that would take them to a land where, according to all reports (and there had been many by then), they could find a better life as well as religious freedom.

The Leiden Separatists bought a small ship, the *Speedwell*, in which they sailed from Holland to Southampton, England, where they met up with the *Mayflower*. Some of the *Mayflower*'s passengers were also Puritan Separatists, but the majority were sent by the London stock company to ensure the venture's success, men such as the military officer Miles Standish (hero of Longfellow's long poem, *The Courtship of Miles Standish*). Both ships set sail from Southampton, but the

The Mayflower, *an English merchant ship before she was hired to transport the Pilgrims*

Speedwell proved unseaworthy and had to be abandoned at Plymouth in Devon, and all her passengers crammed onto an already crowded Mayflower, which set sail once again on September 6, 1620.

Arrival in America Amazingly, the ship and her passengers survived a 66-day journey that was not without storms or near disasters, and land was sighted on November 9. On the 11th, the *Mayflower* dropped anchor at what is now Provincetown on Cape Cod. A meeting was held on board and a famous document, the "Mayflower Compact," was drawn up by the Pilgrim Fathers (as they were only much later called) under the leadership of William Bradford. Under the terms of this agreement, the settlers promised obedience to the minority of Pilgrim leaders and, despite its one-sidedness, it remained in force until the settlement joined with Massachusetts Bay Colony in 1691.

A reconnaissance party then sailed along the coast to Plymouth, with its safe harbor, running water, and cornfields already cleared by the Wampanoag. It also had high ground from which the colonists could defend themselves against possible attacks from Native Americans, Spanish and French traders, or fishermen. On Christmas Day, the men began to build their new homes.

Settling in By the end of that first winter, half of the Mayflower's passengers had died. The weather was harsh, the colonists were weak from the journey, food supplies were low, and crops not yet established. It was a tough time, until the spring came and, with it, friendly contact with members of the Wampanoag people. Like so many other Native Americans, the Wampanoag had been decimated by epidemics of European disease that had come with the traders, but one of the survivors was a man named Squanto. He had been to England (see sidebar opposite) and was prepared to help the colonists.

The Pilgrims and their fellow settlers had come with a diversity of skills and interests, but most were craftsmen and not used to making a living from the land. Nevertheless, with guidance from the Wampanoag and the arrival of more goats, cattle, and other goods with further colonists from England, the Plymouth settlers became self-sufficient within a few years, and by 1640 their numbers had swelled to about 3,000.

181

Top: Miles Standish makes a treaty with the Native Americans
Above: the Pilgrim Fathers give thanks after landing

SQUANTO
In 1605, an English captain, George Weymouth, captured five Wampanoag men, including Squanto, and took them back to Plymouth in England. Here they became friendly with David Thomson, an apprentice to a ship's doctor. In 1607 the doctor, Thomson, and the five Wampanoag joined Sir John Popham's expedition to Sagadahoc, the men acting as intermediaries between the Native Americans and the English. Squanto made several more similar trips.

THANKSGIVING

Thanksgiving Day, celebrated across the country with turkey and pumpkin pie, traditionally originated in the autumn of 1621, when the first colonists invited the Wampanoags to join in a three-day festival of thanksgiving for their first successful harvest. Nineteenth-century romancing turned it into a New England institution, and in 1863, Thanksgiving Day was made a national holiday by President Abraham Lincoln.

A calm evening on Quabbin

▶ Quabbin Reservoir   *138B3*

One of America's largest reservoirs, Quabbin supplies water to half of Massachusetts, and its zigzag form effectively divides the state into eastern and western halves. The reservoir has a 118-mile shoreline and many islands. Some 2,500 homes were lost when it was built, and 7,500 bodies from 34 cemeteries were reinterred. For the tourist, its scenic attributes make it worth a detour: an excellent view is from **Quabbin Summit▶▶** at the southern end, where a tower looks to Mounts Tom, Lincoln, Monadnock, and Wachusett. To locate the tower, follow signs past Winsor Dam. The reservoir offers outstanding freshwater fishing (boat rental is available for anglers), and there are nine trails, including the 3/4-mile summit trail from Quabbin Hill Lookout.

North of the reservoir, at North New Salem, the Swift River's middle branch roars along **Bear's Den▶**, a gorge with rushing waterfalls embraced by granite cliffs which are cloaked with hemlock trees. Supposedly, this was a Native American haunt in 1675 during the wars against the white settlers.

JOHN QUINCY ADAMS

An advocate of strong federal government during his presidency, Adams was previously the U.S. minister in The Hague, Berlin, St. Petersburg and London. As secretary of state to James Monroe, he formulated in 1823 the Monroe Doctrine, which defined any European colonial ambitions in the Western World as a threat to American peace and security. He was also a lawyer and in a landmark case successfully defended the Mendi Africans who were taken aboard the slave ship *Amistad* and mounted a rebellion against their captors (see page 105).

▶ Quincy   *139D2*

Quincy (pronounced "Quinzee") is known as the "City of Presidents" because John Adams (America's second president) and his son, John Quincy Adams (America's sixth), were both born here, in 1735 and 1767, respectively. The **Adams Mansion▶**, a large clapboard house, was home to four generations of the Adams family and now displays family pieces and paintings. In the garden, the 1870 Stone Library contains presidential books and manuscripts. Both John and John Quincy Adams were born in 17th-century saltbox farmhouses nearby, forming, with the mansion, the **Adams National Historical Site**, the earliest surviving presidential birthplace. The **Adams Academy**, built on the site of John Hancock's birthplace, is now the home of the Quincy Historical Society. The National Park Service Visitor Center (opposite City Hall on Hancock Street) has brochures on historic Quincy, with information about the Quincy Homestead, the Josiah Quincy House, the Quarry Museum, and the United First Parish Church and Crypt, where two presidents and their wives are buried. Quincy can be reached from Boston by the Red Line to Quincy Center.

In 1692, the village of Salem, in the Massachusetts Bay Colony, suddenly found itself in the grip of an infamous witchcraft hysteria. It was a brush with the devil that that would leave its mark forever.

Tituba's secret Reverend Samuel Parris came to Salem after working as a merchant in the Caribbean. He brought back a slave girl, Tituba, who was put in charge of Parris's daughter Betty and her cousin Abigail Williams, girls at the impressionable ages of 9 and 11. Innocently, Tituba would tell them stories of her own voodoo culture, so very different from the starchy Puritan ethic the girls were brought up on. They were gripped. Soon they were bringing others into Tituba's "circle"—but for fear of eternal damnation they had to keep it all secret. Betty, however, could not cope with the divided loyalties, and it began to show in her behavior. Abigail, jealous of all the fuss now being made of Betty, mimicked her "fits" and, one by one, the other girls began to writhe and scream similarly.

"Spectral evidence" In 1692, most of the world believed in witchcraft, and to the Puritans of Salem this was the only explanation for the girls' behavior. But who was it who was bewitching them? The hunt was on. Tituba and others were put under pressure, false confessions were made, innocents incriminated. Things got out of control. Prisons were bursting with suspects (even the wife of the governor of Massachusetts, William Phips, was accused), and 19 "witches" were actually hanged. But everything hinged on "spectral evidence," the evidence given by the bewitched girls that they were afflicted by a specter, or the devil, in the image of someone else.

Eventually, in October, Increase Mather and his son Cotton, leading Puritans, and others protested that this meant that it was on the testimony of the Devil that justices were condemning people to death. Governor Phips brought the trials to an end, prisoners were released, and convictions annulled. The girls were discredited—and Tituba was able to renounce her confession.

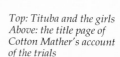

183

Top: Tituba and the girls
Above: the title page of Cotton Mather's account of the trials

THE CRUCIBLE
The names of Tituba, Abigail, and many of the other personalities involved will be familiar from American playwright Arthur Miller's play *The Crucible* (1953), based on the Salem witch trials. A French film, *Les Sorcières de Salem*, was made of the play. A remake of the film, *The Crucible*, was shot in 1995 on location on Hog Island, located off Ipswich, MA. The film stars Daniel Day-Lewis and Winona Ryder.

An all-too-common sight in 1692: a "witch" is arrested

Map of Salem

The Puritan Roger Conant founded Salem in 1626; his statue can be found in front of Salem Witch Museum

▶▶▶ Salem and Marblehead ⠀⠀⠀⠀⠀⠀⠀⠀*139D3*

Salem's notorious witch hunts of the past are only one aspect of the town. Its prosperity, brought about by trading (in particular with China), has left the town with a rich architectural legacy and a particular wealth of Federal-style houses.

That the witch trials (see page 183) amounted to a puritanical persecution of innocent women is hardly remembered here in the ghoulish array of trinkets and souvenirs, all featuring witches in pointed hats. At least the museum-type attractions aim for rather more authenticity.

History Alive! Cry Innocent—The People Versus Bridget Bishop▶ is worth catching (tours daily at 11:30, 1:30 and 3 PM only, Jun–Oct); this theatrical reconstruction of a witch trial is set in the Old Town Hall, with its faded classical grandeur and courtroom atmosphere. The audience plays the role of a 17th-century Puritan jury asked to judge the woman's guilt.

The **Witch Dungeon Museum** also starts with a short two-person theatrical presentation, setting the scene for the persecutions, before embarking on a brisk tour of the reconstructed dungeons.

The **Witch House▶** is a fine example of a mid-17th-century house, with period furniture. It belonged to Jonathan Corwin, one of the witchcraft trial judges. It was here that witches were examined for bodily defects. In the **Salem Witch Museum** (presentations every half hour), 13 tableaus are lit to spin the witchcraft yarn; the dummies are not particularly lifelike and the commentary is over-sensationalized in tone, but the story is gripping.

Trading and Maritime Legacies Founded in 1626, Salem was once America's sixth largest city. So widely was the name of Salem known at the peak of its trading activity (1790–1807) that many overseas merchants thought Salem was a country and America just a part of it. At the **Salem Maritime National Historic Site▶** (free) you can see three surviving wharves (there were once over 50). Elias Hesketh Derby, America's first millionaire, established Derby Wharf (1762), and his brick Georgian home, Derby House, can be visited along with the unfurnished Narbonne-Hale House. In the 1840s, Nathaniel Hawthorne worked as a surveyor in the Custom House (1819): you can peer into his "cobwebbed and dingy" office, still used up to 1937. Behind is the Scale House (1829), where goods were weighed and taxed.

While Hawthorne worked here observing the life of Salem, he lived in a house in the grounds of his cousin's 17th-century mansion, **The House of the Seven Gables▶▶**. A secret staircase, a lookout window for observing ships in the harbor, and numerous odd corners and nar-

Above: The House of the Seven Gables, inspiration for Hawthorne's novel
Left: ship's figurehead in Salem's Peabody Essex Museum

row passages add to the romance of the house that inspired Hawthorne to write his famous novel (1851) of the same name. Hawthorne's birthplace, the Retire Becket House of 1655, and the Hooper-Hathasay House of 1682 are on the same site.

The **Peabody Essex Museum▶▶▶** (*Open* daily, Memorial Day –Oct 31) celebrates three centuries of Salem trade with an outstanding collection of model ships and maritime art, as well as period rooms, pictures of old Salem, witchcraft exhibits, and a splendid array of ships' figureheads. Outside are an 1830s shoe shop and the 1684 John Ward House. The adjacent Andrew-Safford House (1819) was, in its day, the most expensive house ever built (not open).

Chestnut Street▶▶ has been called America's finest street. The Stephen Phillips Memorial Trust House at number 34 and the Ropes Mansion (1727), around the corner at 318 Essex Street, are both open in summer. Salem Common was a pasture and drill ground.

Pioneer Village, a short drive to the south (*Open* late May–mid-Oct), is a re-creation of old Salem, with gardens, farm animals, and crafts as well as costumed actors playing the roles of 17th-century Puritans and acting scenes from Hawthorne's *The Scarlet Letter* (1850).

"Halfway down a bystreet of one of our New England towns stands a rusty wooden house, with seven acutely peaked gables facing towards various points of the compass, and a huge, clustered chimney in the midst...The aspect of the venerable mansion has always affected me like a human countenance, bearing the traces not merely of outward storm and sunshine, but expressive also of the long lapse of mortal life, and accompanying vicissitudes that have passed within."
—Nathaniel Hawthorne, *The House of the Seven Gables* (opening)

...lehead, once a busy .rading port, is today popular with yachtsmen

GETTING AROUND

Salem is easily reached from Boston's North Station; trains are frequent and inexpensive (with discounts for round trips) and take 30 minutes. Trolley buses tour Salem every half hour, and there is also a free shuttle bus. However, the sights can easily be taken in on foot, and Salem is a delightful town for walking. A red line marks the walking route linking the historic sights (but omits Chestnut Street); free brochures are available from the National Park Visitor Center in Museum Place or from the Chamber of Commerce in the Old Town Hall.

TRADE WITH CHINA

The China trade began when Derby's ship, the *Grand Turk*, dropped anchor at Whampoa in 1786. By 1800, traders from Salem and Marblehead were a common sight in Canton, the only Chinese port open to them. All sorts of exotic items turned up in America as a result of this trade. From East Africa came ivory, gold, ostrich feathers, and hippopotamus teeth; from the West Pacific appeared semi-precious corals and mother-of-pearl; from the Far East, ceramics, textiles, tea, coffee, spices, sugar, and Japanese artifacts were landed.

Marblehead▶▶ This handsome coastal town is located just to the east of Salem, and can be reached by bus 441 from Boston or Salem. Like Salem, it prospered on trade. Its tightly knit, irregular 18th-century streets have a salty charm that evokes coastal England. Today, it is a wealthy commuter satellite, known for boating, antique shops, and boutiques.

At **Public Landing** you can join cruises around the harbor and buy lobster, sea bass, and striped bass off the boats. Fort Sewell, a small fortification built for the War of 1812, Fountain Park, and Crocker Park all overlook the bay. Some 600 Revolutionary War soldiers are buried in the **Old Burial Ground**. In **Abbot Hall** (the town hall) hangs Archibald Willard's famous painting, *Spirit of '76*, epitomizing the patriotic spirit of the Revolution. The **Jeremiah Lee Mansion▶** (*Open* summer) has altered little since it was built in 1768; its wooden exterior was made to resemble stone in an attempt to look English.

A causeway road links **Marblehead Neck**, skirted by a loop road; affluent New Yorkers have built summer houses here in various styles such as French château and English Tudor. Chandler Hovey Park is at the northern tip of the Neck and overlooks the bay at Marblehead Light. The best sandy beaches are at Beverly; West Beach has 3 miles of sand, while Dane Street Beach is smaller.

▶ Springfield 138B2

This major industrial city sits at the southern end of the Pioneer Valley (see pages 174–175) and deserves a visit for its museums (*Open* Wed–Sun, 12–4). Combined entry to four of them, all situated by the Quadrangle, is available. The **Connecticut Valley Historical Museum** details the history of the valley from 1636. Dinosaur exhibits, an aquarium, a planetarium, and the story of early aviation are attractions at the **Springfield Science Museum**. **The George Walter Vincent Smith Art Museum** is an excellent collection of Victoriana, armor, Hudson River School paintings, and an outstanding collection of Chinese *cloisonné*. The **Museum of Fine Arts** features French Impressionist works among its European paintings. At **Springfield Armory National Historic Site▶**, Washington set up the first arsenal in America. In 1873, the "Trapdoor" Springfield Rifle was invented here (the model 1903 was used by the U.S. Army in World War I). The arsenal closed in 1968 and now

INDUSTRIAL LEGACY
The Blackstone River Valley close to Worcester was a busy mill district in the 19th century. Mill owners provided jobs, schools, housing, churches, and stores for their workers, who included refugees from Europe seeking religious and personal freedom. Industrial competition from the South eventually spelled economic decline. Some old mill villages survive, such as Hopedale and Whitinsville, while the Willard House and Clock Museum at Grafton honors the Willard brothers, clockmakers in the 18th century.

187

Worcester: museum visitors can choose between armory (left) or fine art (below)

contains perhaps the nation's finest collection of firearms.
In 1891, Dr. James Naismith devised the game of basketball in Springfield. At 1150 West Columbus Avenue, the **Naismith Memorial Basketball Hall of Fame▶** pays homage to the sport's great players, teams, and coaches with reverent displays of photos and mementoes, as well as "virtual reality." Interactive exhibits include the chance to participate in a shootaround (*Open* daily).

▶ Worcester 138C2

A busy industrial and commercial center, and New England's second-largest city, Worcester has two notable museums. The **Worcester Art Museum▶▶▶** (55 Salisbury Street; *Open* Wed–Sun) boasts works from the ancient world, European art from the Renaissance to the 20th century, and American masters including Whistler, Homer, Copley, and Sargent. The **Higgins Armory Museum▶▶**, 100 Barber Avenue (*Open* Tue–Sat 10–4, Sun 2–4), is spectacularly housed in a gallery modeled on the hall of a medieval Austrian castle and displays a good collection of weapons and armor from all over the world. For details of **Worcester Common** shopping outlets, see page 16.

Welcome to the Worcester Art Museum

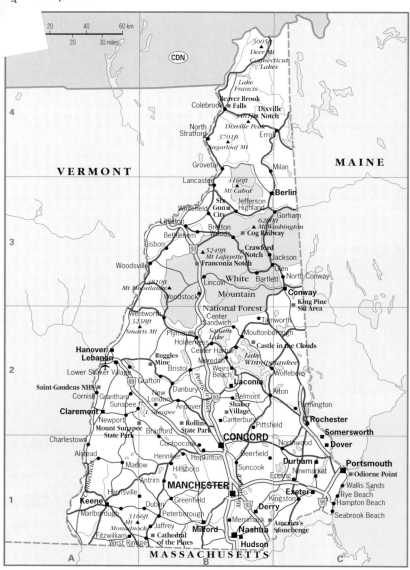

Scale:
20   40   60 km
20   30 miles

CDN

3005ft
Deer Mt
Connecticut
Lakes

Lake
Francis

Beaver Brook
Colebrook   Falls
3481ft   Dixville
Notch
North   Dixville Peak
Stratford   3701ft   Errol
Sugarloaf Mt

VERMONT

Groveton   Milan

Lancaster   4160ft
Mt Cabot   Berlin

St.   Jefferson
Whitefield   Gun   Highland
City   Gorham
Littleton   6288ft
Bretton   Mt Washington
Bethlehem   Woods   Cog Railway
Lisbon
5249ft   Crawford
93   Mt Lafayette   Notch   Jackson
Woodsville   Franconia Notch   Glen
4810ft   Lincoln   North Conway
Mt Moosilauke   White   Bartlett
Woodstock   Mountain   Conway
Wentworth   National Forest   King Pine
3238ft   Center   Ski Area
Smarts Mt   Sandwich   Tamworth
Plymouth   Squam   Moultonborough
Holderness   Lake
Hanover   Center Harbor   Castle in the Clouds
Lebanon   Meredith   Lake
Ruggles   Winnipesaukee
Mine   Weirs
Lower Shaker Village   Bristol   Beach   Wolfeboro
89   Grafton   Laconia
Saint-Gaudens NHS   New   Danbury   Belmont   Alton
Cornish   Grantham   London   Shaker   Farmington
Claremont   Sunapee   Andover   Village
L. Sunapee   93   Canterbury
Newport   Rollins   Pittsfield   Rochester
Mount Sunapee   State Park   Somersworth
State Park   Bradford   CONCORD   Dover
Charlestown   Contoocook   Northwood
Alstead   Henniker   Deerfield   Durham   Portsmouth
Marlow   Hopkinton   Suncook   Newmarket   Odiorne Point
Antrim   Hillsboro   Epping   Wallis Sands
Harrisville   MANCHESTER   Exeter   Rye Beach
Keene   Dublin   Greenfield   Kingston   Hampton Beach
Marlborough   Peterborough   Derry   95   Seabrook Beach
3166ft   Merrimack
Mt   Jaffrey   America's
Monadnock   Milford   Nashua   Stonehenge
Fitzwilliam   Cathedral
West Ringe   of the Pines   Hudson

MAINE

MASSACHUSETTS

A   B   C

*The Union Church and
covered bridge at Stark
(both 1850s) in northern
New Hampshire*

Fall foliage in the White Mountains

NEW HAMPSHIRE The state's triangular form extends 168 miles north to south and 90 miles west to east at its maximum dimensions. In shape and size, it is an inverted form of Vermont, although its population, nudging a million, is almost twice as much.

THE LAND AND PEOPLE By repute, New Hampshire inhabitants are independent, hardworking, conservative, and proud of their state and its history. They are also thrifty, and somewhat suspicious of government. One typical manifestation of this diehard New Hampshire attitude is that there are no income or sales taxes: much state revenue comes instead from "sin tax" on liquor (hence you can only purchase alcohol at state liquor stores) and from tobacco and gambling. Another is that the state is unique in the Union in that any resident has the right to raise an issue at the state capitol for discussion. "Live free or die," words first uttered in the Revolution by Colonel John Stark, form the most cut-and-thrust of all state mottos. New Hampshire was the first state to vote in favor of the Declaration of Independence.

Despite its nickname "The Granite State," New Hampshire does have areas of good, fertile land, particularly in the river valleys. Agriculture, together with forestry, ranks third in the state's economy after manufacturing and tourism. With a decline in the number of dairy farms in recent years have come changes in farming methods, including the replacement of animal-feed crops with strawberries, flowers, and other produce.

► ► ► REGION HIGHLIGHTS

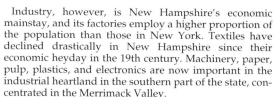

Ask a New Hampshire native if he's lived there all his life and he'll reply "not yet"

Views from the Kancamagus Highway in the White Mountains present some of New England's finest shows of autumn color

"…New Hampshire has One each of everything as in a show-case."
– Robert Frost, New Hampshire (1937).

Industry, however, is New Hampshire's economic mainstay, and its factories employ a higher proportion of the population than those in New York. Textiles have declined drastically in New Hampshire since their economic heyday in the 19th century. Machinery, paper, pulp, plastics, and electronics are now important in the industrial heartland in the southern part of the state, concentrated in the Merrimack Valley.

Tourism is another state money-earner. Locals will tell you that New Hampshire has better maple syrup than Vermont and the best autumn foliage in New England. It certainly does have the distinction of possessing New England's tallest mountains and the merit of having lakes, uplands, forests, and the coast all within an hour or two's drive.

VISITOR HIGHLIGHTS The **White Mountains** in the north of the state are New England's tallest and finest uplands. This prime territory for fall foliage, scenic drives, and hiking has attracted artists, writers, and intellectuals since the early 1800s. Today it is busier than ever, and shopping outlets, motels, and theme parks have sprung up around its edges. As with elsewhere in New England, many of the visitor attractions, however, are only open during the May to October season.

Summer crowds also head for the seacoast and lakes regions of New Hampshire. The state's first colonial settlers came to the coast in 1623 and eked out a living supplying timber to the English. In 1679, New Hampshire became a separate royal colony from Massachusetts. Today, **Portsmouth** continues as a commercial port. The town itself has the state's biggest concentration of historic houses.

Elsewhere, the 18-mile seaboard is given over to recreation. Apart from a short, empty stretch at its northern end, the seaboard is almost entirely developed, with summer cottages, motels, and fast-food outlets culminating in the 3-mile boardwalk at Hampton Beach.

The lakes number about 1,300 in all, including the smaller "ponds." **Lake Winnipesaukee** is the largest and the most obviously commercialized but is still very attractive, with abundant islands and tempting boat excursions.

The **Mount Monadnock region** in the southwest has a bucolic charm belying its nearness to the urbanized parts of New England. Bumpy backroads set a slow pace in the vicinity of Mount Monadnock itself, where the sleepy villages have quintessential white clapboard and trim greens. The mountain itself gives a view over six states and has long attracted visitors; in 1860 there was a "half-way house" and a "summit house."

Events

For further information, contact the state tourist office (see page 266) or alternatively the local chambers of commerce.

January
Loon Mountain Independence Day Weekend, Lincoln.
Jackson Winter Carnival, Jackson.

February
Great Rotary Fishing Derby, Meredith.
Dartmouth Winter Carnival, Hanover.
World Championship Sled Dog Derby, Laconia.

March
Rockingham Park Craft Festival, Salem.
Spring Mania, Attitash Mountain, Bartlett.

April
Aprilfest, Cannon Mountain, Franconia.

May
Sheep and Wool Festival, New Boston.
New Hampshire Lilac Festival, Lisbon.

June
Market Square Celebration, Portsmouth.
Old Time Fiddlers Contests, Lincoln and Stark.
Seacoast Jazz Weekend, Portsmouth.

July
Nascar Winston Cup Race, at NH **International Speedway**, Loudon.
Wolfeboro Antique Fair, Wolfeboro.
Antique and Classic Boat Show, Laconia.

August
League of NH Craftsmen's Fair, Mount Sunapee State Park.
Balloon Rally, Pittsfield.
Attitash Equine Festival, Bartlett.
Candlelight Tour of Historic Homes, Portsmouth.

September
Riverfest Celebration, Manchester.
Seafood Festival, Hampton Beach.
NH Highland Games, Loon Mountain, Lincoln.

October
Harvest Day, Canterbury Shaker Village, Canterbury.
Fall Foliage Festival, Warner.
Sandwich Fair, Sandwich.

November–December
Traditionally Yours, Jackson.

December
Dickens Holiday Celebration, Hanover.
Candlelight Stroll, Strawbery Banke, Portsmouth.
First Night Celebrations, (New Year's Eve) Concord, Portsmouth Wolfeboro, Claremont, North Conway, and Keene.

On the shores of Lake Sunapee, an all-year-round resort

...rbury Shaker ...e, now a museum, ...celibate religious community, relying on conversion and adopting orphan children

A PREHISTORIC MYSTERY
Also known as Mystery Hill, America's Stonehenge comprises chambers with massive capstones, stone walls, standing stones, a sacrificial table, and a "speaking tube." Various monoliths align with the pole star and the summer solstice. What connection all this had to solar and lunar events is uncertain, but its purpose may well have been astronomical and/or ceremonial.

The Shakers believed that every artifact should be perfectly made, to last a thousand years

► America's Stonehenge 188B1

This enigmatic 4,000-year-old site at North Salem may not quite emulate its more famous English namesake but is a genuine prehistoric relic (see sidebar). From Boston, leave I–93 at Exit 3 and take Route 111 east to Island Pond and Haverhill Road. Go south on Haverhill Road to the entrance on the right. (*Open* weather permitting, daily, Apr–Nov; call for hours: tel: 603/893 8300.)

►► Canterbury Shaker Village 188B2

Just north of Concord, this pristine example of a Shaker community, established in the 1780s, is the sixth of 18 such villages in order of founding. The last surviving female inhabitant, or sister, died in 1992, but the village has been preserved intact, with a meeting house (note the separate entrances for men and women), fire station, schoolhouse, herb garden, dwelling house (with a bell cast by Paul Revere), and a remarkably well-preserved steam-powered laundry. The Shakers here were progressive in outlook: they had the first telephone and first car in the area, and converted to electricity in 1910, five years before the statehouse in Concord.

The guided tour takes a look at Shaker inventions, which include the wide-headed brush, an early washing machine, knitting machines, an automatic hayseeding device, and a self-sealing front door. Craft workshops, including herbal crafts, broom-making, and boxmaking, are held in season. For more on the Shaker way of life, see pages 148–149. (*Open* daily, May–Oct; Apr, Nov and Dec, weekends only. Tours last 90 minutes, starting on the hour.)

► Concord 188B1

Not to be confused with Concord, Massachusetts (see pages 168–170), this commercial and administrative center is the state capital of New

Hampshire. Visitors are most likely to come for the **Christa McAuliffe Planetarium▶ ▶** (for times and reservations, tel: 603/271 STAR), named after the Concord astronaut and schoolteacher who died instantly in the ill-fated takeoff of the *Challenger* space shuttle. The planetarium is one of the world's most technologically advanced. It offers a number of programs, in which you may see our galaxy from inside and outside in a simulated voyage through space, and home in on close-ups of the moon and the planets. It holds an Astronomy Day Celebration in May, as well as a monthly SkyWatch.

One of a number of granite public buildings downtown, the **State House▶** was erected by prisoner labor in 1819 and much enlarged subsequently, although the legislature still meets in the original chambers. With 400 representatives, it is the fourth-largest such assembly in the world (after the government assemblies of Britain and India, and the U.S. Congress). Murals and some 200 portraits of New Hampshire dignitaries adorn the inside, as well as 88 tattered Civil War flags in the entrance hall. There are free weekend tours on the hour between 10 AM and 2 PM; during the week you guide yourself with a leaflet available at the desk.

In Eagle Square, close by the State House, the **Museum of New Hampshire History** (*Open* Tue–Sun) is where the renowned 1852 Concord Coach is on display (see sidebar). **The New Hampshire Historical Society** (free), across from the State House, maintains changing displays looking back on the state's past. The Coach and Eagle Trail is a self-guided walk taking in points of interest in the city center (free pamphlets available from the State House and from the Chamber of Commerce, 244 North Main Street). **The League of New Hampshire Craftsmen**, a statewide handicraft association, has its headquarters and a gallery at 205 North Main Street.

Out of the downtown area at 14 Penacook Street at the end of North Main Street, the **Franklin Pierce Manse** (*Open* mid-Jun–Labor Day, Mon–Fri 11–3) was the home from 1842 of the 14th president and contains a number of family pieces. Pierce had a somewhat nondescript political life and a tragic family one: two of his children died in infancy, then his third was killed in a train accident at age 13, two months before his inauguration in 1853. As a consequence of this, his wife could not face public appearances and his cousin had to stand in as the first lady.

Concord's up-to-the-minute planetarium

193

THE CONCORD COACH
Concord's history of coachmaking dates from 1827, when J. Stephen Abbot, coach builder and wheelwright, completed the first Concord coach. He forged a partnership with Lewis Downing, and together they created 14 types of Concord coach, as well as numerous kinds of other recreational and commercial vehicles. Their company produced 3,000 coaches, some of which were used by the Wells Fargo Company in the pioneering days of the West.

Pick your own fruit in Canterbury—and in many other places

Winter, with deep snow in much of the region, still provides entertainment in New England. Christmas and First Night, a New Year's Eve festival that originated in Boston's bicentennial Independence celebrations of 1976, are very special times.

194

Top: Christmas at Faneuil Hall, Boston Above: snow and a welcoming wreath on the door—all part of the spirit of a New England Christmas

CHRISTMAS WREATHS
One small but thriving industry in the economically impoverished area of northern Maine is the making of decorative Christmas wreaths. Based on a particular type of balsam fir, they are sold all over eastern America.

First Night Buttons—passport to Boston's New Year's Eve celebrations

Christmas As soon as Thanksgiving Day is over, Christmas trees, lights, wreaths, and garlands start going up all over the towns and villages. The month of December is filled with festivities, from lantern-lit sleigh rides to readings of Dickens. To highlight just three: in Portsmouth, New Hampshire, there is a Candlelight Stroll around the houses of Strawbery Banke Museum, each decorated in its own period style; lantern-bearing guides in 19th-century costume lead evening tours in Mystic Seaport Village, Connecticut; and Old Sturbridge Village, Massachusetts, celebrates a colonial-period Christmas.

Summer visitors who want to see what a New England Christmas is like should be sure to look inside one of the dozens of Christmas shops that stay open all year round. Plastic trees hung heavy with color-coordinated bows, baubles, enameled cut-outs, and crystal Santas glitter against the fake snow and piped carols. There are rolls of ribbon by the dozen, tiny stars by the yard, garlands, and wreaths ready-made or in kits. Displayed among it all are little groups of "Snowbabies," "Carolers," Annalee dolls (see sidebar on page 196), nutcrackers, and miniature Christmas villages—collections to build up and arrange under the tree or on the mantelpiece. There may even be a Nativity scene.

First Night This colorful and exciting, nonalcoholic community festival has become a well-established tradition that is spreading rapidly to dozens of towns throughout New England and elsewhere. Between the afternoon carnival procession and the midnight fireworks on New Year's Eve, there are scores of different indoor and outdoor "happenings." For the cost of a First Night Button, families and friends, often wearing masks or more elaborate costumes, wander the streets imbibing jazz, dance, theater, puppets, ice carvings, store-front tableaus, and many other entertainments.

1784

Dartmouth College, the only Ivy League college in northern New England

DARTMOUTH'S BEGINNINGS
Dartmouth College was founded in 1769 when the Congregational minister, Eleazar Wheelock, gained a charter from the governor of New Hampshire to educate Native Americans in a log hut. The college's first sponsor was the 2nd Earl of Dartmouth, the secretary of state for the colonies under George III.

▶ **Hanover**   *188A2*

In Hanover, on the Connecticut River, the town center is dominated by the 265-acre campus of prestigious **Dartmouth College▶**, an Ivy League establishment (see pages 22–23). Notable among the college buildings grouped around the maple-shaded green are the colonial-style **Baker Library** (1928) and **Dartmouth Hall** (1784). The **Hood Museum** has a small but choice art collection (*Open* Tue–Sat 10–5, Wed 10–9, Sun 12–5. *Admission* free). The **Hopkins Center** features year-round music performances, plays, movies, and other cultural events.

South of town toward Windsor, the **Saint-Gaudens National Historic Site▶▶**, off Route 12A at Cornish, marks the summer home of Augustus Saint-Gaudens (1848–1907), one of America's foremost sculptors. Many of his works are on display, both in the garden that was his passion and in his studio. Pieces include copies of the *Shaw Memorial*, which stands on Boston Common opposite the State House, and the *Adams Memorial*, installed in Washington, DC. (*Open* last weekend in May to end of October.)

East from Hanover, by Mascoma Lake, is the **Lower Shaker Village**, retaining 13 Shaker buildings of the former nearby Enfield community (1781–1923) and including a crafts shop and a small museum of Shaker artifacts (*Open* mid-May–mid-Oct, and winter weekends). The nearby feast ground on Mount Assurance was chosen for its view of the lake. Farther on, at Grafton Center, a signpost points up a bumpy road to the **Ruggles Mine▶**. This abandoned mica, feldspar, beryl, and uranium mine (see sidebar) is an expensive visit for what is offered, but the site is dramatic. Entrance is through a rock tunnel into a huge open-cut mine, from which a number of manmade caverns and underground ponds can be explored (a flashlight is advisable). (*Open* weekends, mid-May–mid-Jun; then daily until mid-Oct.)

MICA AT THE RUGGLES MINE
The flexible, flaky material known as mica, which is found abundantly in the Ruggles Mine, has high resistance to heat. It was formerly used to glaze stove fronts and lanterns and to carry wires in electric toasters. The owners claim over 150 types of minerals have been found at the mine. Visitors can rent hammers and take home souvenir chunks of rock.

The motif of Annalee's dolls

ANNALEE'S DOLLS
Back in 1934, Annalee Thorndike made her first doll, the first of many thousands of felt and wire creations that, with their hand painted faces and rosy cheeks, have gained something of a cult status. Near Meredith in the Winnipesaukee region is the Annalee Doll Museum and shop, on the original manufacturing site. The museum exhibits some pre–World War II specimens, including the first doll ever produced (in 1934); early examples can fetch $2,000 nowadays. The gift shop sells a variety of mice in top hats, Christmas shepherds, baseball players, and fishing boys.

Lake Sunapee is popular for water sports

►► Lake Sunapee
188B2

The Sunapee area offers unspoiled lake and mountain scenery and a good alternative for those who find Lake Winnipesaukee too commercialized. The state beach on Lake Sunapee is a narrow sandy strip, ideal for families with small children as the water is shallow and the beach slopes very gently. The M/V *Mt Sunapee II* cruises the lake, with two narrated tours daily (tel: 603/763 4030). The **John Hay National Wildlife Refuge**, Newbury, is a former estate of a diplomat's summer mansion, with fine grounds sloping to the lake and containing rare alpines.

Mount Sunapee►► towers over the lake. Its ski lift operates all year, and the summit café offers a huge panorama encompassing Mad River Glen (73 miles) and Mount Washington (75 miles). Walks from the top include the 1,000-yard trail to a cliff high above spectacularly situated Lake Solitude. At the base of the chair lift is the site of the League of New Hampshire Craftsmen's Craft Fair in August.

Mount Kearsarge► (2,937 feet), in Rollins State Park, has a straightforward trail up its south side (reached by road from Warner). The walk up takes 20–30 minutes; the view from the top takes in the White Mountains. **Mount Kearsarge Indian Museum** (Exit 8 off Route 89 near Warner) exhibits baskets, fishing artifacts, canoes, and quiltwork of the Native Americans of the region (*Open daily, May–Oct; Nov and Dec, weekends only*).

►► Lake Winnipesaukee
188B2

New Hampshire's largest lake is the center of a busy vacation area whose fortunes were boosted considerably by the movie *On Golden Pond*, filmed at adjacent Squam Lake. Its shoreline is very irregular and the charming views ever changing, although the small Victorian resort communities that fringe it are of limited interest. The best way to appreciate it is to take a cruise on the M/S *Mount Washington* (May–Oct; tel: 603/366 5531).

Ellacoya State Beach is suitable for families, with a narrow sandy strip; the water is clean, and there is a boat launch for lightweights. **Weirs Beach**, with the main

Aerial view of Moultonborough in the Lakes Region

SPEEDWAY
New Hampshire International Speedway (tel: 603/783 4931) is a big state revenue earner on Route 106 north of Canterbury. Races take place in the 75,000-seat stadium.

steamer pier, is the most commercialized point on the lake. It is a far from sedate boardwalk village thick with fast-food stands, motels, and family-oriented action (see sidebar), but retaining a quaintly antique array of 1950s homemade slush kiosks and amusement arcades. One of New England's last drive-in movie theaters (an endangered species) is here, too. **Meredith Bay** hosts a summer theater, while **Center Harbor** has a Children's Museum for ages two to ten.

The **Science Center of New Hampshire▶** (*Open May 1–Nov 1*), off Route 113 near Holderness, is a wildlife sanctuary for rescued animals of New Hampshire. It is nicely done, with a ¾-mile trail leading past enclosures. Live animal demonstrations with a naturalist take place twice daily, and there are lots of hands-on activities for children, including microscopes and quizzes. In addition to the main trail, there is a 1-mile trail up to Mount Fayal, which offers a view of **Squam Lake**. From July through September, the center also runs nature cruises on the lake for sightings of loons and other wildlife (for details, tel: 603/968 7194). Cruises are also operated by Squam Lake Tours (tel: 603/968 7577).

Quieter, traditional towns include **Center Sandwich** and **Wolfeboro▶**. Both have crafts shops and historical museums. The nearby **Castle in the Clouds▶**, built in 1911–1914 for millionaire Thomas Plant, is a turreted hilltop house with whimsical interior features, including an octagonal elm-paneled dining room. However, it is the setting that is most memorable. The shuttle bus which takes you up also visits the Castle Springs mineral-water bottling plant. Be prepared for crowds.

At **Tamworth** is the Barnstormers Theater, New Hampshire's oldest professional summer theater. Tamworth itself glimpses Chocorua Lake, while nearby **White Lake State Park** has a beach with canoe and rowboat rentals.

FAMILY FUN AT WEIRS BEACH
The Winnipesaukee Railroad runs diesel trains along the lakeside from here, with dinner specials in the evening. There are also two open-air water parks, one called simply Water Slide; pay for a batch of rides, or for two hours, or for the whole day. The Surf Coaster lies away from the beach and is pricier, but it also has a wave machine surf coaster. It also runs a miniature golf course. Across the road, another company operates go-karts and a baseball pitching machine.

Seaplane rides are a popular way of enjoying the autumn foliage

Andrew Wyeth is one of several artists with New England connections on show at the Currier Gallery

ROUTES UP MOUNT MONADNOCK

Numerous routes lead up the mountain from Monadnock State Park headquarters at Jaffrey, where free maps are available. The most popular and easiest are the White Cross and White Arrow trails (3–4 hours there and back). The Pumpelly Trail is the longest, at about 5 hours' walking time. The Spelman Trail, which heads up a breath-taking series of schist rock ledges to reach Pumpelly Ridge, ascends 1,000 feet in half a mile and is the steepest. The Red Spot Trail is perhaps the most scenic. For a very full but rewarding day's walking, make a circuit by taking any trail via Bald Rock to the summit and return via Pumpelly Ridge.

▶ Manchester 188B1

In the 19th century, the thriving Amoskeag Mill made Manchester the world's largest cotton cloth-producing center. Today, it is a commercial and manufacturing city, but the **Currier Gallery of Art▶▶** makes the city worth a visit. The collection includes European and American masters, with paintings, sculpture, and decorative art from the 13th to 20th centuries (*Open* daily, except Tue; late night on Fri). The gallery also organizes tours of the 1950 Zimmerman House, designed by Frank Lloyd Wright (Fri–Sun; reservations only, tel: 603/626 4158).

South of town is the **Robert Frost Farm▶** at Derry, the poet's home from 1900 to 1911 (see page 209). Here he "wrote more than half of my first book, much more than half of my second and even quite a little of my third." He later visited it to find it a scrap yard, and it was only after his death that his daughter Lesley Frost Ballantine restored it. The locality was the setting for Frost's "Stopping by Woods on a Snowy Evening." (*Open* daily in summer, weekends in spring and autumn.)

▶▶ Mount Monadnock Region 188A1

Mount Monadnock▶▶▶, America's most climbed peak, rises to a modest 3,165 feet, but by virtue of its isolation from New England's other high spots it gets one of the grandest views in the Northeast. The surroundings are relatively unfrequented and make a good getaway from the Boston area for those seeking accessible, low-key relaxation. Walking, kayaking, canoeing, covered bridge spotting, looking at fall foliage, skiing, and antique hunting lead the pursuits.

Only reached on foot, the mountain that stands alone on the plain demands a substantial walk to the top (see sidebar). Rock formations to look for include the Imp, the Sarcophagus (a boulder transported and dumped on Pumpelly Ridge by glaciers in the Ice Age), and the Doric Temple (a set of composite stone blocks). The summit view on a clear day takes in points more than 100 miles away, and extends to the White Mountains, to the Boston skyscrapers, and over every New England state.

Peterborough is home to the MacDowell Colony, begun by composer Edward MacDowell (1861–1908), whose best-known works include his second piano concerto and the piano solos *To a Wild Rose* and *New England Idyls*. After his death the Colony was for 40 years directed by his widow; it offers artistic seclusion to artists, composers, and writers, but only a small part is open to the public. Those attracted here have included Leonard Bernstein,

Thornton Wilder, Aaron Copland, and Virgil Thomson. Wilder's play, *Our Town*, was set in Peterborough and became one of the cornerstones of American drama. Theatrical traditions are maintained by the Peterborough Players with their summer theater and the Marionette Theater (tel: 603/924 7585), which specializes, most unusually, in opera performed by marionettes to recorded music. Fans of vintage diners should seek out the Peterborough Diner in Depot Street. **Miller State Park▶▶**, off Route 101 east of Peterbor-ough, has road access for vehicles to the summit of Pack Monadnock (2,300 feet), plus picnic sites and a summit loop trail. You can walk up (nearly 1 1/2 miles) by following the Wapack Trail from Route 101.

Blink and you'll miss **Dublin**. Along its sleepy main street is the headquarters of the *Yankee Magazine* and *Farmers' Almanac*, two famous New England–based publications; tours of the premises are given on weekdays. West of town is Dublin Pond, the haunt of blue herons and featuring a town beach with water slides, sailing, windsurfing, and swimming. Close by, Friendly Farm (*Open* daily in summer, weekends in autumn) operates a petting farm for children, with a range of farmyard animals and milking demonstrations. Nearby is **Harrisville▶**, with a pretty pond and a cluster of old mill cottages; Harrisville Designs demonstrates old weaving methods (*Open* Tue–Sat. *Admission* free).

Keene is a commercial center rather than a tourist town but has some dignified 19th-century homes. The Horatio Colony House Museum, at 199 Main Street, is a pleasing Federal-style house of 1806. The Children's Museum has displays on different parts of New England, including colonial life and a "typical" village.

West of Keene by Route 9, an easy ¾-mile loop trail follows Wilde Brook through deep **Chesterfield Gorge** (*Open* weekends. *Admission* free). **Rhododendron State Park▶**, at Fitzwilliam, comes into spectacular bloom in mid-July and has views of Mount Monadnock. **Fitzwilliam** itself has a concentration of antiques shops, while at **West Rindge** Ed's Country Auction offers rural antiques, domestic junk, and copious local color (Saturdays in summer at 10 am; winter at 6 PM). Near Rindge is the **Cathedral of the Pines▶** (*Open* year round, 9–5; see sidebar).

THE WAPACK TRAIL
A 21-mile hiking trail leads from the base of Mount Watatic, near Ashburnham, MA, to the slope of North Pack Monadnock in Greenfield, NH. The trail takes a skyline route with views of Boston, the White Mountains, and Vermont on the way. Yellow triangle markers and stone heaps show the route.

CATHEDRAL OF THE PINES
Begun to commemorate Lieutenant Sanderson Sloane, shot down over Germany in 1944, this out-door interdominational place of worship became a national memorial in 1957. With its charming backdrop of Mount Monadnock, it focuses on a 2,000-seat "cathedral" shaded by tall white pines. The altar contains stones donated by every president since Truman, and the stone lectern contains sand and rock from every battlefield where Americans have fought. The Memorial Bell Tower, with bas-reliefs designed by Norman Rockwell, was the first memorial in the U.S. devoted to womankind.

199

Mt. Monadnock, seen from Dublin

Over 80 percent of New England is covered in forest. The woods, a mixture of hardwoods and softwoods, are home to an exciting variety of wildlife species. Seeing moose or beaver can be a vacation highlight, and in summer the sound of songbirds is sensational. There are also areas of enchanting alpine flora.

"BRAKE FOR MOOSE..."

"...It could save your life." So read the road signs in New Hampshire. Every year there are scores of collisions between moose and cars on forest roads. A moose can severely damage not only the car, but quite possibly the driver, too. If you see a moose at the side of the road, try not to startle it and go carefully—moose are unpredictable. Dark brown in color, they are difficult to see in the dark.

POISON IVY

Poison ivy is common throughout eastern North America and is poisonous to touch. Its leaves have three leaflets, green turning to red/purple, and it has white berries. If you so much as brush against the plant, its poison can cause blistering and great discomfort (it can even rub off from a dog's coat onto your leg). Clothes worn a year after contact can cause poisoning. Don't go into undergrowth and always wear socks and long pants if you are going near wild vegetation.
If you brush against it, wash its poison off quickly; don't scratch the infected area or rub your eyes. Severe allergies are rare.

New England has two National Forests: the White Mountains National Forest, which covers much of New Hampshire and creeps over the border into Maine, and the Green Mountain National Forest, in Vermont. Both are laced with trails. Away from the coastal strip, Maine is also heavily forested—and dotted with thousands of lakes. Its most northerly areas are predominantly softwood, managed by timber companies. The softwoods are mainly pine, spruce, and fir, while sugar maple, yellow birch, aspen, and paper birch are New England's dominant hardwoods.

Forest fauna The largest of the forest animals are moose, black bear, and white-tailed deer. The deer are ever-present, and hunting them is an autumn ritual. The black bear stands almost 3 feet high and is fairly frequently seen making its clumsy way through the woods of Maine, New Hampshire, and, occasionally, Vermont. They are usually harmless (but see sidebar, far right). The animal that attracts most attention, however, is the moose. There are numerous organized moose-watching trips (information available locally), and you may well see moose as you drive around (they like the salt that runs off the roads), particularly in northern Maine, the most northerly parts of the White Mountains, and along the Kancamagus Highway. Baxter State Park is one of the best places in New England for moose. The most likely time of day to spot moose is at dawn or dusk, especially near ponds or marshes. A full-grown male moose can be 6 feet tall at its shoulders, weigh over half a ton, and has huge antlers as well—give such an animal a wide berth. Moose are most ungainly creatures, with a long,

White-tailed deer are a fairly common sight

pendulous snout and a hairy dewlap. They eat grasses and often stand in lakes.

Smaller forest animals include raccoon, chipmunk, marten, woodchuck, and porcupine. Red squirrel, coyote, red fox, lynx, muskrat, skunk, and snowshoe hare are fairly common. Beaver activity in rivers and lakes is always fascinating. Their lodges (houses of sticks and mud) are up to 6 feet high, and the dams, similarly built, are amazing constructions. The beaver's favorite food is bark—watch for sticks that have been neatly stripped and gnawed. The beavers themselves are usually seen at dusk or dawn, giving themselves away with a slap of their tails as they dive.

Mountain birds Even if you cannot identify all the songbirds, you will enjoy the songs that fill the woods in spring and summer. Many of the birds are migratory. The most common include blackpoll and Nashville warblers, ruby- and golden-crowned kinglets, pine siskin, raven, phoebe, and chickadee, the state bird of Maine and Massachusetts and a member of the tit family. The loon, a diver sometimes heard calling from the lakes of New Hampshire, is reputedly the oldest bird species on earth.

Alpine flora There are over 8 square miles of alpine zone in the White Mountains. On Mount Washington the treeline occurs exceptionally low, at 1,400 feet. Climb it (see page 208) and you will notice the trees become more and more stunted. Dense mats of vegetation called *krummholz* (German for "twisted tree") cover the ground.

Above the treeline, in the alpine zone, 100 different alpine flowers that are unique to Mount Washington, Labrador, and the Arctic grow among lichens, sedges, and mosses. The dwarf cinquefoil (Potentilla robbinsiana) is endemic to Mount Washington. Other alpine flowers that may be found here and in the alpine areas of the Katahdin range in Maine's Baxter State Park include mountain aster, alpine violet, alpine bearberry, moss plant, mountain brook saxifrage, and goldthread.

This young moose is one of many that inhabit the remote northern forests

BEAR ESSENTIALS
Black bears are shy, preferring to stay away from people and unlikely to do any harm. Nevertheless, it is wise to be careful with food, as the smell attracts them and this is when injuries may occur.
● Never feed bears.
● Don't leave food scraps lying around or throw them into a camp-fire.
● Store food (and any clothes soiled with food) in sealed containers in the trunk of the car or in a tree (so the bears don't damage your car).

FRAGILE FLORA
Remember that some of the flowers that have adapted to the biting winter winds and the poor soil take up to 25 years to flower for the first time, so watch where you put your feet. The best time to see wild flowers is from mid-June to August.

Settled in the 1630s, Strawbery Banke was named after the strawberries that once grew wild there

STRAWBERY BANKE
In its early days, Strawbery Banke was a prosperous merchants' center. Later, the Puritans came and, in 1653, changed the name to Portsmouth, which sounded less frivolous. Now the grid of old streets of the 1690s has been restored. The 42 houses show the lifestyles of its inhabitants through the ages.

NEW HAMPSHIRE CRUISES
Cruises to the nine islands constituting the Isles of Shoals and whale-watching trips are popular excursions. Operators around Portsmouth include:
● Portsmouth Harbor Cruises (tel: 800/776 0915).
● The Isles of Shoals Steamship Co. (tel: 800/441 4620).
● New Hampshire Seacoast Cruises (tel: 603/964 5545).
● The Atlantic Fishing Fleet, which operates the Atlantic Queen II (at Rye Harbor; tel: 603/964 5220).

▶▶ Portsmouth and the coast   *188C1*

Portsmouth Occupying the northern end of New Hampshire's short coastline, **Portsmouth▶▶** was the most important colonial town north of Boston. It has an English look, with a fine legacy of red-brick 18th- and 19th-century houses, many built for prosperous sea captains. Along the waterfront you can see one of the swiftest flowing navigable rivers in the world.

The original colonial settlement in the harbor was **Strawbery Banke▶▶**, one of New Hampshire's leading historic attractions (see sidebar). All but one of the houses, plus a reerected four-seater privy, stand on their original sites. (*Open* May–Oct for self-guided tours, and two weekends in December for Candlelight Strolls, which also take place one night in August.)

Portsmouth Historical Society, with the Society for the Preservation of New England Antiquities, maintains a number of 18th-century houses (*Open* Jun–Oct) scattered around town (the Portsmouth Trail connects the sites). If you intend to visit more than one, pick up a Portsmouth Passport for reduced admission.

In 1962, the **Warner House▶▶** (ca1716) became the first house in the country to be registered as a National Historic Landmark (following the restoration of the White House in Washington, DC, an action that promoted an awareness of house preservation). It was Portsmouth's first brick house, the work of John Drew, an English builder. The house retains numerous English features in its paneling and furniture. Folk-art murals date back to the time of construction; one of them (once covered up) shows English patriotic sentiment with its portrayal of a redcoat. Outstanding among the furnishings is a Portsmouth-made high chest on the upstairs landing.

The **Moffat Ladd House▶** (*Open* daily), a three-story blue and white building of 1763, stands amid pretty English-style gardens with grass steps. In them William Whipple, a signatory of the Declaration of Independence, planted what is now the state's tallest horse chestnut tree. The house has fine Portsmouth furniture, eye-catching wallpaper that was hand painted in Paris in 1819, and a tunnel in its kitchen that supposedly led to the wharf! Its spacious entrance hall is modeled on the English style. The **Wentworth Gardner House**, located at 50 Mechanic Street (*Open* Tue–Sun, 1–4), is a Georgian structure of 1760, and is noted for the quality of its interior carved woodwork, tiled fireplaces, and painted wallpaper.

Two other houses have historical connections: the **Tobias Lear House** (*Open* Wed, 1–4) was the birthplace of George Washington's private secretary, Colonel Tobias Lear, while the **John Paul Jones House** was the lodging of the Revolutionary commander Jones while his frigate *Ranger* was being refurbished in the port.

A state-of-the-art interior of 1807 is found in the **Rundlet-May House** (owned and operated by SPNEA—see page 68), featuring a contemporary roasting oven, Portsmouth furniture, and foreign wallpaper, while the Governor John Langdon House of 1784 (also an SPNEA property) has fine carving, Portsmouth furniture, and landscaped grounds.

In Albacore Park, Market Street, is the **USS** *Albacore*, a navy submarine in service from 1953 to 1972 (see sidebar).

Horse-and-carriage tours of the old town start from the church. The **Children's Museum** at 280 Marcy Street provides a variety of hands-on activities for youngsters of all ages (*Open* daily, except Monday outside summer and school vacations).

The Coast Just out of town, **Odiorne Point State Park►** covers 350 acres of duneland, the largest tract of undeveloped land on the 18-mile New Hampshire coast, and provides views of the harbor. The World War II fort here is one of a number of historic harbor defenses. The Science Center (free) features aquariums showing tide pool and salt marsh ecology. There is also a fine drive on Route 1B to **New Castle Island►** (also known as Great Island), which has old homes, forts, and lighthouses. The remainder of the New Hampshire coast is almost entirely built up, except for a few patches of marshy hinterland, but there are good state beaches at **Wallis Sands**, **Jenness**, and **North Hampton**. **Hampton Beach** has a long sandy beach but is very commercialized with an extensive boardwalk, amusements, and fast-food outlets. **Water Country**, New England's biggest water park, is on Route 1, some 3 miles south of Portsmouth.

PORTSMOUTH FURNITURE
Portsmouth's proximity to vast stands of inland timber and its ice-free harbor made it a major center of shipbuilding, house construction, and furniture-making in the 18th century. The town prospered, the ships' captains built grand mansions, and a market for quality furniture was born. Foreign influences molded taste and fashion in furniture, notably through the skills of immigrant craftsmen from England. New styles were born; reversed curves, scrolled pediments, and cabriole legs appeared. Black walnut was the rage; stained maple was a simulation. John Gaines III and Joseph Davis led the way with flamboyant styles, Gothic and Chinese pieces appearing in the 1760s.

203

REVOLUTIONARY SUB
The USS *Albacore* is one of a number of submarines to have been built in the Portsmouth naval shipyard, founded in 1800 as the first U.S. government shipyard and still in use. During her 19 years in service, the vessel never fired a weapon. She was a prototype submarine which boasted new hull design, sonar system and dive brakes. A memorial garden nearby pays tribute to crew and officers who perished in submarine service.

Portsmouth's waterfront: boats have taken visitors to the Isles of Shoals from here since the mid-19th century

Map

VERMONT

Moore Reservoir

Connecticut

Johns

3

Jefferson

White Mountain National Forest

Cascade

Moose Brook State Park

Santa's Village

2

Jefferson Highlands

Gorham

Androscoggin

Six Gun City

Whitefield

Randolph

Shelburne Birches

Comerford Dam

Moore Dam

Forest Lake State Park

16

Littleton

93

Monroe

Bethlehem

302

Twin Mountain

Presidential Range

5797ft

Cog Railway

Mount Washington Auto Road

MAINE

Fabyan

6289ft

Mt Washington

Franconia

3

Bretton Woods

Mt Washington Hotel

Glen Ellis Falls

Lisbon

Robert Frost Place

4062ft

White Mountain

Silver Cascade

Pinkham Notch

Bath

Cannon Mt

Old Man of the Mountains

Crawford Notch State Park

Woodsville

Easton

Franconia Notch State Park

Jackson

3268ft

North Haverhill

The Basin

The Flume

Pemigewasset

302

Storyland

Heritage

New Hampshire

Glen

Benton

Clark's Trading Post

National Forest

Saco

Echo Lake State Park & Cathedral Ledge

Pike

Lost River

Lincoln

112

4646ft

Mt Carrigan

Attitash

Bartlett

North Conway

4810ft

Loon Mt Ski Area

Russell-Colbath House

Alpine Slide

Conway Scenic Railroad

25

North Woodstock

Pemi Overlook

KANCAMAGUS

3701ft

Rocky Gorge

Lower Falls

302

Glencliff

Woodstock

Mt Kancamagus

HWY

Passaconaway

Conway

2929ft

Lake Tarleton

Sabbaday Falls

Champney Falls

Albany

Conway Lake

Gilmans Corner

Warren

3320ft

Mt Kineo

Waterville Valley

4016ft

16

Stinson Lake

93

Thornton

Mad

Chocorua

Silver Lake

Wentworth

Campton

Hemenway State Forest

Cheever

Rumney

White Lake State Park

Ossipee Lake

See drive pages 206–7

Baker

Pemigewasset

Squam Mountains

Sandwich

0   10   20 km

Plymouth

Squam Lake

25

0   10 miles

204

EARLY CONSERVATION DAYS

The Weeks Act was passed in 1911 and intro-duced the National Forest system. The White Mountains were the first such forest area to be designated, affording pro-tection after the removal of many trees in the region. The soil erosion and washdown that had occurred had worried politicians who spent vacations here, and political pressure for change followed.

▶▶▶ The White Mountains   *188B3*

The White Mountains are the highest and most dramatic uplands in New England. This is the region's finest area for mountain walking and in season draws crowds to its ski slopes and fall foliage display. The main areas for accommodations are the purely functional resort towns around the White Mountains proper. These places are well geared to tourism but not strong on atmosphere.

North Conway is highly rated by many for its outlet shopping malls (also known as Mount Washington Valley), which get particularly busy on rainy days in high

Winter in the White Mountains: Echo Lake

The Mount Washington Cog Railway puffs its way up an uncomfortable but scenic 1¼-hour ascent over fragile-looking viaducts and up 37-degree gradients

season. **Woodstock** and **Lincoln** are the best bases for exploring the Kancamagus and Franconia areas. **Bethlehem** is particularly noted for its architectural gems.

White Mountain sights Mount Washington►►►, New England's tallest (6,288 feet) and extremely windswept mountain, soars high above the rest of the Presidential Range. Numerous hiking routes lead up the slopes, but the most popular ways up are by the toll road (guided tours by van also available) and the **Mount Washington Cog Railway►►**, the world's oldest tourist railway (May–Oct; for reservations, tel: 603/278 5404, or 800/922 8825; note that you only have 20 minutes at the summit to ensure a return seat). At the summit, the view extends to Boston and the Atlantic Ocean. There was once a succession of grand hotels at the top; today only the Tip Top House survives (preserved as a museum; *admission* free), while the rest is a stark miscellany of antennas and small buildings, together with an observatory and a small museum.

The **Robert Frost Place►**, in a remote spot near Franconia, is the humble 50-acre farmstead where the New England poet (see page 209) dreamed he "could live cheap and get Yankier and Yankier." The tiny house contains original manuscripts and Frost's own writing table.

Clark's Trading Post►, near Lincoln, was set up by a family of avid collectors in the 1920s. The complex includes a reconstructed New England Street, the museum (with working music boxes, vintage slot machines, and peep shows), and a topsy-turvy "haunted house." Black bears perform three times daily, while the railroad around the grounds gets held up by "bandits."

At Glen, **Heritage-New Hampshire**, a look at the state's past using tableaus of selected historical tidbits, is like walking through a huge stage set. Actors explain their lives—one as a trapper, another in a mockup of 18th-century Portsmouth. It finishes with a simulated train ride. Next door is **StoryLand**, a well thought out children's theme park. There is a Mexican village, and rides that include flying clogs and a log-boat trip down water slides.

Two other theme parks, both at Jefferson, are **Santa's Village**, including "Santa's summer home" with similar rides to StoryLand, and **Six Gun City**, with a water slide and Wild West adventure. **Whale's Tale** (Route 3, North Woodstock) is a water park. **Attitash Alpine Slide**, at Bartlett, features "wet and wild water slides," plus a scenic chair lift, horseback riding, and a golf driving range.

Continued on page 208.

"Men hang out their signs indicative of their respective trades; shoemakers hang out a gigantic shoe; jewelers, a monster watch; and the dentist hangs out a gold tooth; but up in the mountains of New Hampshire, God Almighty has hung out a sign to show that there He makes men."
– Attributed to Daniel Webster, on the Old Man of the Mountain, Franconia Notch.

THE WORLD'S WORST WEATHER
Because of a funnel effect, Mount Washington gets the full brunt of three continental storm systems. The fastest winds ever recorded (231m.p.h.) have occurred here: a 10m.p.h. breeze farther down becomes an 80m.p.h. blast at the top. Some 175 feet down, the ground is permanently frozen. These unusual conditions give rise to 63 alpine flower species. The mountain has claimed many lives: below the summit, on the right of the railway, a wooden sign and stone marker show the spot where 23-year-old walker Lizzie Bourne died of exhaustion in 1855.

Drive

The White Mountains

See map on page 204 (yellow route).

This 94-mile loop tour is perhaps the most scenic mountain drive in New England. It takes in the Kancamagus Highway and Franconia Notch and provides opportunities to drive up to the magnificent lookouts on Cathedral Ledge and Mount Washington. Watch out for moose, which often stray onto the roads, and keep the gas tank full.

From North Woodstock, take Route 112, the **Kancamagus Highway**▶▶▶, famous for its fall foliage, and with choice but scattered views. Beyond **Loon Mountain ski area**, with its gondolas and outdoor activities, there are particularly fine roadside panoramas from the Pemi Overlook (with its view of mounts Kancamagus, Osceola, and Loon) and from Kancamagus Pass Overlook (with Mount

Covered bridge over The Flume in Franconia Notch

Kancamagus prominent). Numerous trails start from the road, including a short path to **Sabbaday Falls**▶, a trio of waterfalls tumbling and twisting into a deep chasm, and another to **Champney Falls**▶.

**Passaconaway Historic Site:
Russell-Colbath House** (*Open* Jul–Aug 9–4:30, but may vary. *Admission* free) is a tiny cottage formerly occupied by Ruth Colbath, the "hermit woman" postmistress whose husband walked out without explanation one night. She waited 39 years for him and left a light burning each night, but died in 1933 before his return. The Swift River flows over great boulders at **Rocky Gorge**, where a short loop trail leads to Falls Pond. A short distance east, also by the road, Lower Falls is designated for swimming and picnicking. At the next left turn take Dugway Road, leaving Route 112 to dodge the traffic jams of North Conway. **Conway** has a pair of covered bridges.

Turn left to Echo Lake and **Cathedral Ledge**▶▶▶. The small lake (a state park with a small, roped-off swimming area) is magnificently situated beneath the huge granite outcrop of Cathedral Ledge, a popular cliff for rock climbing. A road ascends the top of the ledge, and a path leads out to a dizzy view.

Farther north, via Glen, is the Summit of **Mount Washington ▶▶▶** approached on foot, by toll road, or by cog railway. Retrace your drive to Glen, then follow Route 302 to the **Mount Washington Hotel,** New England's largest wooden building, the last surviving of 15 grand hotels in the White Mountains and still laced with period atmosphere (see pages 40–41).

To the west, the **Franconia Notch road** (I–93) **▶▶▶** carves its way through awesome scenery. The drama unfolds fully from above: take the cable car up **Cannon Mountain ▶▶**, where the 1⁄2-mile Rim Trail looks down 2,500 feet into the valley and into New York State. By the cable car station is the **New England Ski Museum** (*Open* daily; Fri–Tue in winter. *Admission* free), with displays of archive photographs and equipment of various periods, plus a multiscreen slide show about skiing history.

From I–93 you can glimpse the famous **Old Man of the Mountains**, a rock outcrop some 40 feet tall that displays the uncanny profile of a human face. There is roadside parking for northbound traffic, and a short trail from a parking lot to Profile Lake for southbound traffic. **The Basin ▶**, a 30-foot-wide pothole, was gouged out by glacial meltwater and is one of a number of attractive features passed on the popular Cascade Brook Trail. Better known still is **The Flume ▶▶**, a dark, steep-sided chasm that keeps cool on the hottest of summer days and becomes laden with 30–40 feet of ice in winter, when the wooden walk-ways are dismantled. A fine waterfall tumbles into its far end.

At North Woodstock, it is worth a detour west on Route 112 to **Lost River ▶▶** (closed winter). The boardwalk trail, through caves cre-ated by tumbled boulders and along a series of waterfalls, is tortuous and exciting, and requires good footwear. The river disappears at points into the caves, which can be explored by ladder. This remote

Take a trip on a cable car for bird's-eye views

Glorious color is guaranteed in the autumn

spot was discovered by two brothers on a fishing trip, when one fell into the top entrance of a cave and had to be rescued.

New Hampshire

Zealand Notch is between Whitewall Mountain to the east and Zealand Ridge to the west, which provides a magnificent walk up to the 4,580-foot summit of Mount Guyot

PLANNING AND PREPARATION

National Forest information centers have free leaflets detailing the main trails and sell hiking maps. The De Lorme Trail Map gives an overview of trails, with 250 descriptions. For serious hiking, the Appalachian Mountain Club (AMC) publishes the definitive guide to mountain walks and maintains a network of mountain huts. Reservations recommended (tel: 603/466 2727; website www.outdoors.org); admission free. Shelters are open on a first come, first served basis. Since even the easy trails tend to be rocky, good boots with tough soles are recommended.

HIKE HINTS

● Drinking stream water is discouraged, as the parasite giardia is prevalent. This causes symptoms similar to dysentery.
● Parts of the White Mountains are designated as wilderness areas, where no vehicles, fires, bicycles, or radios are allowed, and camping must be at least 200 feet from the trail.
● The Appalachian Trail is marked in white on rocks and trees. Side trails into it are blue; other trails are yellow. Two blazes together denotes a junction. A pile of sticks across a trail means that that trail is closed.

Continued from page 205.

White Mountain walks The White Mountains are amply laced with trails of all degrees of difficulty. The Presidential Range has the highest summits. **Mount Washington** is popular but must not be underestimated; a recommended ascent is from Pinkham Notch and up Tuckerman's Ravine. Ask at the Appalachian Mountain Club (AMC) here first about conditions. Another rewarding hike is the **Zealand Trail** to the Zealand Falls AMC hut (3–3½ hours there and back). From the AMC building at Crawford rail depot on Route 302, an easy climb up **Mount Willard** follows a well-graded trail, an old carriage road, which takes in ledges and cliffs above Crawford Notch Zealand Campground (allow 2–2½ hours).

Along the Kancamagus Highway, photogenic **Mount Chocorua** can be approached from the trailhead leading to **Champney Falls**. The less demanding 3-mile **Boulder Loop Trail**, starting at Covered Bridge Campground, offers views from high rock ledges. Easier still is the Lincoln Woods Trail from Hancock Campground, which follows the course of an old railroad and gives river views before reaching Franconia Falls (allow 4 hours).

Northeast of Glen, Town Hall Road leads into Slippery Brook and becomes a dirt road. Farther on is the trail encircling lonely **Mountain Pond**, set beneath Slope Mountain. One of the best ridge walks above the treeline is along the **Franconia Ridge Trail**, reached from Lafayette Campground on I–93 (allow 5 hours). Ascend via the Falling Waters Trail and climb Mount Lincoln (5,089 feet); descend via the Bridal Path. **Mount Kearsarge North** (3,268 feet) is a 2,700-foot climb, north of North Conway, taking roughly 3 hours each way.

For a very arduous day's walking (for experienced and fit hikers only), an exceptionally fine route is from Route 16 south of Gorham up **Mount Jefferson**.

Further ideas for short walks are covered in the drive on pages 206–207.

The poet Robert Frost is best known for his simple themes, his language, and his rhythms. His appeal lies in his sharp observation of daily rural scenes, which he describes in conversational language, but with delicacy and a hint at deeper meanings. In setting and in character, his poetry is deeply rooted in New England.

ROBERT LEE FROST
MAR. 26, 1874 — JAN. 29, 1963
HAD A LOVERS QUARREL WITH THE WOR

HIS WIFE
ELINOR MIRIAM WHITE
OCT. 25, 1873, — MAR. 20, 1938
TOGETHER WING TO WING AND OAR TO

Early days Robert Frost's father, William, a teacher and newspaper editor, was a New Englander. His mother, Isabell Moodie, also a teacher, was born in Scotland, of Orkneyan origin. Robert was born on March 26, 1874, in San Francisco, where his father was working on a newspaper, but after his father's death he was taken back to New England, age 10.

Frost's mother was to exert a strong influence, teaching him and his sister and encouraging the enjoyment of literature. He briefly attended both Dartmouth College in Vermont and, later, Harvard, but left to teach and to write poetry. In 1900, he began working on a farm in Derry, New Hampshire, given him by his grandfather (see page 198). Farming was to be a recurring theme of his life, one never taken very seriously as a living, but something that brought him close to nature and, in particular, botany.

"The voice of New England" Some of Frost's best-known poetry was written in Derry, but he received no recognition there. In 1912, he moved with his wife, Elinor Miriam White, and their children to Britain, to live in Beaconsfield, Buckinghamshire. During this time, two collections of poems written in Derry, *A Boy's Will* and *North of Boston*, were published in Britain, and to great acclaim.

After the outbreak of World War II, Frost returned with his family to America, unexpectedly famous. He bought another farm, in Franconia, New Hampshire (see page 205), and began a long association as teacher and poet-in-residence with several academic institutions, including Amherst College in Massachusetts.

Four times Pulitzer Prize winner, Robert Frost died in Boston in 1963, almost 90 years of age.

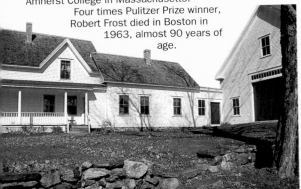

Top: the poet's grave in Bennington
Above: Robert Frost on his 85th birthday
Below: the Robert Frost Farm in Derry

"I'd like to get away from earth awhile
And then come back to it and begin over.
I'd like to go by climbing a birch tree,
And climb black branches up a snow-white trunk
Toward heaven, till the tree could bear no more,
But dipped its top and set me down again.
That would be good both going and coming back.
One could do worse than be a swinger of birches."
– From "Birches"

Yachting is big in Rhode Island, and Newport in particular

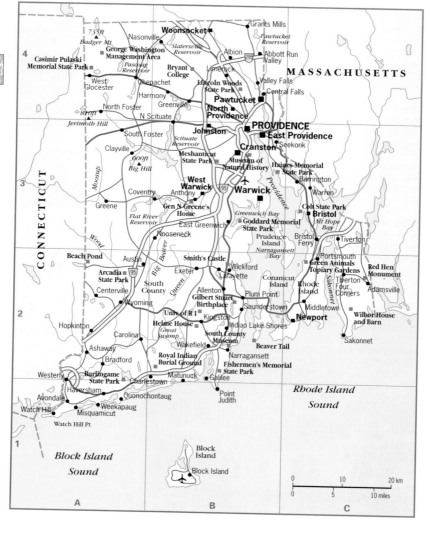

RHODE ISLAND Officially, this is Rhode Island and Providence Plantations, the state with the longest name but the smallest area, roughly 48 miles by 37 miles at its maximum dimensions. The state capital, Providence, lies at the northern end of Narragansett Bay, a scenic 28-mile inlet that is speckled with islands and that almost splits the state in two. The hinterland is low lying. To the east it is densely urbanized and industrialized, while to the west it is more rural, with pockets of solitude such as the 2,600-acre Great Swamp. But it is the intricate coastline, measuring 419 miles, that most attracts visitors. Rhode Island is one of the finest sailing areas on the East Coast, and the state proudly proclaims itself as "America's first resort." Its major island, Block Island, has an open terrain with cliffs and a rolling countryside that remind some visitors of Scotland.

The state's remarkable architectural legacy includes 20 percent of all the nation's registered National Historic Landmarks. Most famous of all are the Newport mansions, the summer "cottages" of magnates of the coal and railroad age, but there are also fine earlier survivors. Both Newport and Providence have impressively intact colonial districts. A ferry service enables Providence, Newport and Block Island to be enjoyed without a car.

EARLY DAYS Rhode Island began as a haven in a time of religious intolerance. Roger Williams, a clergyman, founded the state in 1636 after being expelled from the Puritans' Massachusetts Bay Colony for his heretical views. Williams and his followers established a settlement on the banks of the Moshassuck River and named the place Providence, as God's providence was thought to have led them there. In 1644, he traveled to England and gained a charter, reinforced in 1663, uniting the various settlements in the area as the Colony of Rhode Island and Providence Plantations. The charter gave the inhabitants a degree of independence and "full liberty in religious commencements." Hence the state became a sanctuary for religious refugees. Jews and Quakers came to Newport, and made a significant contribution to the town's success. The Native American population declined after 1676, when an unsuccessful attempt by Philip, king of the Wampanoags, led his people, the Narragansetts and Nipmucks, in a war against the English colonists.

Rhode Island was the first colony to declare its independence from Britain (May 1776) but the last to become a state (1790); it celebrates May 4th as well as July 4th. Providence became a commercial center with the boom in shipping and trade. The China trade, pioneered by John Brown of Providence, and the notorious Triangle Trade (see page 34) enhanced the state's prosperity. In 1793, the opening of Slater's Mill at Pawtucket touched off the

move to the mass production of textiles, a landmark in America's industrialization. Skilled immigrant workers, notably from Britain, Ireland, Italy and French Canada, heralded an expansion of the cities and the emergence of the state's tradition of industrial excellence.

Events

March
Irish Heritage Month, Newport: month-long, citywide celebration of Irish Heritage.

April
Blithewold Gardens & Arboretum Annual Spring Bulb Display, Bristol.

May
May Breakfasts, over 100 statewide.
Gaspee Days, Warwick: arts and crafts festival, with colonial encampment.

June
Used Boat Show, Newport.
Quonset Air Show, North Kingstown.
Festival of Historic Houses, Providence: private houses and gardens specially open for tours.
Annual Great Chowder Cook Off, Newport: best chowder competition.
Annual Newport Outdoor Art Festival.
Block Island Race Week.
Annual Big Easy Bash, West Greenwich.
Festival of Historic Houses, Providence.
Convergence Art Festival, Providence.

July
Bristol 4th of July Parade: the nation's oldest (1785).
Newport Music Festival: two weeks of classical music in the mansions.
Miller Lite International Hall of Fame Tennis Championships, Newport: major professional men's grass court tennis tournament.
Wickford Art Festival: Wickford one of the East Coast's oldest, largest, and best.
Black Ships Festival, Newport: celebration of American-Japanese trade, with sumo wrestling and kite flying.
South County Hot Air Balloon Festival, Kingston.

August
Charlestown Chamber Seafood Festival.
Newport Folk Festival: the best and biggest in the country.
JVC Jazz Festival, Newport.
WaterFire, Providence.

September
Cajun & Bluegrass Music and Dance Festival, West Greenwich: nonstop Louisiana Cajun music extravaganza.
Annual Tuna Tournament, Galilee.
International Boat Show, Newport.
Heritage Festival, Providence.
Providence Waterfront Festival.
Annual Taste of Rhode Island, Newport.
Waterfront Festival, Providence.

October
Newport Harvest-by-the-Sea Festival: month-long celebration.
Octoberfest, Pawtucket.
Annual Autumnfest, Woonsocket.
Columbus Day Festival, Federal Hill, Providence.

November
Montgolfier Day Balloon Regatta, Providence.

December
Christmas in Newport: much of the town and several mansions lavishly decorated, candlelight tours and concerts.
Festival of Lights, Wickford Village.
First Night Providence, family-oriented citywide arts and entertainment celebration.

Fishing boats on their moorings in Galilee

▶▶ Block Island
210B1

Block Island is something of an underrated getaway. Formed of rock debris dumped by two glaciers in the Ice Age, the island has 200-foot clay cliffs, 365 glacial ponds, and an open terrain. Known by Indians as Manisses ("Island of the little God") and mentioned by the Italian explorer Giovanni da Verrazano in 1524, the island was explored by and named after the Dutchman Adriaen Block before being settled by the English in 1661.

In the 19th century, Block Island became a weekend pleasure resort, but by the 1960s much of it was boarded up and its Victorian charm lay crumbling and forgotten. Today, it has been spruced up, but not overdone; the Victorian character is jealously preserved, and nightlife is distinctly sleepy. There are more bicycles than cars outside the main town, and its attractions are deliberately low-key. In fact, the island is nowhere near as busy as Martha's Vineyard or Nantucket. The authorities are promoting the island for "green" tourism as it has appeal for naturalists and for hikers, with coastal and inland trails; but beware of the deer ticks, for Lyme Disease (see page 263) is prevalent.

The island is 7 miles by 3 miles at its maximum dimensions, and is small enough to bike around at leisure (bicycles can be rented at the port). Alternatively, taxi drivers will give a tour for about $20 (the older drivers tend to have the best anecdotes), or you can see the island on horseback. **Black Rock Point**, at the island's southern tip, and **Clay Head** (with trails), at the northeastern end, have fine cliffs. The Greenway Trails are recommended for flora and fauna, and there are guided nature walks for visitors during the summer.

The main town is officially called **New Shoreham**, but is usually known as Block Island, and has a small beach. Beaches on the south coast have no undertow (unlike those on the mainland) and are ideal for families. **Corn Neck**, at the north end, has the longest beach. Surfers should head for the south coast, while **Chaqum Pond** is the place for windsurfing.

GETTING TO BLOCK ISLAND
The fastest ferry crossing is from Galilee (1 hour 10 minutes). Other ferries operate from Providence, New London (Connecticut), and Montauk (Long Island); for car reservations, tel: 401/783 4613. Flights can be taken from Westerly (New England Airlines, tel: 401/466 5881, or 800/243 2460).

213

BLOCK ISLAND WILDLIFE
In 1991, the Nature Conservancy listed Block Island among the 12 "Last Great Places" in the Americas, and 23 percent of the island is now held for nature conservation. The island is the home of the rare northern harrier and is one of only two habitats in the U.S.A. for burying beetles and regal fritillary butterflies. May brings out the snow-white flowers of the shad bush, while autumn sees a spectacular bird migration of some 150 overwintering species.

A FREAK VIEW
West Side Baptist Church on Block Island is the only church in the U.S.A. from where you can see the sun both rise and set over the Atlantic Ocean.

A view along the dramatic Mohegan Bluffs toward Southeast Lighthouse, at the southern end of Block Island

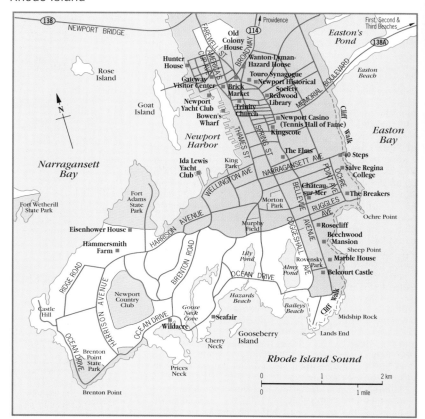

Newport Bridge, leading over Narragansett Bay

▶▶▶ Newport

210C2

With the combined attractions of its historic summer mansions and colonial architecture, its jazz festival, its sailing and regattas, its golf, its beaches, and its nightlife, Newport has a lot to offer visitors. Although the town gets busy on summer weekends, accommodations are plentiful, with a large concentration of B&Bs.

Newport is an important lobster town; lobsters can be bought fresh off the boats at Aquidneck Lobster Co. in Bowen's Wharf near the harbor, at the hub of the town's crafts and gift shops. The three main beaches are called, unsurprisingly, First Beach, Second Beach, and Third Beach. Additionally, there are a couple of small beaches off Ocean Drive. Parking fees at the beaches are expensive, but it is only a mile or so to bike out from the center of town. Good views of the ocean can be had from the 3½-mile **Cliff Walk▶▶**, which snakes above rocky shores and beaches and offers fascinating glimpses of some mansion backyards and gardens. Good shoes are needed to walk it in its entirety. Just outside town is a major naval base. Allied navies come to the Naval War College to carry out both war games and preparations for the real thing (much of the 1990 Gulf War was planned here).

Newport in its early days was a center for religious tolerance, thanks to the liberal attitude of Roger Williams

ENIGMA VARIATIONS
The provenance of the curious building in Newport's Touro Park is obscure. Various explanations claim that it has Viking origins, that it was built in conjunction with the solstice, that it was a beacon, that privateers stored their booty in it, that giants with green eyes and red hair erected it, or that it was a windmill. However, carbon dating in 1993 indicated that the structure dates from either the 16th or early 17th centuries.

215

AMERICA'S OLDEST TAVERN
Threatened with demolition in the 1950s, Newport's White Horse Tavern, dating from the 17th century, was fortunately rescued and still survives as the oldest tavern in the U.S.A. Churches on either side had objected to the renewal of its liquor license; to get around this, a state law was specially passed to the effect that only taverns built before 1700 with a church on either side can obtain a new license!

A FORESIGHTED PLEA
"These old houses and old doorways are a stock-in-trade for Newport, and there is a decided question whether the so-called march of progress, which prompts the tearing down or extensive remodeling of old structures, will in the long run pay the owners as well as if they were put in repair and their features preserved, so that in years to come they may continue to attract strangers who are interested in the old and quaint."
– *Newport Daily News*, April 15, 1910.

(see page 211), the founder of Rhode Island. In colonial times, Jews and Quakers made it their home, and this cultural diversity was instrumental in the town's success.

Colonial Newport Despite devastation in the Revolutionary War and a long period of neglect, colonial Newport still survives to a remarkable extent: there are 200 buildings over 200 years old (the biggest such concentration in the country). Until the late 1960s, the town looked drab and many houses were tar-covered. Although many buildings were torn down, 60 were saved by Operation Clapboard, a campaign to encourage people to buy and renovate a historic house, and Newport's dreamed-of facelift became a reality. Pineapple motifs are found on many of Newport's older buildings, the fruit being a symbol of hospitality in the state (sailors returning from the tropics used to display a pineapple in their windows to show they had returned safely and were receiving visitors).

Today, **Town Green** looks like a typically timeless New England green, dominated by **Trinity Church▶** (1726), which still has box pews and a galleried interior. In fact, the green was a 20th-century beautification scheme: houses were moved here after buildings were cleared.

In **Touro Park** is the town's most celebrated enigma, an open-sided stone structure in the center of a green (see sidebar). Nearby is the library, opened in 1748 and the oldest in the U.S.A. It is a classical, wooden building, designed to resemble stone.

The **Touro Synagogue▶ ▶** is the oldest Jewish place of worship in the country and dates from 1763. A century earlier, Portuguese and Spanish Jews, fleeing religious persecution, found sanctuary in Newport. The elegant interior is a real surprise and contains the famous letter from George Washington to warden Moses Seixas extolling religious tolerance.

Aerial view of The Breakers, showing the cliff walk that skirts its grounds

NEWPORT CASINO

This American Renaissance period piece began in 1880 as a social and residential club, gaining popularity with old-money families as lawn tennis boomed. The Newport Casino hosted the U.S. National Tennis Championships (later to become the U.S. Open) from 1881 to 1914, and is still the center for major competitions as well as court tennis (real tennis) and bowls tournaments. The 13 grass courts are the only ones in the nation available for public use. Tournaments held today include tennis, sumo wrestling, bowls, and croquet. For more information, tel: 401/849 3990.

At 54 Washington Street is **Hunter House** (1748), a colonial-era house open to the public. It has period furniture made locally and a charming old-world garden.

At 17 Broadway, the restored **Wanton-Lyman-Hazard House** (1675) is Newport's oldest colonial house (*Open* Thu–Sat in summer). In Thames Street is the **Museum of Newport History▶**, a treasure house commemorating Newport's remarkable past, with exhibits on fishing, crafts, religion, and social history. The **Doll Museum**, at 520 Thames Street, has over 600 antique and modern dolls (*Open* Wed–Mon).

The **Newport Casino▶ ▶** has never had anything to do with gambling, taking its name from the Italian for "little house" (see sidebar). Inside the casino is the **Tennis Hall of Fame▶ ▶**, the world's largest tennis museum and a shrine to the tennis greats, where new additions undergo an induction ceremony. In addition to the displays of vintage tennis equipment, there are entertaining interactive videos featuring quizzes and comparisons of the game techniques of the stars.

The Mansions In the 19th century, Newport became a summer playground for the elite. Mansions modeled on Italian *palazzi*, French châteaus, and English stately homes appeared along **Bellevue Avenue▶ ▶ ▶** and **Ocean Drive▶ ▶ ▶**. No expense was spared as European craftsmen were employed and the rooms were packed with costly objets d'art. First came the old-money families; later, the new-guard Vanderbilts and others added flamboyance and entertained in their fabulous "summer cottages."

Today, numerous mansions are open to the public. It is best to select a few contrasting types, then drive or bike along Bellevue Avenue and along the 9½-mile Ocean Drive to enjoy the scenery. The Preservation Society of Newport County maintains eight properties (*Open* daily in summer, with several also open on weekends in winter; reduced admission if visiting more than one property, including the five mansions on Bellevue Avenue). For further details, tel: 401/847 1000.

Kingscote▶, a gray clapboard Victorian Gothic house of 1839, is notable as being Newport's first "cottage" and is more modest than its successors. The house contains family pieces of William Henry King, a China trade merchant. McKim, Mead, and White, architects of the Newport Casino, added the dining room.

The Elms▶▶ (1901), a French Renaissance château built by Horace Trumbauer for a Pennsylvania coal magnate, was modeled on the Château d'Asnières near Paris.

Château-sur-Mer▶▶ (1852) was the first truly grand cottage, with its French-style mansard roof. Inside, a wall-painting of the Tree of Life accompanies the staircase, with overhead paintings of sky, birds, and foliage. This was a year-round rather than a summer residence and was enlarged by Richard Morris Hunt in the 1870s, his first commission in the High Victorian grand manner, although he later reverted to French and Italian styles.

The Breakers▶▶▶, on Ochre Point Avenue, was designed by Richard Morris Hunt for Cornelius Vanderbilt and took 2,500 workers two years to complete in 1895. It was modeled on a 16th-century Italian *palazzo*, with French additions, and no expense was spared. The music room was constructed in Paris and shipped over, and there is a huge hall of Caen marble. The grandest gesture in an architectural medley of styles is the formal dining room, festooned with gilded garlands of fruit and cherubs, decorated with wall paintings and alabaster pillars, and lit by chandeliers. It is perhaps testament to the Vanderbilts' wealth that the house was only seen as the "summer cottage," used for about 10 weeks each year, and that, accordingly, the youngest daughter inherited it.

Rosecliff▶▶, a graceful building of 1902, was modeled by Stanford White on the Grand Trianon palace at Versailles and features a Court of Love and a heart-shaped staircase. The Great Gatsby was filmed here.

NEWPORT ÝPRACTICALITIES
In the Newport Gateway Visitor Center there is a free direct-dial service connecting with hotels. Walking tours of colonial Newport also begin here. Bicycle rental and tours are available from Ten Speed Spokes at 18 Elm Street (tel: 401/847 5609). Some of the best views of Newport are from the water, and cruises tour the harbor, offering excellent views. Viking Cruises operate from Goat Island (tel: 401/847 6921) and from Sayer's Wharf.

217

The Ballroom at Rosecliff, the grandest of all ballrooms in Newport, where leading socialites were entertained and many dazzling soirées were held

THE COAL MAN'S RETREAT

In 1894, Pennsylvania coal magnate Augustus van Wickle gave his wife Bessie a steam yacht for her birthday. They cruised into Narragansett Bay and set their hearts on owning a summer retreat at Bristol, north of Newport. Their first house burned down in 1906, but their new 45-room "cottage," Blithewold, survives and is open to the public. It is a delightful amalgam of English manor, colonial, and Dutch styles. Bessie filled the grounds with exotic trees and flora.

At the Astors' **Beechwood Mansion▶** (1856), costumed guides treat visitors as though they were guests at a dinner party with the Astors in the 1890s and play the part of servants and debutantes. Special events include tea-dance tours, grand parties, cotillions, and murder mystery tours. The house lacks the physical glamour of many of the others, but many visitors prefer this livelier approach.

Marble House▶▶ (1892) was the first of the "gilded era" houses and was modeled on the Grand and Petit Trianons at Versailles. Although smaller than The Breakers, it is even more ornate. It was built for William Vanderbilt by Richard Morris Hunt, who was also involved in designing the pedestal of the Statue of Liberty and New York Public Library. A whimsical Chinese Tea House stands close to the Cliff Walk.

Belcourt Castle▶▶ (1891), modeled on the Louis XIII hunting lodge at Versailles, has an intimate half-timbered courtyard and 60 rooms filled with European treasures, including 13th-century stained glass and a 13,000-piece crystal chandelier from Imperial Russia.

Hammersmith Farm, a "mansion" of interest for its links with J.F.K.

Hammersmith Farm▶, on Ocean Drive, can be reached by taking a Viking Cruises tour (see sidebar on page 217) or by a short drive or bicycle ride. Built in 1887–1889, it gained worldwide prominence in the 1950s when Jacqueline Bouvier and John F. Kennedy had their wedding reception here. It later functioned as the Summer White House, and Kennedy's presidential desk can be seen. Compared to the other mansions it is somewhat a return to normality, its décor having a luxurious 1940s and 1950s look. It is still a working farm, the only one in Newport, and is rated the best wedding locale in the U.S.

Along **Ocean Drive▶▶▶** are the America's Cup Museum and the summer home of the New York Yacht Club, where hundreds of regattas are held each year. Apart from Hammersmith Farm, the mansions here are private; look for "Normandy," designed in the style of a Normandy farmhouse.

North of town, at Portsmouth, is **Green Animals▶▶**, a bewitching topiary garden featuring 21 animal creations ingeniously formed from privet and yew and numerous other geometrical boxwood figures, as well as a toy museum. For **Blithewold▶▶** see top sidebar.

NEWPORT FIRSTS

● In 1803, Newport was the first town in the U.S.A. to have its streets installed with gas lighting.
● A Newport man was the first person brave enough to eat a tomato (the fruit was previously thought to be poisonous).
● The town's synagogue was America's first (1763), as was its ferry (1657), open golf tournament (1895), and free public school (1640).

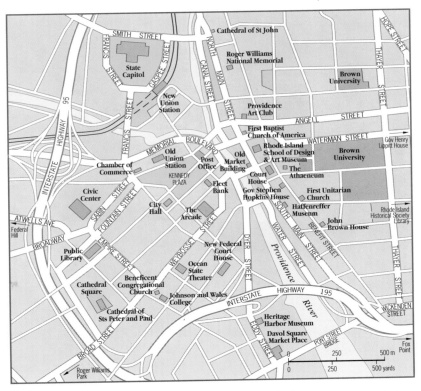

▶▶ Providence

210B3

Easily reached by commuter train or bus from Boston, Providence is well worth a visit as an example of a city renaissance. Founded by Roger Williams in 1636, it prospered as a China trade and Triangle Trade seaport. Its downtown is still compact enough to explore on foot and has a skyline graced by church spires, the State House and the art deco Fleet Bank—a mini-skyscraper known as the Superman Building. The presence of both **Brown University**, founded in 1764 and centered on College Green, and the **Rhode Island School of Design (RISD)** lend the downtown area a college-life air, with plenty of cafés, funky boutiques, nightclubs and numerous bookshops along Thayer, Hope and Wickenden streets. At the fore of the recent climate of change has been the ongoing rejuvenation of the river, with the creation of walkways and a park; in summer gondolas operate and outdoor concerts take place. In an attempt to rejuvenate the whole downtown shopping area, artists have been enticed with tax-free incentives; many stores stand empty still. At 65 Weybosset Street, **The Arcade**, the nation's oldest covered shopping mall (1828), is a three-tier Greek Revival structure which houses food stalls and shops.

Marble marvel: the smallest state boasts a state house as imposing as any

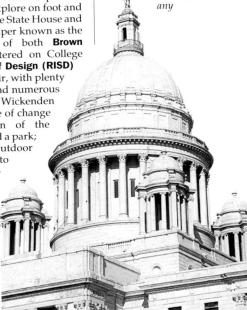

The **State House▶ ▶** (free tours Mon–Fri, 9:30–3:30), built of Georgia marble, was modeled on the Capitol at Washington, DC, and boasts the world's fourth largest self-supporting marble dome. Gilbert Stuart's famous portrait of George Washington hangs in the Executive Chamber, while the 1663 Charter granted by Charles II is displayed at the entrance to the Senate.

Set on College Hill close to downtown, historic East Side displays fine colonial, Federal, Greek Revival and Victorian domestic architecture, 19th-century industrialists' mansions and steep cobbled streets. Its pride and joy is **Benefit Street▶ ▶ ▶**, the city's "mile of history." Restoration began in the 1950s with the founding of the Providence Preservation Society, which bought up houses and pushed

The Carrie Tower, a landmark of Brown University's campus

for conservation laws. A fine view extends from **Prospect Terrace**, a park where Roger Williams is buried on Congdon Street. Elsewhere along Benefit Street peep inside the **Old State House**, with its tiny general assembly room, and the **Athenaeum▶**, a Greek Revival building of 1838, where Edgar Allen Poe met Sarah Helen Whitman (she is thought to have inspired his poem *Annabel Lee*). The **First Baptist Church▶** (1775) has a magnificent 185-foot steeple, a galleried interior and a Waterford crystal chandelier. The Browns, who endowed Brown University, were Baptists and intended it to be a Baptist ministry school; it has become an eminent and ultra-liberal Ivy League university, but some commencement ceremonies are still held in the church.

At 224 Benefit Street, the **RISD Art Museum▶ ▶** has an outstanding collection which includes paintings by U.S. masters, French Impressionists and modern artists. Highlights among artifacts of the ancient world are a wooden Buddha (ca1150) from Japan and a 4th-century Roman mosaic (*Open* Wed–Sun 12–5, Fri 10–8). Foremost among the historic houses open to view is the **John Brown House▶ ▶**, built at 52 Power Street in 1786 for a wealthy China trade merchant, and later extended. It contains John Brown's chariot of 1782 (the earliest American-made vehicle in existence) and a spectacular turn-of-the-century bathroom with tiled murals of water nymphs (*Open* Tue–Sat 10–5, Sun 12–4, plus Mon holidays; Jan and Feb, Fri–Sun only). Other museum attractions include the **Haffenreffer Museum of Anthropology** in South Main Street, with numerous Native American artifacts, and the **Heritage Harbor Museum** opening by 2000—to feature a museum of immigration and an exhibition on diners (see panel on page 221).

Federal Hill is the Italian quarter, with lively festivals and good restaurants, at its most animated around Atwells Avenue. South of downtown, **Roger Williams Park** is a Victorian creation with bandstand concerts and lakes. It contains a natural history museum

TOURS OF PROVIDENCE
Guided walking tours start from the old schoolhouse at 21 Meeting Street, while trolley tours start from Kennedy Plaza. Cruises on the *Bay Queen* start from Warren and take in Narragansett Bay (tel: 410/245 1350).

BIRTH OF A BOOM
North of Providence is the Blackstone River Valley, once a hive of textile mills and the cradle of the American Industrial Revolution—the catalyst for huge social change later in the 19th century. The nation's first mass production of cotton yarn using waterpowered machines took place in 1793 at Slater's Mill in Pawtucket. Samuel Slater had been a manager at Arkwright Mills in Derbyshire, England and brought technical know-how with him. The mill now functions as a museum and gives demonstrations.

and planetarium, as well as a zoo with over 600 animals including a wetlands area with native New England species.

► South County   210A2

South County makes up Rhode Island's southwestern corner. Swimming and beaches are the main draw of the coast itself, although wildlife reserves here and in numerous inland wetlands attract naturalists.

Sedate **Watch Hill** is both a fishing port and resort town, with long beaches. Its Flying Horse Carousel, built in 1867, is the oldest in America. Lively family fun is provided at Misquamicut, where **Water Wizz** offers amusements, miniature golf, a giant water slide, and a roller-skating rink. There are several beaches between the resort towns of **Charlestown** and **Narragansett**. Near the latter, the **South County Museum►** displays a range of reconstructed New England buildings, including an old-time store and a cobbler's shop (*Open* May–Oct, Wed–Sun).

The quaint community of **Wickford►**, off scenic Route 1A, has a pretty view of the harbor and abounds in antiques, crafts, and specialty shops. John Updike set his novel *The Witches of Eastwick* here. Look for signs on Route 1A for the **Gilbert Stuart Birthplace**, near Saunderstown (*Open* Apr–Oct, Thu–Mon) the home of the artist who created the portrait of George Washington seen on dollar bills. At Wakefield, the **Washington County Jail** (1792) has changing local history exhibits and original jail cells and rooms (*Open* May–Oct, Tue, Thu and Sat 1–4. *Admission* free).

221

Native American monument, Narragansett

THE BIRTHPLACE OF THE DINER
Rhode Island can claim to be the true birthplace of that uniquely American institution, the diner. The semi-mobile cabins that can still be seen throughout the U.S. (there is a fine surviving example in the center of Providence, just off Kennedy Plaza) had its origins during the early Industrial Revolution in the Blackstone Valley, when workers were fed by horse-drawn food carts.

A MARINE FEAST
Bargain-priced fresh lobsters can be bought at Galilee, near Point Judith, when the boats come in at around 4–5pm. Take a plastic bag.

Galilee: fishing is important all along Rhode Island's coastline

Vermont

CDN

Lake Memphremagog

5

Alburg
Swanton
Lake Carmi
Newport
Derby
Norton

89
Enosburg Falls
3862ft Jay Peak
Hazens Notch
Brownington
3330ft Gore Mt
Island Pond

Hyde Log Cabin
St Albans
Bakersfield
Lowell
Orleans
Barton
Lake Willoughby
Bloomfield

4

Grand Isle
Fairfax
Jeffersonville
Craftsbury Common
Glover
91
Bread and Puppet Museum
East Burke

Lake Champlain
Milton
Smugglers Notch
4393ft Notch
Morrisville
Greensboro
Lyndonville
3268ft Burke Mt

Winooski
Essex Junction
Mt Mansfield
Hardwick
Danville
Burke Mt

Burlington
Stowe
Concord

Shelburne
Ben and Jerry's Ice Cream Factory
Cabot
St Johnsbury

Waterbury
Peacham
Lower Waterford

Shelburne Museum
4081ft Camels Hump
MONTPELIER
Groton

3

Rokeby
Ferrisburgh
Barre
Wells River

Vergennes
4134ft Mt Ellen
Northfield
Granite Quarries

Bristol
Lincoln
Brookfield Gulf
Williamstown Gulf

Chimney Point
Morgan Horse Farm
3822ft Bread Loaf Mt
Moss Glen
Brookfield

Middlebury
Texas Falls
Randolph Gap
Chelsea
Bradford

Leicester
Hancock
Bethel
Justin Smith Morrill Homestead

Shoreham
Goshen
Green Mountain National Forest
Sharon

Sudbury
Brandon

Orwell
Pittsford
Norwich

Benson
Marble Exhibit
Proctor
Killington
White River Junction

Wilson Castle
4241ft Killington Peak
Woodstock
Quechee Gorge

2

Fair Haven
Rutland
Bridgewater

Poultney
Wallingford
Plymouth Notch
3143ft Mt Ascutney
Windsor

Danby
Felchville

Pawlet
Ludlow
Weston
Perkinsville
Springfield

Dorset
3167ft Bromley Mt
Londonderry
Chester

Manchester
Hildene
Magic Mt

3816ft Big Equinox
Grafton

Arlington
Green Mountain Nat Forest
3937ft Stratton Mt
Jamaica
Bellows Falls

1

Park McCullough House
3461ft Haystack Mt
Newfane
Townshend

Bennington
West Dover
Putney

Green Mountain Park
Wilmington
Marlboro
Brattleboro

Harriman Res
Brigham Young's Birthplace

0 20 40 60 km
0 10 20 30 miles

See drive pages 240–1

NEW YORK

NEW HAMPSHIRE

Connecticut River

White River

Otter

Green Mountains

Green Mountains

MASSACHUSETTS

A B C

*Vermont retains the
character of a retreat
from the busier outside
world*

The Northeast Kingdom in the autumn

VERMONT Vermont is a survivor, a rural state of mountains and forests, much of it quite unspoiled. The landscape is folded; its very name, derived from the French words for green mountain, is descriptive enough for much of the year (although the forests you see today have taken over after cleared farmland was abandoned a century or so ago). Towns are distinctly on the small side; even Burlington is far from being a buzzing metropolis, and Montpelier, the state capital, has a village-like quietness at night. A few days' driving around the state will leave memories of quiet, winding roads and huge red barns, of handpainted signs pointing out ATM machines and homemade maple syrup outlets, of fashionable designer shops and country stores. Vermonters thrive on crafts, music, and literature, and are strongly involved in the visual arts of painting and sculpture. The events calendar always looks busy.

THE RURAL HERITAGE In the second quarter of the 19th century, Vermont was the wool capital of the world. Spain had been forced to sell off a large part of its herds of sheep in 1811 to pay off Napoleonic War debts, and many of the sheep came here. Wool production only declined in Vermont after the Civil War, when the railroads in the West allowed sheep from Wyoming and Montana to dominate the wool trade. Foreign competition from Australia accompanied this downturn.

Vermont

Right: red barns and silos are a common sight

"They hewed this state out of the wilderness, they held it against a foreign foe, they laid deep and stable the foundation of our state life because they sought not the life of ease but the life of effort for a worthy end."
– President Theodore Roosevelt, 1902.

FIRSTS IN THE NATION
Vermont was the first state in the U.S.A:
● to manufacture a postage stamp (at Brattleboro, 1846).
● to offer troops in the Civil War.
● to found a Boy Scout Club (at Barre, 1909).
● to install a chair lift (at Mount Mansfield, 1940).
● to abolish slavery (1777).

The first pumpkins of the season: they must be picked before the frosts arrive

Today, cows and sheep no longer outnumber the inhabitants, but dairy farming is by far the largest agricultural industry. Fruit and vegetable farming, producing hardy crops which can survive the harsh winters, also takes place. Other industries include granite and marble extraction.

The fragile character of "Vermontness" has been preserved, but only just. Proximity to the Big Apple and to Boston might change all that, although large advertising signs are banned in this last bastion of rural perfection. A state law lays down ten tough environmental conditions to be met by all new large developments, including a requirement that new structures should not adversely affect the "aesthetics, scenic beauty, historic sites, or natural areas" of the vicinity.

VERMONT FOR VISITORS The southern part of Vermont, with its relatively affluent communities of Bennington, Manchester, and Woodstock, is seductive vacation territory. Northern Vermont is appreciably quieter and emptier, except for the area around Burlington and Shelburne. The Northeast Kingdom (the northeast corner of the state) is less sophisticated, ideal for those who like to make their own discoveries.

For hikers, the 260-mile Long Trail crosses the state from the Massachusetts line to the Canadian border, via the Green Mountains and Mount Mansfield (4,393 feet), the highest peak in Vermont. Vermont's towns are distinctly on the small side; even Burlington is far from being a buzzing metropolis and Montpelier, the state capital, has a village-like quietness at night. A few days' driving around the state will leave memories of quiet, winding roads, huge red barns where the cattle herds winter, of hand-painted signs advertising home-made maple syrup outlets, of smart designer shops contrasting with country stores and hippy survivals. Vermonters thrive on crafts, music and literature.

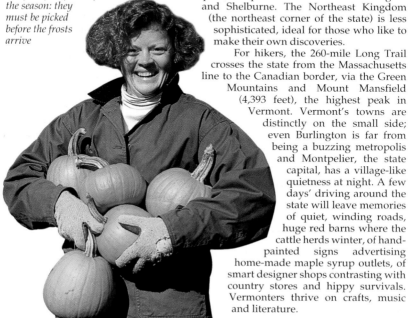

Events

For further information on any of the following events, contact the state tourist office (see page 266) or alternatively the local chambers of commerce.

January
Ice Harvest, Brookfield.
Winter Carnival, Stowe: top winter event.

February
Stratton Winter Carnival, Stratton.
Fisk Trophy Race, Woodstock: oldest continually run ski race in the U.S.

March
Maple Festival, Woodstock.
U.S. Open Snowboarding Championships, Stratton.

April
Vermont Maple Festival, St. Albans.

May
Champlain Valley Quilt Show, Shelburne.
Spring Farm Festival, Woodstock.
Lilac Weekend, Shelburne: 400 lilacs in full bloom.

June
Balloon Festival and Crafts Fair, Quechee and Essex.
Discover Jazz Festival, Burlington.
Lake Champlain Balloon and Craft Festival, Champlain Valley/Essex Junction.

July
Bennington Museum Antiques Show.
Fiddlers' Contest, Hardwick.
Marlboro Music Festival, Marlboro College (ends August).
Old Time Farm Day and Grand Old Fourth Celebration, Shelburne.
Vermont Mozart Festival, various locations (ends August).
Vermont Quilt Festival, Northfield: largest quilt event in New England.

August
Antique and Classic Car Rally, Stowe.
Bennington Battle Day Celebration.
Vermont Antique Dealers' Association Antiques Show, Stratton.
Vermont Craft Fair, Manchester.
Vermont State Fair, Rutland (ends September).

Autumn color comes to the Northeast Kingdom

September
Antique and Classic Car Show, Bennington.
Champlain Valley Exposition, Burlington: dairy days and funfair.
Harvest Festival, Shelburne.
National Traditional Old-Time Fiddlers' Contest, Barre.
Northeast Kingdom Fall Foliage Festival, various locations (ends October).
Stratton Arts Festival, Stratton Mountain (ends October).
Apple Days, Brattleboro: hayrides, cider pressing and apple pie contest.

October
Apples and Crafts Fair, Woodstock.
Northeast Kingdom Foliage Festival, various locations.
Foliage Craft Fair, Stowe.
Mount Snow Craft Fair, West Dover.

November
Thanksgiving Weekend Craft Show, Killington.
Vermont Hand Crafters Craft Show, Burlington.

December
Wassail Christmas Festival, Woodstock.
Prelude to Christmas, Manchester.

225

Vermont

The archetypal New England clapboard church, Bennington's Old First Church

THE BATTLE OF BENNINGTON

On August 16, 1777, British General Burgoyne sent Hessian and Indian troops to capture military supplies stored in Bennington as part of his attempt to split the colonies in two in an advance down the Hudson River. Brigadier General John Stark countered by sending two detachments to head off the British. The battle actually took place at Walloomsac Heights (now in New York State), 5 miles from Bennington; it began at 3 PM and two hours later the British were forced to retreat. The British failure to procure supplies resulted in defeat at Saratoga two months later, and in surrender on October 7.

GRANDMA MOSES (1860–1961)

Born in New York State, Grandma Moses lived in Virginia and later in Bennington. As an artist she was self-taught, and her primitive, even child-like style, which captured the public imagination, is immediately identifiable. Typically her work shows village scenes or hill landscapes with tiny figures. She was perhaps more significant for recording a particular time and region in America's past than for her gifts as an artist.

▶ Barre

222B3

Pronounced "Barry," this is a blue-collar town adjacent to the **Rock of Ages ▶**, the world's largest granite quarry, which covers a 50-acre site. Self-guided tours from the visitors' center (Mon–Fri) give a view of the quarry, where huge blocks are lifted by derricks, and of the manufacturing division and the finished products. **Hope Cemetery**, established in 1895, has choice examples of memorials crafted from Barre granite.

▶▶ Bennington

222A1

Tucked into Vermont's southwest corner, Bennington is doubly famous for its college and for the Battle of Bennington, a turning point in the Revolution (see sidebar). A bronze panther marks the site of the Catamount Tavern where Ethan Allen and the Green Mountain Boys plotted against the British for the capture of Fort Ticonderoga. Allen's house was beside the **Old First Church** (1805), whose magnificent steeple dominates the old village, up the hill from the modern town. The beautifully sited churchyard has a good number of fine carved tombstones. Among these are the graves of Revolutionary War soldiers from both sides, as well as the resting place (follow the arrows) of the poet Robert Frost (see page 209), whose epitaph records "I had a lover's quarrel with the world."

The entire district of Old Bennington is worth taking in for its crisp examples of Federal-style homes. At the far end, the **Bennington Battle Monument**, a 306-foot memorial tower, rises close to the site of the storehouse that sparked the battle. An elevator whisks you up Vermont's tallest structure for a view over three states.

Bennington Museum► (*Open* daily) has a collection of Grandma Moses paintings (see sidebar), as well as numerous examples of Bennington glassware and pottery, plus musical instruments, Revolutionary War exhibits, and the oldest Stars and Stripes flag in existence.

Route 67 passes the **Park McCullough House►** (*Open* May–Oct) on West Street, North Bennington, a cheerful yellow 35-room Second Empire Victorian mansion. Built as a summer cottage in 1875 and occupied by four generations of one family up to 1965, it retains original furnishings and even the owners' clothing, diaries, and 37,000 documents. It hosts regular music recitals.

Also on Route 67A, **Bennington Center for the Arts** is an exclusive, liberal, and progressive institution where plays, readings, and an August music festival are presented. South of town, **Southern Vermont College** is the home, from May through October, of the professional Oldcastle Theatre Company (tel: 802/447 1267).

Joseph Cerniglia Winery, New England's largest, is on scenic Route 103 and offers free tastings.

► Burlington   *222A4*

Set beside Lake Champlain on the state's western border, Burlington is a university town whose population increases drastically in the autumn and that hosts numerous arts and music events. Apart from the considerable attractions of Lake Champlain, the largest city in Vermont is a place worth stopping at for its shops. It has a range of "environmental" stores, sidewalk cafés, and the pedestrianized area of Church Street Marketplace. Of the town's four beaches, North Beach is the best.

Lake Champlain►►, 128 miles long and up to 12 miles wide and the largest body of fresh water in the U.S.A. outside the Great Lakes, lies between the Hudson River and New York to the south and the Richelieu River and Montreal to the north. Lake views can be enjoyed from a number of points on the shore, notably Red Rocks Park in South Burlington and Sand Bar State Park at Milton (where there are windsurfer and boat rentals). To appreciate the lake's shoreline and sunsets, try a cruise on the *Spirit of Ethan Allen* from Burlington (tel: 802/862 8300).

The **Lake Champlain Maritime Museum►**, near Vergennes (*Open* May–Oct), has historical and maritime displays, boat-building demonstrations, and a working forge. On Grand Isle, **Hyde Log Cabin** dates from 1783 and is one of the country's oldest log cabins. Built by surveyor Jedediah Hyde, Jr., whose family stayed here for 150 years, the interior houses maps and memorabilia.

CHAMP
Lake Champlain has its own version of Scotland's Loch Ness Monster, known as Champ. This creature gets occasional "sightings." In 1982, the Vermont House of Representatives passed a resolution to protect the beast from "any willful act resulting in death, injury, or harassment."

ACROSS THE LAKE
The ferry from Burlington to Port Kent, NY, is handy for visits to Ausable Chasm (*Open* mid-May to early October). This sandstone gorge with its rapids and whirlpools surging beneath 200-foot cliffs can be seen from a boat ride and a ¾-mile walkway. Further south, on Route 74, a ferry gives access to the New York side at Fort Ticonderoga, begun in 1755 by the French to block the British and now mostly reconstructed and marketed for the tourist industry. Between mid-May and mid-October, costumed guides explain the history, and cannon firing and period music supply the background atmosphere.

227

The lively Church Street Marketplace, Burlington

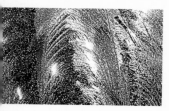

New England's long, cold winters bring plenty of snow, and New Englanders certainly know how to make the most of it. Resorts, though generally small, offer great variety; locals flock to them at weekends. To make the most of a full week you may wish to sample a range of places or activities.

FURTHER INFORMATION
● The brochure Skiing in New England is available from Discover New England (see page 266).
● Maine Handicapped Skiing assists those with disabilities with programs at Sunday River; tel: 207/824 2440; fax: 207/824 0453.
● The American Skiing Company's Magnificent Seven Pass covers Killington VT, Mount Snow VT, Sugarbush VT, Sugarloaf ME, Sunday River ME, Attitash Bear Peak NH and The Canyons in the Rockies.

ICE CLIMBING
Frozen waterfalls are targets for ice climbers. Novices are taught how to use an ice axe and might try a 30° climb. Contact the International Mountain Climbing School, PO Box 1666, North Conway, NH 03860 (tel: 603/356 7064; e-mail: guides@ime-usa.com).

Many gondolas are open to non-skiers

Downhill (Alpine) skiing and snowboarding You can ski in all six New England States, but Vermont, New Hampshire and Maine are the prime downhill destinations. Snowboarding has gained massive popularity with teenagers in particular; beginners will find themselves falling a lot, but learning is rapid. Some areas have dedicated snowboard parks, with jumps and half-pipes. You can hire skis, boots and snowboards at all resorts, and childcare is available; the standard of instruction is high.

Weekends, Christmas and President's Week in February are peak times. Snowmaking guarantees good conditions from November to April in many areas. After dark, some slopes stay open for night skiing, or you can try out tubing—hurtling down a run on a rubber innertube—or take a guided snowshoe walk. During the day you may like to try a horse-drawn sleigh ride.

From Stowe, you can take high-speed gondola up Mount Mansfield—which has steeper top-to-bottom runs plus easier terrain on Spruce Peak nearby, or ski over to Smuggler's Notch, the premier family winter resort. Killington (now linked to Pico) is New England's biggest resort and ranks top for nightlife. Its season runs from October to June, and there are more than 100 miles of trails, the highest from 4,241 feet. Stratton, the birthplace of snowboarding, is a single mountain with a full range of runs, and an attractive resort at its base. Wachusett is the closest ski area to Boston and is excellent for children, beginners and intermediates. Massachusetts' main skiing is in the Berkshires, including Jiminy Peak.

The White Mountains ski areas each have enough skiing for three days or so (if you plan to stay longer the Ski New

Hampshire Pass is useful). Of these, Bretton Woods is best for families and beginners, while Waterville Valley, Attitash Bear Peak and Loon are all-rounders—Loon has plenty for non-skiers including an animal park and a skating rink—and Cannon attracts intermediates and experts.

Maine's resorts, out of range for day trips from Boston or New York, avoid the weekend crowds. Sunday River encompasses eight mountains, three miles across, and has the largest snowmaking system in New England; it includes long easier runs with views all the way. A few days here can be combined with Sugarloaf, where the treeless summit offers the highest skiing in New England (2,820 feet vertical from the 4,237-foot summit), and superb views over three states and Canada.

Cross-country (Nordic) skiing Much of this sport's appeal lies in its sense of freedom: you can take prepared trails at your own pace and stop wherever you like. Cross-country on flat trails is easily mastered, but even experienced downhill skiers should have some instruction in the technique for steeper descents. Passes and equipment rental are less expensive than for downhill skiing.

Stowe is the birthplace of American cross-country, and includes four interlinked areas constituting New England's premier network. The original one, Von Trapp, has glorious views toward Mount Mansfield as well as wooded trails leading up through conifers and birches to a tiny log cabin where skiers are greeted with an open fire and bowls of soup. In addition to the many cross-country centres, the Catamount Trail gives scope for long-distance skiing through the length of Vermont (for information: Catamount Trail Association, PO Box 1235, Burlington, VT 05401; tel: 802/864 5794).

In the White Mountains there are fine views of the Presidential Range from Bretton Woods and Great Glen—both good for beginners—as well as from the more challenging trails at Jackson, New Hampshire's main cross-country area.

In Maine, Sunday River and Sugarloaf both lie below the downhill resorts of the same name; Sugarloaf has especially fine views and some rewarding trails for beginners. Acadia National Park offers of coastal skiing on its carriage roads.

SNOWMOBILING
Dedicated snowmobile routes exist all over northern New England, with large networks in the White Mountains and in the Rangeley Lakes area of Maine (from where you can ride into Canada), as well as Vermont. Equipped with chains and skis, these exciting machines have impressive traction and are easy to drive; youngsters aged 12 to 18 must have instruction. Some snowmobiles are two-seaters.

229

Several resorts have dedicated snowboard parks but most ski slopes are also open to snowboarders

▶ Manchester 222A1

Pristine-looking old Manchester Village, with its white houses and marble sidewalks, has been a pleasure resort and spa since the 1850s. Nowadays the village merges into Manchester Center, often something of a traffic jam owing to the popularity of its outlet shopping and crafts and country stores.

On the southern fringes of the village is **Hildene**▶▶ (*Open* mid-May–Oct), a 24-room Georgian Revival mansion, the home of Robert Todd Lincoln, son of Abraham and Mary Lincoln. Mary discovered this elite mountain village retreat, and the Lincolns spent the summer here in 1863 to recuperate in the midst of the Civil War. Robert made Hildene his home, and his descendants lived here until 1975. Today, the house, with its family furnishings and memorabilia, offers interesting insight into the lives and times of the Lincolns. Highlights include landscaped grounds and a self-playing Aeolian organ. Also in Manchester is the **American Museum of Fly Fishing** (*Open* May–Oct), with the rods and reels of President Eisenhower, Bing Crosby, and other celebrities.

Manchester lies beneath the commanding peak of **Mount Equinox**▶▶ (3,835 feet). The highest point in the

230

COVERED BRIDGES
Spanning rivers and streams all over the region, wooden covered bridges, built from the 1830s onward, are now recognized as historic landmarks. Pretty structures, often painted in reds, greens, and blues, and by the nature of their setting almost inevitably highly picturesque, they are collected by photographers (particularly in the fall foliage season). Their *raison d'être* seems to be to protect the wooden bridge from the weather, particularly snow—though some say they prevented horses from taking fright. They are usually named after their builder or the river they cross.

Manchester, with its upscale stores, is popular as a base for fishing and other outdoor sports

Taconic Mountains, it is reached by the Skyline Drive toll road and has a mountaintop inn. On the way up the views unfold spectacularly; you pass Little Equinox Mountain and a Carthusian monastery built in 1960.

At Arlington, south of Manchester, the **Norman Rockwell Exhibition** comprises reproductions of the famous illustrator's work (see page 150). A 15-minute film show is included. Northwest on Route 30, **Dorset▶** is a showcase village in a conspicuously attractive setting and with a summer playhouse (tel: 802/867 5777).

▶ Middlebury and the Green Mountains   *222A3*

Middlebury is a small but bustling college town, picturesque and unfussy, dominated by the four-tiered, wedding-cake steeple of its Congregational Church. Crafts are popular, with the nonprofit Vermont State Craft Center based with other craft outlets in the old mill complex in Frog Hollow. On Park Street, the Sheldon Museum (displaying furniture and decorative arts) has been open since 1882.

Out of town on Route 23, past a rare two-way covered bridge, the **Morgan Horse Farm** (*Open* May–Oct) still breeds the famous Morgan horses and gives tours of its stables (see sidebar). Farther north is **Vergennes**, with over 100 craft and other shops in its Factory Marketplace. At Ferrisburgh is **Rokeby▶** (*Open* May–Oct, Thu–Sat), a fascinating 11-room Quaker family home that was once a focus of abolitionist activity and a stop on the Underground Railroad.

West of **Orwell** is a relic of the Revolutionary War: Mount Independence, a peninsula jutting into Lake Champlain that was fortified to defend against a British attack from Canada. The visitors' center fleshes out the historical background, and trails lead past blockhouses, a stockade, and the remains of batteries.

The **Green Mountain National Forest** describes an area of densely wooded, rounded hills covering much of western Vermont. Much of it is unspoiled and offers countless opportunities for walking. On Route 125, the 1-mile **Robert Frost Trail** begins close to the site of his summer cabin: Frost's verses are placed along the route, which crosses damp bogs and passes through scrub and woodland. **Silver Lake**, east of Leicester, has a 2½-mile shoreline interpretive nature trail, and there is a shorter circuit around the nearby **Falls of Llana** (both in Branbury State Park). More dramatic hikes include the hour-long walk to **Sunset Ledge** from Lincoln Gap, east of Lincoln. **Bristol Ledges** (1,825 feet) is the highlight of a 1-mile trail above the pleasant town of Bristol and provides views of the village and of Lake Champlain. More ambitious is the 3–4 hour walk on the Long Trail to *Mount Abraham* from Lincoln Gap, with its rocky 4,006-foot summit rising above the timberline.

Kingsland Bay, on Lake Champlain northwest of Vergennes, and **Lake Dunmore** in Branbury State Park are good for swimming.

231

Visitors to Morgan Horse Farm can see where these sturdy working horses are trained

Vermont

The golden dome of the State House, Montpelier, seen against the early autumn sky

MOUNTAIN GREENERY
As you ascend Mount Mansfield, notice the changes in vegetation as the climate gets harsher. The typical New England trees are found lower down (sugar maple, yellow birch, and beech). Further up the slope are pine, white birch, red spruce, and balsam fir, and finally tundra. At the summit is the largest community of arctic-alpine flora in Vermont.

"Vermont's Finest" is a Ben & Jerry's ice cream

▶ **Montpelier**   *222B3*

Vermont's state capital is scarcely more than a country town graced by the golden dome of the State House. A good local view of the town can be obtained by climbing from Elm Street to Winter Street and up into Hubbard Park, where a stone tower in the woods affords an all-round panorama. Life continues at an amiable pace in a town small enough to make a relaxing base. Alongside the alternative lifestyle of the Horn of the Moon Café, on Langdon Street, Montpelier has the New England Culinary Institute, a large insurance industry, and a high proportion of lawyers.

The **State House**▶ (*Open* weekdays. *Admission* free) has been restored to its original 1859 appearance internally and is the third building on its site. The first State House became too cramped, while its 1838 successor was the victim of an exploding stove. Brochures for self-guided tours are available. Next door, the **Vermont Museum** (*Open* Tue–Sun), run by the Vermont Historical Society, has well-displayed, changing exhibitions about various aspects of state life.

Ben & Jerry's Ice-Cream Factory▶▶ (see also page 234), near Waterbury on Route 100 north of I–89, has become Vermont's biggest visitor attraction. The free samples are the lure; although the tour omits the factory on Sundays, the samples are larger. The tours are very popular: you may have to wait hours, but there are kids' activities (face-painting and the like) and ice cream to be eaten. Cow souvenirs of the wackiest kind proliferate in the gift shop. There is also a Hall of Fame, featuring the ink-scrawled napkin used by former school friends Ben Cohen and Jerry Greenfield to plan their ice cream pickups on their marathon promotion journey ("Scoopathon") across the U.S.A., giving free samples of their super-premium ice cream as they went. It proved a hugely successful public relations venture. From humble beginnings in an abandoned filling station in Burlington in 1978 on an $8,000 investment, their ice cream business has soared.

Other Vermont specialties are produced at the Morse Farm maple sugar plant, outside Montpelier, and the Cold Hollow Cider Mill, on Route 100.

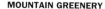

▶▶ Mount Mansfield and Stowe   *222B4*

Vermont's highest peak, Mount Mansfield (4,393 feet) rises amid some of the state's grandest scenery. At the Stowe Mountain Resort, on Route 108 some 6 miles north of Stowe, are the toll road and gondola up the mountain. The toll road winds up the slopes for 4½ miles (bicycles are not allowed) and is open from May to October. Farther north along Route 108, at Spruce Peak on the right, a chair lift gives access to the Alpine Slide, a summer sled ride. At **Smugglers Notch**, the road rises to 2,162 feet, with 1,000-foot cliffs on either side. During the War of 1812, when trade with Canada was forbidden, much cattle smuggling took place here.

Stowe, the main skiing and recreation center for the area, has a wide choice of high-class dining and lodging. Many of the hotels in the town have an Austrian appearance, including the Trapp Family Lodge, still owned by the Trapps of *The Sound of Music* fame, although the original structure has been replaced. The Stowe Recreation Path gains lovely riverside views, and leads to a covered bridge.

▶ Plymouth Notch   *222B2*

This tiny and remote hamlet was the birthplace and home of "Silent Cal," Calvin Coolidge (1872–1933), president of the United States between 1923 and 1929 (see page 42). Today, the hamlet is part museum, and one ticket covers all the sites. The modest homestead that was the **Coolidge Birthplace** is much as it was, with a quilt and a miniature chest of drawers he made himself; the **Coolidge Homestead** is the family's later home. The visitors' center tells of the president's life, while the (still-functioning) store displays a "Drink Moxie" sign—a memento of his favorite drink. Upstairs in the latter building, the **Coolidge Hall** served as the Summer White House: the nation's affairs were conducted with a staff of two from this humble place. The huge barn next to the visitors' center houses a collection of family carriages.

The village **cheese factory**, built in 1892, offers handmade cheddar-like products, including an extra-sharp cheese matured for two years. Cheesemaking takes place from Monday to Wednesday, when visitors are welcome to watch the process.

(see page 42)

MOUNT MANSFIELD
The remarkable resemblance the mountain has to an upward-facing head has meant that each protuberance is named accordingly on the map: the Forehead, the Adam's Apple, the Chin, and the Nose. Native folklore speaks of the mountain as a sleeping giant. The Chin, reached by a 1¼-mile trail, is the true summit.

Stowe: a classic landmark

SILENT CAL
A dinner party guest once jested, "Mr. President, I have made a bet with my friends that I can get more than two words out of you this evening." Coolidge replied "You lose."

233

Out of Vermont's rolling hills and lush valleys come a range of distinctive products. There are the famous traditional cheeses (including cheddar, colby, and Monterey jack); there are McIntosh apples and there is cider; there is honey, chocolates, and hams. And then there is maple syrup, and Ben & Jerry's.

LIQUID GOLD

Maple syrup is sold in a variety of grades: Fancy, or Grade A Light Amber (delicate flavor, light color); Grade A Medium Amber (the most popular); Grade A Dark Amber (stronger flavor, dark color); and Grade B (robust color and flavor, good for cooking). You can sample them all at the New England Maple Museum in Pittsford (see page 235) or the Maple Grove Maple Museum and Factory in St. Johnsbury (see page 236). During the maple-sugaring season (March and April), visitors are welcome at farms listed in the brochure *Maple Sugarhouses Open to Visitors*, available from Vermont Department of Agriculture, 116 State Street, Montpelier, VT 05620-2901 (tel: 802/828 2416).

234

Vermont farm produce includes maple syrup (below) and cider (right)

Vermont's finest All over Vermont there are black-and-white cows. A good many are the Holstein (Holstein-Friesian) cows grazing in the fields; others are Woody Jackson's Holy Cows. Woody Jackson is an artist, and his famous symbols of Vermont appear on anything from mugs and boxer shorts to the T-shirts produced for Ben & Jerry's.

Ben & Jerry's makes Vermont's Finest All Natural Ice Cream, in over 30 "euphoric flavors." But making great ice cream (and frozen yogurt) is only part of the Ben & Jerry's story that has so captured the public imagination. For Ben Cohen and Jerry Greenfield, serving the community is just as important as making a profit: 7.5 percent of pretax profits go to nonprofit organizations working for progressive social change, and half the proceeds of the Waterbury factory tours (see page 232) go to Vermont charities. So popular have Ben and Jerry found their ice cream to be, that they have now taken them abroad, notably to Britain.

Maple syrup See steam billowing up from the sugar houses that dot the Vermont landscape and you know spring has arrived. Ideally the temperature will be about 40°F in the daytime, but there will still be a light frost at night. Under these conditions, sap rises up the sugar maple tree (*Acer saccharum*), and the sugar farmer gets "a good run"—any warmer and the tree bursts into bud and the sap stops rising.

The farmer drills holes in the trunk, into which he fits spouts through which the sap drains, either into galvanized buckets or into long plastic pipes that feed directly into a holding tank in the sugar house. The buckets (up to three per tree) take several hours to fill, and about 40 gallons of sap will have to be boiled down to make one gallon of syrup.

▶ Proctor   *222A2*

Proctor and its larger neighbor, Rutland, are at the heart of Vermont's marble-producing district (see sidebar). **Rutland** has plenty of budget accommodations serving the huge **Killington** ski area (see pages 229 and 243). Massive blocks of rock are cut and dressed at the Vermont Marble Company, whose **Marble Exhibit** (*Open* daily May through October) displays the virtues of marble here in the form of a marble chapel (complete with Leonardo da Vinci's *Last Supper*, also in marble) and a series of bas-reliefs depicting every U.S. president.

Wilson Castle▶, south of Proctor, was built in 1874 by Dr. Robert Johnson for his wife Sarah, who had set her heart on living in a castle in the Green Mountains. Unfortunately, the marriage broke up just as the 32-room castle was being completed. It is still lived in and feels like it, with a welcome lack of roping off. Despite being an architectural hodgepodge with Dutch gables and French Renaissance-style mansards, and turrets, it is a good example of an opulent Victorian status symbol, with stained glass and painted ceilings. European and Far Eastern antiques adorn an interior dramatically bathed in golden light (*Open* daily late May– mid-Oct, 9–6).

North of Pittsford on Route 7, the **New England Maple Museum** is at the back of a huge gift shop selling syrup by the gallon, maple candy, and numerous other Vermont specialties. The exhibition shows the many maple sugar-making methods used through the ages, with murals, utensils, and the most complete collection of old sugar-making equipment known ; there is also a short film and free samples of the various grades of maple syrup.

235

One of dozens of Victorian stained-glass windows in Wilson Castle

A sculptor works in Vermont marble

ST. JOHNSBURY'S ATHENAEUM

This pristine Victorian-style art gallery is the oldest unaltered example of its kind in the U.S.A. It was presented to the townspeople by businessman Horace Fairbanks in 1873 to house *Domes of Yosemite*, a major work by Albert Bierstadt of the Hudson River School of artists, whose works form a major part of the collection. Critics despaired of "a profound loss to civilization," claiming that the painting would be "doomed to the obscurity of a Vermont town where it will astonish the natives." Nevertheless, its installation drew visitors from all over the world.

St. Johnsbury and the forests, hills, and valleys of the Northeast Kingdom that surround it

▶▶ St. Johnsbury and the Northeast Kingdom   *222C4*

The modestly sized town of **St. Johnsbury▶**, known locally as St. Jay, harbors a few surprises. One is its main street itself, a fetching Victorian survival, with its brick mansions and granite churches. Another is the room at the back of the town library housing the celebrated **Athenaeum▶▶** art museum (*Open* during library hours *Admission* free; see sidebar). Also on the main street, the **Fairbanks Museum and Planetarium** is yet another Victorian period piece; the museum houses natural history exhibits, tribal artifacts, and dolls in its old-fashioned barrel-vaulted hall. The tiny **Maple Grove Maple Museum and Factory** is a sweet-smelling, sticky place where you can watch the sugar-making process and see maple candies being packed—and find your shoes sticking to the floor.

St. Johnsbury is a good base for excursions into the three northeastern counties that comprise the remote-feeling **Northeast Kingdom▶▶**. North of the town, **Burke Mountain** (3,267 feet) is accessible by toll road and affords 120-mile panoramic views. **Lake Willoughby▶**, beside Route 5A, is popular for windsurfing, boating, and fishing, and swimming for those hardy enough. Hikers can take the 7-mile circular route up adjacent **Mount Pisgah** (2,751 feet). Adventurous naturalists might care to seek out **Victory Bog**, a huge wetland preserve harboring rare plants, as well as moose and black bears. The rural character of the area is exemplified by the **Bread and Puppet Museum▶**, south of Glover on Route 122 (see sidebar). There is also the farmers' **Co-operative Creamery** (closed Sun and Jan) at Cabot, which makes a renowned sharp cheddar cheese.

Craftsbury Common▶, conspicuously attractive and high up on a ridge road (part of a planned military route to Canada built in the 1780s), was painted white for the filming of Alfred Hitchcock's 1955 movie *The Trouble with Harry* and has stayed that way ever since. Route 14 north of here and the unclassified road southwest to Route 15 give a good idea of the quiet beauty of the Northeast Kingdom. Willey's General Store at nearby **Greensboro** is one of the best stocked in Vermont; its outside wall serves as the local bulletin board.

The SS Ticonderoga is preserved at the Shelburne Museum

BREAD AND PUPPET
Glover is the home of the Bread and Puppet Theater troupe, founded in New York in 1974. Its rickety looking barn, a free "museum," displays the giant Expressionist-style puppets, masks, and props used in previous shows and pageants. Sourdough bread is given to audiences, symbolizing that theater is as much a necessity as bread. Performances in the field across the road attract audiences of 20,000-strong. Some camp out the night before. The troupe regularly tours the U.S.A. and Europe.

At **Brownington**, an out-of-the-way hamlet in the far north where the paved road turns to a dirt one, is the **Old Stone House**, the former county grammar school built by Reverend Alexander Twilight, a black minister, in the 1830s. It now houses a local history museum (*Open* daily, Jul–Aug; mid-May–mid-Oct, Fri–Tue), run on a shoestring, with everything donated by locals. Across the road, a path to the right of the church leads to an excellent view.

"I did not want to create a village...I was anxious to create something in arrangement and conception that had not been tried."
—Electra Havemeyer Webb, founder of the Shelburne Museum.

►►► Shelburne   222A4

At Shelburne is the remarkable **Shelburne Museum►►►** (*Open* late May–mid-Oct; limited winter schedule), an astonishing collection of buildings, reassembled and packed with Americana and American folk art, which was the creation of Mrs. Electra Havemeyer Webb. Her love of everyday objects started as a hobby, the collection being housed in a public museum when the first building, a schoolhouse, was moved here in 1947. Other structures then followed, including a general store, jail, inn, and covered bridge. The wide-ranging collection of objects—over 80,000 items in nearly 40 buildings—means there is something for most tastes. Allow a full day to see it properly (tickets are valid for two consecutive days). Do not miss the comprehensive quilt collection, the 1890 private rail car, the *Ticonderoga* (America's last surviving vertical beam sidewheel steamboat, once in service on Lake Champlain), and the Electra Havemeyer Webb Building (a stylish New York apartment adorned with Impressionist paintings).

To the north, **Shelburne Farms►** was an agricultural experiment set up with Vanderbilt money (see sidebar). Today, it plays a semi-educational role in demonstrating stewardship and farm animals, with a family-oriented, hands-on activity area, cheese-making, a farm trail, 90-minute tours, and farm animals.

Also of interest are the **Vermont Teddy Bear Co.** on Route 7, and **Vermont Wildflower Farm**, in Charlotte.

A FARM OF THE FUTURE
Shelburne Farms was founded in the late 19th century by Dr. William Seward Webb and Lila Vanderbilt Webb as a grand agricultural experiment. Dr. Webb purchased 32 farms and hired the services of landscape architect Frederick Law Olmsted, designer of Central Park in New York City, and forester Gifford Pinchot, known in the U.S. today as the father of forestry. Architect Robert H. Robertson designed the three main buildings on the property. The Shelburne House, once the Webb's family residence, is now a comfortable inn and restaurant (*Open* mid-May–mid-Oct).

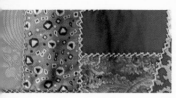

Quilts and rugs, weather vanes and whirligigs, trade signs and decoy ducks, baskets, boxes, and wooden toys—New England's myriad antiques shops, its dozens of crafts shops, and many of its museums are stuffed with examples, old and new, of these folk crafts.

STENCILING

Kitchen utensils, containers, walls, and pieces of furniture were commonly painted and decorated with motifs. Some of these patterns were applied with stencils, and itinerant stencilers would work from pattern books, using milk-based paints in dusky shades.

238

DO-IT-YOURSELF

Visitors interested in patchwork and quilting will enjoy a browse in the many shops that sell everything needed. Keepsake Quilting (Senter's Marketplace, Center Harbor, New Hampshire; catalogue available) claims to be America's largest quilt shop, with thousands of small prints as well as plains. Paints for stenciling can be found in crafts supply shops but are also readily available in many hardware stores.

Right: a spinner practices an ancient craft
Top: crazy quilting

SPRUCE GUM BOXES

Lumbermen whiling away the evenings in the logging camps of Maine, New Hampshire, and Vermont used to carve little wooden boxes for a wife or sweetheart to hold a gift of spruce gum. These were often in the shape of books and fitted with a slide at one end, and typically carved with hearts and a cross.

Quilts and coverlets Winters have always been hard in New England, and the early colonists certainly needed the quilted bed coverings that had long been traditional in Europe. Fabric was in short supply, so the tradition of piecing scraps of leftover fabric together was an economic necessity. Some patchwork designs crossed the Atlantic with the early settlers: "Log Wood," used in the north of England, for instance, became known as "Log Cabin," and some Pennsylvania quilts, made by settlers from Germany, used designs known in Europe since the Renaissance. Other patterns, such as "Bear's Paw," were clearly inspired by new experiences. As material

became more available, small pieces were appliquéd onto larger areas, often representing the farmhouse, its occupants, and animals, so that the quilt was a personal journal of its creator's life. Old quilts are collectors' items, while modern ones are sold widely across New England.

The colonial coverlet, woven in cotton in overshot patterns, traditionally in blue and cream, is another craft that dates back hundreds of years. Popular as throws, modern versions of these cotton blankets in various, usually pastel colors may be found in numerous crafts outlets.

Baskets and boxes Market baskets, half-bushel and bushel baskets, fish baskets, berry baskets, clothes baskets, sewing baskets, feather baskets (in which to collect feathers until you had enough to stuff a pillow)—in the days before containers were made of mass-produced material, the Native Americans made baskets in dozens of shapes and sizes, traditionally using the brown ash (*Fraxinus nigra*). The Native Americans are still noted for their basketry, though now it is made for the tourist trade. Glass beads may have been replaced by plastic, and colored strips are no longer dyed with berries, but basketry is an unbroken tradition, passed from generation to generation. The Shakers, who made a unique contribution to

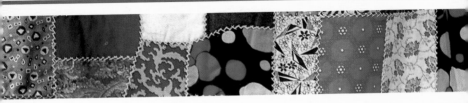

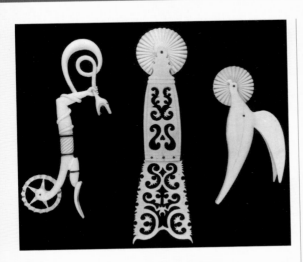

American crafts, were famed for their baskets as well as for their oval boxes and furniture (see pages 148–149).

Carving Native Americans introduced the early colonials to the use of duck decoys in hunting. Made at first of skin and feathers, they were later made from wood, carved and painted more and more realistically until the decoy became a traditional art form. The Shelburne Museum in Vermont has the largest decoy collection in the world.

New England's was a seafaring and a farming community, dependent on the weather, and many buildings would have a weather vane on the roof, cut from metal or carved in wood in a variety of shapes. Along the coast, fish, mermaids, or ships were popular designs, while a farm building would often be topped by a cow or sheep. A variant, the "whirligig," had paddles that kept it turning in a wind; the noise it made, they say, kept the moles at bay. So sought after are these traditional pieces of folk art now that thieves have been known to go to the extent of dropping a line from a helicopter to grab an antique off a roof. Reproductions are popular, decorative items.

Boat-builders turned their skills to woodcarving, too, and some made magnificent figureheads for the ships they built. Woodcarvers produced signs to hang outside shops, painted to advertise their specialty. They also made little models of subjects dear to them: a maple-sugaring scene, a team of working horses, or farmers chain-sawing.

Scrimshaw jagging wheels or pie-crimpers

SCRIMSHAW
Dating from the whaling boom of the early 19th century is the type of carving called scrimshaw. Using a sail needle or jackknife, sailors out at sea carved exquisitely detailed designs on whalebone or teeth, which they then etched in black. There are many examples of scrimshaw in maritime museums and the old captains' houses.

CIGAR STORE FIGURES
The Shelburne Museum in Vermont (see page 237) has a room full of these carved figures. Up to 6 feet high, they normally depicted Native Americans, wearing or carrying the tobacco leaves that they introduced to the colonials.

Weather vanes are now more decorative than functional

Southern Vermont is prime territory for crafts, from the fancifully ornate to such simple items as these turned dishes at the Weston Bowl Mill

Drive

Southern Vermont

See map on page 222 (yellow route).

This is a tour of southern Vermont's choicest rural retreats. Allow a very full day to sample the crafts shops and village atmosphere, and maybe to take in a walk in Townshend State Park.

Start from **Manchester▶** (page 230). A few miles east, Bromley Ski Area stays open all year round and operates an alpine slide and a chair lift up to a 360-degree lookout, with views stretching over five states. There are a number of hiking trails from the summit.

Then stop off at **Weston▶**, home to the Vermont Country Store, to browse in its quintessentially Vermont-style crafts shops, of the homespun rather than the designer variety. Clustered around the green and village bandstand are the old sawmill, now housing a tinsmith's workshop and a display of antique tools, and the Weston Playhouse, Vermont's oldest professional summer theater (tel: 802/824 5288). Just to the north, in an appealingly ramshackle old sawmill that began life in 1902, the Weston Bowl Mill carries inexpensive wooden products, while southward the Toy Works stocks wooden toys, marionettes, and more. The Farrar-Mansur House (*Open* Memorial Day–Columbus Day) is a former colonial tavern.

Chester▶ is quiet and prosperous looking, with some classic old-fashioned shops, including a drug-store with an enamel sign and the famously offbeat Inn at Long Last along its main street. The National Survey Charthouse ("Clear, correct, complete" boasts its motto) has a stock of world maps and excellent local hiking maps, as well as art supplies. A rare group of stone houses are found a mile out of Chester by turning off the main street by the Jiffy Mart. Rising from a bridge, immaculate

Covered bridge at Brattleboro

Grafton▶ ▶, a former wool-making and soapstone quarrying village, was rescued from part dereliction and is now one of Vermont's best-looking villages. It makes a point of having plenty of nothing to do, though there are a historical society and natural history museums. Craftswatchers can observe a smithy at work and see cheddar cheese being made at the Grafton Village Cheese Company. A covered bridge can be seen in Townshend Road. On Route 35 to Townshend, the road

town, is more of a cultural than a rural center. The Museum and Art Center in Union Railroad Station opens May to October. Connecticut River Tours offers cruises on the *Belle of Brattleboro* (Wed–Sun in summer and at foliage time; tel: 802/254 4565).

Maple syrup stalls accompany Route 9 west. **Marlboro College**, a liberal arts establishment that is one of America's smallest colleges, with just 260 students, hosts a major summer chamber music festival, founded in 1951 by the legendary Rudolf Serkin,

The Old Tavern Inn, in the pristine village of Grafton

is briefly unpaved. Continue 2 miles west of Townshend on Route 30, past the **Scott Covered Bridge**▶ on the left, then turn left across the dam to **Townshend State Park**▶ (fee payable). Here you can walk 1,100 feet up Bald Mountain, which rises above the treeline and affords fine views of Mount Monadnock and West River Valley. The 1.8-mile trail has both steep and gentler routes. Nearby, Townshend Dam (free entry) offers swimming and canoeing from a man-made sand beach.

Newfane offers a touch of grandeur around its green, with its county court-house, Congregational Church, and old inns. **Brattleboro**, a red-brick administrative and manufacturing

which attracts big names. Its Tyler Gallery is a showcase of regional artistic talent (*Open* Mon–Fri during the school year; free).

Westward, the road climbs to **Hogback Mountain**▶, giving an extensive view south, with the prominently pointed Haystack Mountain (3,420 feet) visible to the northwest. Close by, the slopes of Mount Olga offer pleasant walks in Molly Stark State Park. **Wilmington** is a small resort town on the main road, but there are quieter accommodations nearby in the Mount Snow resort area to the north. Continue west to **Bennington**▶ ▶ (see page 226) before turning north to explore **Arlington** and enjoy the spectacular scenic drive up **Mount Equinox**▶ ▶ (see page 230) on the way back to Manchester.

FOR BUDDING SCIENTISTS
The Montshire Museum of Science at Norwich (north of Windsor) is a leading children's attraction in central Vermont. Sited on the Connecticut River, it has nature trails outside, plus an aquarium and a snake show, plus a bubble room and tunnels to explore. Emphasis is firmly towards hands-on activities. It is open daily, 10–5.

A fisherman faces the challenges of the Quechee Gorge

ALONG THE RIVER
The Connecticut River flows 250 miles along the Vermont–New Hampshire border. The river was the waterway along which numerous early settlers came to these parts.
North Star Canoe Rentals (tel. 603/542 5802) offer canoeing to the covered bridge and to the Sumner Falls from Cornish, NH, as well as winter sleigh rides.

► Windsor 222B2

Windsor has the longest covered bridge in New England, spanning 460 feet over the Connecticut River and the border with New Hampshire. On Main Street are the Vermont State Craft Center and the former Elijah West tavern, known as the **Old Constitution House** (*Open May–Oct, Wed–Sun*). Vermont's constitution was signed here in 1777, and a historical display relating to this accompanies period furnishings, toys, and artifacts. From June through September and at fall foliage time a train runs from Bellows Falls to the Chester area for watching the foliage. On South Main Street, the American Precision Museum, housed in an 1846 armory and machine shop, is a tribute to historic technical innovations.

North of Windsor, **White River Junction**, once a busy railroad junction with 50 passenger trains daily and an eight-track crossing, has tours of Catamount Brewery. Southwest of Windsor, **Mount Ascutney►** (3,144 feet) can be ascended by following hiking trails from Routes 44, 44A, and 131, or by taking the 3.8-mile toll road. Its summit, a 1/2-mile walk from the parking lot, looks over the Green and White Mountains, as well as Mount Monadnock and Lake Sunapee in New Hampshire.

You get a good idea of the rural feel of Windsor County by taking Route 106 through Felchville, with its miniature-looking buildings, then along the flat valley bottom, past cornfields and maple syrup outlets. Stoughton Pond

lies just off the main road and has swimming, a picnic site, and a nature trail in very pretty surroundings. Perkinsville is grander but quite unspoiled, with white chainlink fencing around its green.

►► Woodstock 222B2

A self-consciously pretty village at the heart of Vermont, with its own covered bridge and numerous handsome Federal-style homes, Woodstock has captured the public imagination as epitomizing that elusive quality called "Vermontness." However, the crowds of visitors and the concentration of boutiques, galleries, and designer shops have also given it the veneer of a sophisticated all-year resort. Money was poured into Woodstock and the overhead wires buried by the Rockefellers, who had family ties with the Billings Farm and Woodstock Inn. The **Dana House Museum** in Elm Street offers a glimpse inside one of Woodstock's many well-preserved Federal-style architectural gems.

To get to the **Billings Farm and Museum▶** (*Open May 1–Oct 31*), follow Elm Street out of the village and turn right past the bridge on River Road. This premier local attraction provides a rare chance to look around a working farm, with butter-making, crafts, and milking demonstrations. Established in 1871, the farm has had an outstanding Jersey herd since the 1880s, and in the pristine milking parlor each cow's name, birthday, pedigree, and honors are recorded above its stall. The museum offers preserved artifacts and a film, while a renovated 1890s farmhouse gives a glimpse of a well-to-do farming household. The **Vermont Raptor Center**, 1½ miles from town on Church Hill Road, displays around 26 species of owls, hawks, and eagles that, owing to their injuries, cannot survive in the wild.

Route 4 east of Woodstock crosses the **Quechee Gorge▶ ▶**, dubbed the "Little Grand Canyon" of the Ottauquechee River. The 165-foot chasm can be looked into from the road bridge itself or from the half-mile trail to the bottom. An old riverside mill in the former textile village of **Quechee** is home to Simon Pearce Glass, where you can watch glassblowers and potters at work. The Theron Boyd House, very much a survival of the pre-electric era, is open to the public and worth a visit as it is the state's oldest unaltered dwelling.

West of Woodstock lies **Bridgewater**, offering tours of the Mountain Brewery, makers of Long Trail Ale, and **Killington**, the largest ski area in Vermont. Summer attractions at the latter include tennis, golf, a playhouse (tel: 802/422 9795), and a music festival. Easily accessible by chair lift, 4,241-foot Killington Peak has a nature trail, enabling study of its mountain plants, and views extending to the Adirondacks and White Mountains.

Woodstock offers chic shopping (below) and a look at 19th-century agriculture (above)

243

EUREKA: A SCHOOL
At Springfield, Eureka Schoolhouse stands next to an 1870 covered bridge and is Vermont's oldest one-room schoolhouse. Completed in 1790, it was abandoned in 1900 and underwent wholesale restoration in 1968. It is now open to public view (*Open* Memorial Day–Columbus Day).

CHILDREN'S MUSEUMS
● Connecticut Manchester, Mystic Seaport, New Haven, and Niantic.
● Rhode Island Pawtucket.
● Maine Portland
● New Hampshire Portsmouth Londonderry, Keene; Science Center at Manchester.
● Massachusetts Boston; Dennis and Falmouth on Cape Cod; Acton, Dartmouth, Easton, Foxboro, and Holyoke.

AMUSEMENT PARKS
● Connecticut Quassy Amusement Park, by Lake Quassapaug, Middlebury.
● Maine Funtown, Saco, biggest children's park in southern Maine; Aquaboggan Water Park, Saco.
● Massachusetts Riverside Park, Agawam, near Springfield, largest amusement park in New England; Water Slide and Family Fun Center, Westport, near Fall River; on Cape Cod, Cartland, Wareham (buddy and indy-style carts, bumper boats); Water Wizz (wet and wild thrills and spills), Wareham.
● New Hampshire Plenty around Weirs Beach, Lake Winnipesaukee (see sidebar, page 197), and at Hampton Beach on the coast. In the White Mountains, Santa's Village, Six Gun City, Whale's Tail water slide, Attitash Alpine Slide, StoryLand.

One way of getting supper: an improvised fishing expedition

New England for children

The Great Outdoors In summer, take a whale-watching cruise or lobster-trapping outing (see pages 164 and 116); join a moose search or a sunrise beaver-spotting canoe trip (see pages 200–201); go for a swim, a sail on a lake, or take a picnic on a walk in a forest park. There are rental facilities on many rivers for canoeing and rafting.

In the mountains and forests of the northern states there is excellent mountain biking (ski lifts carry the bikes to the mountaintop), and there are miles of bicycle trails on Cape Cod National Seashore (see page 13). At many ski resorts you can take a cable car to the top of the mountain for a spectacular view (especially in the autumn). In some places (such as Bromley Mountain in Vermont and Attitash Bear Peak in New Hampshire) you can take a chair lift up and a slide down. In the winter, there is the whole gamut of snow sports (see pages 228–9), and as for spectator sports, there are hockey and basketball games galore to watch.

Museums and Attractions "Hands-on" is the buzz word. Children's museums can be found throughout the region (see sidebar) and many others have special rooms, exhibits, or events for children. Listed below are just some of the dozens of attractions featured in official state guides. Aquariums and a selection of amusement parks are listed separately in the sidebars.

CONNECTICUT
Mystic Seaport and **Norwalk Maritime Aquarium** are popular with older children who like ships, history, and the sea. The Denison Pequotsepos Nature Center near Mystic has non-releasable birds of prey and seven miles of trails. In the Connecticut River Valley, the **Steam Train and Riverboat** combines a train ride with a riverboat cruise. The **Science Center of Connecticut**, West Hartford, has hands-on exhibits and a planetarium. You can see inside a lighthouse by visiting the **Old Lighthouse Museum** in

Stonington, handle a live python in the discovery room of the **Peabody Museum**, New Haven—where you can also visit the Connecticut Children's Museum—and dissect a model human body at the **Children's Museum of South Eastern Connecticut** in Niantic (see page 107).

MAINE

The four-level **Children's Museum** in Portland is one of the best of its kind in New England—meet Mr. Bones, the bicycling skeleton, and read the news on television. The **Maritime Museum** at Bath has a variety of interesting exhibitions in its restored shipyard buildings. The **Seashore Trolley Museum** at Kennebunkport has the world's largest street and railway car collection, while at **Boothbay Railway Village** (see page 121) you can take a train ride through gnome-inhabited woods. **York's Wild Kingdom**, on Route 1, is a zoo and amusement park. Try to visit a lighthouse.

MASSACHUSETTS

In and around Boston The city is so visually exciting that most children will get a thrill out of just being there: take them up one of the skyscrapers (**Prudential Skywalk** or **John Hancock Observatory**), enjoy the free entertainment of Faneuil Hall Marketplace, ride the swan boats in the **Public Garden**, take in **Harvard Square**, visit the **Mapparium** and USS *Constitution* in **Charlestown Navy Yard**. Older children will find **Filene's Basement** fun for bargain shopping. The comprehensive **Computer Museum** has superb hands-on displays, while the **Children's Museum**, the **New England Aquarium**, and the **Museum of Science** are all big crowd pleasers. Sports fans can take tours of Fenway Park and the FleetCenter (see pages 68 and 81). On a hot summer's day, take a boat trip from Long Wharf to Georges, the largest of the Boston Harbor Islands, for a picnic. Water taxis go from there to the other islands, where you can explore old forts.

At **Salem** on the North Shore (see page 184) you can go into a jail cell, attend a mock trial, and do some gravestone rubbing at the **Salem Wax Museum**. At Plymouth (see pages 177–79), **Plimoth Plantation** and the *Mayflower II* make an expensive but unforgettable outing. The New **Bedford Whaling Museum** is one of the best.

THE SPRINGFIELD AREA AND THE PIONEER VALLEY

History really comes alive at **Old Sturbridge Village**, a re-creation of life in the 1830s (see pages 173). Young dinosaur experts will insist on seeing the quarry of dinosaur tracks at **Dinosaur Land** in South Hadley and on meeting *Tyrannosaurus Rex* in the **Springfield Science Museum**. See page 175 for the **Words and Pictures Museum** in Northampton, in the Pioneer Valley, and see the sidebar for the **Basketball Hall of Fame**.

History comes alive at Old Sturbridge Village

FOR THE SPORTS ENTHUSIAST

Young basketball fans will want to try their skill at the Basketball Hall of Fame in Springfield, Massachusetts; tennis players should visit the Tennis Hall of Fame in Newport (see page 216); the action-packed New England Sports Museum in Lowell and Boston gives a hands-on taste of everything sporty (see page 75).

AQUARIUMS

● New England Aquarium, Boston.
● Marinelife Aquarium, Mystic, CT.
● Maine Aquarium, Saco, ME.
● Aqua Circus Aquarium and Zoo, West Yarmouth, Cape Cod, MA.
● Maritime Museum, Norwalk, CT.

Boston Common's very famous ducklings

VACATION READING
Small children will love
Robert McCloskey's
1940s classic *Make Way
for Ducklings* (available in
several languages), the
endearing story of a
mother duck looking for a
home for her family by
Boston's Charles River.
Bring the book to life by
taking a guided walk from
Boston Common along the
route described in the
book, with readings and
stops to feed the
ducklings' descendants.
Children leapfrog the
bronze duck sculptures in
the Public Garden.

CAPE COD AND THE ISLANDS Here are miles of sandy white beaches for windsurfing, swimming, and sailing. At Brewster is the excellent **Cape Cod Natural History Museum** (see page 155), while the Wellfleet Bay Sanctuary has programs for the under-sixes and canoe trips for the over 12s (who must be accompanied by an adult).

NEW HAMPSHIRE

At the **Ruggles Mine**, near Grafton, you can tap away with a hammer and explore the old mine. **Christa McAuliffe Planetarium**, Concord, is one of the world's most advanced, while **New Hampshire International Speedway**, near Canterbury, is the biggest venue of its kind in New England. **Clark's Trading Post** is a museum, railroad, and bear show. StoryLand at Glen is a theme park for younger children. Not to be missed is the cog railway up **Mount Washington** (see page 205). In Portsmouth, on the coast, children can join in workshops in some of the **Strawbery Banke** buildings (see page 202).

RHODE ISLAND

Roger Williams Park in Providence hosts a zoo, natural history museum, and planetarium, and there's boating in the park. Older children will learn about the factory age at the **Slater Mill Historic Site**, birthplace of the American Industrial Revolution (see pages 36–7), at Pawtucket, while younger ones will enjoy a trip on the canal. Many of the **Newport Mansions** will impress young and old alike. For Newport's **Tennis Hall of Fame** in the Casino, see sidebar on page 216.

VERMONT

Fun is the word, too, at **Ben & Jerry's ice-cream factory** (see pages 232 and 234). Take in a visit to a maple syrup museum and sample the candy at **New England Maple Museum**, Pittsford, or **Maple Grove Maple Factory**, St. Johnsbury. The **Shelburne Museum** (see page 237) is one for all ages. Birds of prey are sheltered at the **Vermont Raptor Center**, near Woodstock, while at Norwich the Montshire Museum of Science, is an excellent hand-on museum (see panel, page 242).

A Ben & Jerry's could well be the highlight of the day

Travel Facts

Arriving

Airports
Boston's Logan Airport is the inter-national terminal for New England, and terminals C and E have the usual assortment of car rental desks and tourist information facilities (*Open* 8 AM–9:30 PM, Monday to Friday; 11 AM–9:30 PM weekends) as well as a hotel reservation desk covering the whole of New England (no commis-sion charged to customers; open daily, 8:30 AM–11:30 PM).

A number of smaller airports are handy for destinations in other parts of New England. **Bradley International Airport**, in Windsor Locks, Connecticut, north of Hartford, is con-venient to southern Massachusetts and all of Connecticut. **Theodore Francis Green State Airport**, just outside Providence, Rhode Island, is another major airport. Additional New England airports served by major carriers include those in Manchester, New Hampshire; Portland and Bangor, Maine; Burlington, Vermont; and Worcester, Massachusetts. Among U.S. airlines serving the region are: **American** (tel: 800/433 7300), **Continental** (tel: 800/525 0280), **Delta** (tel: 800/221 1212), **Northwest** (tel: 800/225 2525), **TWA** (tel: 800/221 2000), **United** (tel: 800/241 6522), and **US Airways** (tel: 800/428 4322).

Getting into Boston
Excellent public transportation gets you into downtown Boston. From Logan Airport's terminal building, leave the main exit and cross to the courtesy bus stop, where buses marked with a circled T provide a free shuttle service to the Airport sub-way station, on the Blue Line (see pages 52–53). From here it is a few

stops to the downtown area. Alternatively, the Airport Water Shuttle carries passengers to Rowes Wharf in the Financial District (last service 8 PM; no service Saturdays or Sunday morning). A courtesy bus (with frequent service) picks passen-gers up at stops outside the terminal building. The Water Shuttle takes only a few minutes to cross Boston Harbor and provides good views of the Tea Party Ship, the Bunker Hill Monument, and most of the city's tallest buildings.

On weekdays, a nonstop Logan Express shuttle van (tel: 800-23 LOGAN) operates from the airport to South Station in the Financial District. Taxis are available at all terminals; in

1998 fares to downtown Boston and Cambridge averaged about $10–18 compared to 85¢ on the subway, $10 on the water shuttle, and there are buses to South Station (tickets $6).

If you are renting a car at the airport, remember to carry some cash—you will need to pay a toll at the Sumner Tunnel in order to reach Boston.

What to bring
The principal rule on weather in New England is that there are no rules. A cold, foggy morning can and often does become a bright, 60-degree after-noon. A summer breeze can suddenly turn chilly, and rain often appears with little warning. Thus, the best advice on how to dress is to layer your clothing so that you can peel off

The Connecticut Valley Railroad is one of only two steam railways in New England

socks, and waterproof shoes or boots.

Casual sportswear—walking shoes and jeans—will take you almost everywhere, but swimsuits and bare feet will not: shirts and shoes are required attire at even the most casual venues. In Boston, the most cosmopolitan New England city, you may want to dress up. Jacket and tie are required in better Boston restaurants, at a number of inns in the Berkshires, and in the occasional more formal dining room elsewhere.

In summer, bring a hat and sunscreen. Also pack insect repellent—and use it! Recent out-breaks of Lyme disease all over the East Coast make it imperative (even in urban areas) that you protect yourself from ticks in early spring through the summer.

Pack an extra pair of eyeglasses or contact lenses in your carry-on luggage. If you have a health problem that requires a prescription drug, pack enough to last the duration of the trip. Pharmacies, especially in rural areas, may be closed on Sunday. Don't pack prescription drugs in luggage that you plan to checkin, in case your bags go astray. Pack a list of the offices that supply refunds for lost or stolen traveler's checks.

249

or add garments as needed for comfort. Showers are frequent, so pack a raincoat and umbrella. Even in summer, you should pack long pants, a sweater or two, and a waterproof windbreaker, for evenings are often chilly and the sea spray can make things cool on a whale-watch or deep-sea fishing trip. If you'll be walking in the woods, bring heavy boots and expect to find mud. Winter requires heavy clothing, gloves, a hat, warm

A ride around Faneuil Hall Marketplace provides an easy introduction to Boston

Essentials

Climate and seasonal considerations

New England's climate is characterized by warm summers, pleasant if somewhat unreliable spring and autumn seasons, and extremely cold winters.

Spring can bring glorious weather, with warm days and cool nights; there are fewer tourists than in summer and autumn, so room rates are lower. Maple sugaring takes place in northern New England. Inland, April is "mud season," while blackflies (whose bites are not so much painful as annoying) proliferate in late May and early June in parts of the north.

Memorial Day is the start of the migration to the beaches and the mountains, and summer begins in earnest on July 4. Those who are driving to Cape Cod in July or August should know that Friday and Sunday are the days weekenders clog the overburdened Route 6.

More museums and houses open their doors in summer than any other time of year. July and August see the coastal and lake resorts crowded and the roads clogged with traffic. The events calendar is packed with festivals.

Fall foliage attracts visitors from all over the world, making autumn the busiest season; hotel rates are high and the famous foliage areas, such as the Berkshires, White Mountains, and Green Mountains, become very busy.

Winter invariably brings snow to many parts of New England

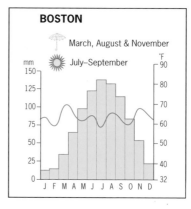

BOSTON

March, August & November
July–September

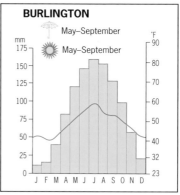

BURLINGTON

May–September
May–September

The first scarlet and gold colors emerge in mid-September in northern areas; "peak" color occurs at different times from year to year. Generally, it is best to visit the northern reaches in early October and then move southward as the month progresses.

Conversely, the coast sees fewer

crowds after Labor Day. The days are mild, the nights cool. There are also plenty of events, such as country fairs and crafts markets, at this time, and roadside produce stalls are a common sight.

A marked lull occurs after the leaves fall in late October, but much happens at Christmas and First Night (see page

> ❏ "There is a sumptuous variety about the New England weather that compels the stranger's imag- ination—and regret...in the spring I have counted one hundred and thirty-six different kinds of weather inside four-and-twenty hours."
> – Mark Twain, speech given in New York City, December 22, 1876. ❏

194). Winter brings enough snow to many areas to make New England a major winter sports destination (see pages 228–9), and when natural snow is lacking, the region has the greatest snowmaking capacity in the U.S. TV and radio weather forecasts and ski reports in New England keep people informed about seasonal matters.

An Automatic Teller Machine (ATM)

Money matters

Cash machines Many automated teller machines (ATMs) are tied to international networks such as Cirrus and Plus. You can use your bank card at ATMs to withdraw money from an account and get cash advances on a credit-card account if your card has been programmed with a personal identification number (PIN). Check in advance on limits on withdrawals and cash advances within specified periods. On cash advances, you are charged interest from the day you receive the money from ATMs as well as from tellers. Transaction fees from ATM withdrawals away from your home turf may be higher than for withdrawals at home. For specific Cirrus locations in the United States and Canada, call 800/424 7787. For U.S. Plus locations, call 800/843 7587 and press the area code and first three digits of the number you're calling from (or of the calling area where you want an ATM).

Wiring money You don't have to be a cardholder in order to send or receive a MoneyGram from American Express for any sum up to $10,000. To send a MoneyGram, go to a MoneyGram agent in a retail or convenience store or American Express travel office and pay up to $1,000 with a credit card and anything over that in cash. You are allowed a free long-distance call in the U.S. to give the transaction code to your recipient, who need only present identification and the refer- ence number to the nearest MoneyGram agent to pick up the cash. MoneyGram agents are in more than 70 countries (call 800/926 9400 for locations). Fees range from 3 percent to 10 percent, depending on the total and how you pay. You can also use **Western Union**. To wire money, take either cash or a cashier's check to the nearest office or call and use MasterCard or Visa. Money sent from the United States or Canada will be available for pickup at agent locations in 78 countries within minutes. Once the money is in the system, it can be picked up at *any* one of 22,000 locations (call 800/325 6000 for the one nearest you).

Sales tax Except in New Hampshire, sales tax is added to certain items, including meals and lodging. Connecticut sales tax is 6 percent; Rhode Island, 7 percent; Massachusetts, 5 percent (except clothing purchases under $150, which are not taxed); Vermont, 5 percent; and Maine, 6 percent.

Opening times

Many museums close on Monday and on public holidays (particularly Christmas, New Year's Day, and Thanksgiving). Smaller museums and many houses open between Memorial Day and Labor Day or mid-October. Attractions often open 10 AM–5 PM (or 4PM if guided tours are given); few places open before noon on Sunday.

Information on hours is given for guidance only. We have tried to ensure accuracy, but things do change. Check locally before your visit.

Public holidays

Roads and attractions are often busy, and accommodations get booked up during New England's holiday weekends. The busiest holidays are New Year's, Memorial Day, July 4,

Labor Day, Thanksgiving, and Christmas. In addition, there are a number of holidays (listed below) that are celebrated in just some of the New England states. Stores usually remain open on these days, but some attractions and services (particularly those that are maintained by the state) are closed.

January 15: Martin Luther King Jr. Day.
February 12: Lincoln's Birthday (Vermont only).
Monday nearest April 19: Patriot's Day (Massachusetts only).
Last Monday in April: Fast Day (New Hampshire only).
First Tuesday after the first Monday in November: Election Day (New Hampshire, Rhode Island, and Vermont only).

Tours and packages

Fully escorted tours and independent packages take the hassle out of planning and provide a better idea of how much a vacation will cost. Year-round, escorted tours are usually sold in three categories: deluxe, first-class, and tourist or budget class. The most important differences are the price

The Fourth of July is celebrated with fireworks, pageants, and parades

and the level of accommodations. Top operators in the deluxe category include Maupintour (Box 807, Lawrence, KS 66044, tel: 800/255 4266)

Tauck Tours (11 Wilton Rd., Westport, CT 06881, tel: 800/ 468 2825). In the first-class category are: **Brush Hill/Gray Line** (39 Dalton Ave., Boston, MA 02199, tel: 617/ 236 2148); **Caravan** (401 N. Michigan Ave., **Chicago**, IL 60611, tel:401/728 3805, 800/832 3656 or groups 800/852 5655);

Collette Travel Service Tours (162 Middle St., Pawtucket, RI 02860, tel: 312/321 9800 or 800/227 2826); **Globus** (5301 S. Federal C., Littleton, CO 80123, tel: 303/797 2800 or 800/221 0090);

New England/Mt. Snow Vacation Tours (Box 560, West Dover, VT 05356, tel: 800/742 7669);

Parker Tours (255 Executive Drive, Plainview, NY 11803, tel: 516/349 0575 or 800/833 9600);

Trieloff Tours (15550A Rockfield Bvd, Irvine, CA 92618, tel: 800/248 6877 or, in CA, 800/432 7125).

Most itineraries are jam-packed. To judge just how fast-paced the tour is, review the itinerary carefully.

Independent packages are offered by tour operators who may also do escorted programs and by any number of other companies—from large, established firms to small, new entrepreneurs. Airline operators include:

American Airlines Fly Away Vacations (tel: 800/321 2121),

Continental Airline's Grand Destinations (tel: 800/634 5555),

TWA Getaway Vacations (tel: 800/438 2929), and

United Airline's Vacation Planning Center (tel: 800/328 6877).

Also look into Americantours International East (347 5th Ave., 3rd floor, New York, NY 10016, tel: 212/683 5337 or 800/340 7284).

Wherever you are staying in the summer months, there's usually a festival nearby: (above) jazz in Burlington, and (below) the Maple Festival in St. Albans, VT

Getting around

Because the six New England states form a relatively compact region with an effective network of interstate highways and other good roads linking the many cities, towns, and recreational and shopping areas which attract visitors, a car is the most convenient means of travel. Yet driving is not without its frustrations; traffic can be heavy on coastal routes and beach-access highways on weekends and in midsummer, and Newport in summer and Boston all year long are inhospitable to automobiles. Each of the states makes available, free on request, an official state map that has directories, mileage, and other useful information in addition to routings. The speed limit in much of New England is 65 miles per hour (55 in more populated areas).

Roads

Apart from the heavily congested roads of downtown Boston, driving in New England is a pleasurable experience.

Country roads are obviously more interesting for touring, but can be slow going, with speed limits down to 25 m.p.h. at some curves (look for the signs) and police radar checks enforcing the law at the most unlikely spots. Signs are not especially good in New England, with turns appearing without prior warning; the problem seems particularly bad in Massachusetts.

Visitors to New England often encounter rotaries (traffic circles) for the first time. Designed to keep traffic moving through busy or complicated junctions, rotaries often have the exact opposite effect. Traffic already on the rotary has the right of way, and you can only enter the rotary when there is a clear break on the left. Once on the rotary, stay in the inside (left) lane unless you are getting off at the next exit, but remember that this traffic rule—like most driving etiquette—is ignored by many Boston drivers.

Car rentals

All major car rental companies are represented in New England, including **Alamo** (tel: 800/327 9633), **Avis** (tel: 416/964 2051, 800/879 2847 in Canada), **Budget** (tel: 800/527 0700), **Dollar** (tel: 800/800 4000), **Hertz** (tel: 416/620 9620, 800/263 0600 in Canada), **National** (tel: 800/227 7368), and **Thrifty** (tel: 800/367 2277).

Depending on season and location, unlimited mileage rates typically range from $40 to $45 per day and $160 to $180 per week for a small car, or $55 to $60 per day and $200 to $250 per week for a large car. This does not include tax, which varies from state to state.

Be aware that picking up the car in one city and leaving it in another may entail substantial drop-off charges or one-way service fees.

The cost of a collision or loss-damage waiver (*see below*) can be high, also. Some rental agencies will charge you extra if you return the car before the time specified on your contract; ask before making unscheduled drop-offs. Fill the tank when you turn in the vehicle to avoid being charged for refueling at what you'll swear is the most expensive pump in town.

Major international car rental companies have programs that discount their standard rates by 15 percent–30 percent if you make the reservation before departure (anywhere from 24 hours to 14 days), rent for a minimum number of days (typically three or four), and prepay the rental. More economical rentals may come as part of fly/drive or other packages, even

LOVER$ LANE

25 M.P.H.

Mopeds for rent on Martha's Vineyard—a good way to get around

255

bare-bones deals that combine only the rental and an airline ticket.

Before you rent a car, find out exactly what coverage, if any, is provided by your personal auto insurer and by the rental company. Don't assume that you are covered. If you do want insurance from the rental company, secondary coverage may be the only type offered. You may already have secondary coverage if you charge the rental to a credit card. Only Diners Club (tel: 800/234 6377) provides primary coverage in the United States and worldwide.

In general, if you are involved in an accident, you are responsible for the automobile. Car rental companies may offer a collision damage waiver (CDW), which ranges in cost from $5 to $16 a day. You should decline the CDW only if you are certain you are covered through your personal insurer or credit card

company. In many states, laws mandate that renters be told what the CDW costs, that it's optional, and that their own auto insurance may provide the same protection.

Hazards

Snowplows keep roads reasonably clear in winter, but even so the roads can still be treacherous; cat litter or sand can be put down to ease the car out if stuck in the snow! Snow tires are essential for winter driving.

During the winter, pay attention to highway signs warning about "Low-Salt Areas." Concern about salt filtering into drinking water supplies has led highway maintenance departments to take alternative—and often less effective—measures for keeping roads clear of ice. Exercise similar caution if you see signs indicating that a "Bridge Freezes Before Road Surface."

Springtime uncovers one of New England's more unpleasant winter side effects—potholes and frost heaves. Road surfaces expand and contract after a winter of heavy freezes and sudden thaws. The result is a series of craters, fissures, and cracks in the asphalt.

Beware of moose, which like the salt that runs off the road and are seemingly oblivious to traffic; colliding with one

Driving in Downtown Boston can be hair-raising for visitors and is best avoided if at all possible

can cause a fatal accident. Moose are particularly prevalent in the White Mountains and inland Maine. Also keep an eye out for deer. If you collide with a skunk it may spray your car; the pungent smell is no joke.

Parking
Boston and other large New England cities have public parking lots and garages as well as the usual parking meters, but demand for spaces often exceeds supply on weekdays. A better bet around Boston is to park near one of the outer stops on the MBTA (see pages 52 and 258), and from there take a train or subway into the city.

Traffic lights
Massachusetts was one of the last states to adopt a policy of "right turn on red." This stubborn refusal has left a legacy of "no right turn on red light" signs at some junctions, so don't take this maneuver for granted.

School buses
Remember that New England pioneered the idea of enforced traffic stops (on both sides of the road) when a school bus stops. This law is strictly observed—even around Boston. Watch for flashing lights on the bus or even stop signs that pop out from the cab.

Biking
In Boston, the **Dr. Paul Dudley White Bikeway**, approximately 18 miles long, runs along both sides of the Charles River. **The Bicycle Workshop** (259 Massachusetts Ave., Cambridge, tel: 617/876 6555) rents bicycles, fixes flat tires while you wait, and delivers bicycles to your hotel. Elsewhere in New England, there are plenty of opportunities for the bicyclist, with ready-made bike trails on Cape Cod and in the Pioneer Valley, for example, and scenic country roads in the Berkshires and northern Vermont; biking is also a feasible option in and around Newport. Mountain biking is very popular (particularly in the White Mountains), and ski resorts often offer this facility when the snows have gone. The loop road in Acadia National Park is scenic (although traffic gets busy in summer), and there is not a lot of distance to cover. Nantucket and Block Island are excellent for exploring by bike; Martha's Vineyard has dangerous roads (too narrow to accommodate traffic safely) but some bike paths.

Free information is available from the Maine Publicity Bureau (Box 2300, Hallowell 04347, tel: 207/623 0363 or 800/932 3419), the Massachusetts Office of Travel and Tourism, the

New Hampshire Bureau of Trails (Box 1856, Concord, NH 03302, tel: 603/271 3254), and the Vermont Travel Division. Other sources include **Maine Sport** (Rte. 1, Rockport, ME 04856, tel: 207/236 8797 or 800/722 0826), and **Vermont Bicycle Touring** (Box 711, Bristol, VT 05443-0711, tel: 802/453 4811). Cycle route maps are available from the Adventure Cycling Association, P.O. Box 8308, Missoula, MT 59807-8308.

Hiking

Country walking for pleasure is mainly confined to state and forest parks, where ready-made trails are well marked. There is usually an indication of the time needed, and the length and difficulty of the walk, and free maps are generally available. The finest areas in New England for walking are the White Mountains and Acadia National Park, although there are many smaller parks with one or two outstanding trails. Naturalists particularly enjoy the trails in the wilds of Baxter State Park in Maine.

Many of the best routes are mentioned in this book. Because of the prevalence of tree cover, good views can be hard to find; you often see nothing until the summit. Ask locally which routes go above the timberline. Long-distance walks include the **Appalachian Trail**, which stretches for 2,035 miles between Georgia and Maine, and Vermont's 260-mile **Long Trail** over the Green Mountains and Mount Mansfield.

A range of practical walking guidebooks covers the region. For further information contact the **Appalachian Mountain Club** (AMC), Box 298,

Left: Signposts and road numbers can leave some first-time visitors scratching their heads

Gorham, NH 03581 (tel: 603/466 2721), the Berkshire Region Headquarters, 740 South St., Pittsfield, MA 01202 (tel: 413/442 8928), the **White Mountains National Forest**, 719 North Main Street, Laconia, NH 03246 (tel: 603/528 8721), or the **Green Mountain National Forest**, 231 North Main Street, Rutland, VT 05701 (tel: 802/747 6700).

Boating and sailing

In most lakeside and coastal resorts, sailboats and powerboats can be rented at a local marina. Newport, Rhode Island, and Maine's Penobscot Bay are famous sailing areas. Lakes in New Hampshire and Vermont are splendid for all kinds of boating. The Connecticut River in the Pioneer Valley and the Housatonic River in the Berkshires are popular for canoeing.

257

A coastal bicycle trail gives the freedom to look around as you travel

Public transportation

Selected train trips Commuter rail services from Boston and New Haven are inexpensive, and tickets can be bought immediately prior to travel. Long-distance Amtrak services can fill up and should be booked in advance. Some basic trips are suggested here.

● **Amtrak** (tel: 800 USA-RAIL). Northeast Corridor: Boston South Station, Providence, Mystic, New London, Old Saybrook, New Haven, New York, Philadelphia.

● **Metro-North** (tel: 800/METRO INFO; in New York, tel: 212/532 4900). New York (Grand Central), Rowayton, South Norwalk, New Haven, with connections to New Canaan, Danbury, and Waterbury.

● **MBTA Commuter Rail** (tel: 617/374 1234). Boston North Station to Fitchburg via Concord (MA); Rockport via Salem (for bus to Marblehead), Manchester (MA), Gloucester; Ipswich.

The "T" is useful for traveling between Boston and the North and South Shores

Boston South Station to Providence.

Selected bus trips Boston services leave from South Station in downtown Boston and/or Logan Airport.

Services vary in frequency and are periodically altered or withdrawn completely; check before traveling.

Bus companies tend to be organized regionally; for example:

● **Concord Trailways** (tel: 800/639

Trolley tours operate in Boston

3317) covers much of New Hampshire and parts of Maine, including Concord NH, and Maine to Bangor via Camden.
- **Plymouth and Brockton** (tel: 508/746 0378) serves Cape Cod (including Provincetown).
- **Bonanza Buses** (tel: 800/556 3815): Connecticut, Rhode Island; the Maine coast, the Berkshires (from New York), Cape Cod for ferries to the islands. Includes Providence, Fall River, Portsmouth, Portland, Bangor.
- **C&J Trailways** (tel: 800/258 7111: the coastal towns of New Hampshire and Maine, including Newburyport and Portsmouth.
- **Peter Pan Trailways** (tel: 800/343 9999); western Massachusetts and Connecticut, covering Amherst, Hartford, Foxwoods, Old Sturbridge, Lowell, New Haven and New York.
- **Greyhound International** (tel: 800/231 2222); Hartford, Springfield; long-distance routes across the USA.
- **Vermont Transit Lines** (tel: 617/526 1801 or 802/864 6811); numerous towns in Vermont, New Hampshire and Maine, notably Lowell, Montpelier, Burlington, Brattleboro, Portland, Portsmouth, Augusta and Bangor.

Selected ferry trips See gazetteer entries for Block Island (page 213), Martha's Vineyard (page 160), Nantucket (page 162), and Provincetown (page 159). One option is to tour Rhode Island by ferry from Providence, stopping at Newport and continuing to Block Island (Interstate Navigation, tel: 401/783 4613).

Regional flights Boston's Logan Airport and many of the smaller airports mentioned in the "Arriving" section (see page 248) are ideal jumping-off points for flights to other parts of New England. Flying is the most expensive travel alternative within New England, but the savings in time can make a getaway weekend possible.
Major carriers within the New England region include:
- **Cape Air** (tel: 800/352 0714).
- **Delta** (tel: 800/345 3400).
- **Island Airlines** (serving Nantucket,

Most trains running in much of the north of the region will be those on tourist railways

tel: 800/698 1109).
- **Northwest Airlines** (tel: 800/224 2525).
- **US Airways** (tel: 800/428 4322).
  In addition, short-hop charter flights or scenic aerial tours can be arranged at many of the small rural airports.

Canny planning
Public transportation can help you overcome the busy times of year. For example, during conventions in downtown Boston, consider commuting from an outlying town such as Concord, Salem, or Quincy, all of which are pleasant bases with good accommodations, and excellent transportation links enabling you to be into Boston in a short time. Bus, train, and air services also take the hassle out of trying to plan a circular car tour of New England, but beware of one-way drop-off charges (see page 254).
  You could further dodge the crowds by visiting New England in spring, by visiting the coast in autumn or even winter, by venturing into the mountains in the summer, or by going to the busier resorts during the week and saving money on hotel bills by staying in Boston at the weekend.

Communications

Language

New England has seen more centuries of immigration and assimilation into the "melting pot" than just about any other part of the U.S. Each incoming ethnic group, whether French Canadian, Irish, Portuguese, or Hispanic, has left a lasting mark on the way New Englanders speak.

Nevertheless, visitors to New England expect locals to speak like the Kennedys. That accent, with its characteristic broad *A*'s and ignored *R*'s, is at its most pronounced around Boston and along the New England coastline. Some linguists maintain that it is close to the accent of those original settlers from the eastern part of England. Distinctively "English" pronunciations of words such as "half," "can't," "aunt," and "path" are beginning to be lost in the face of the mass media, but each generation of Bostonians learns to "pahk the cah in Hahvid yahd."

The accent of western New England played a large role in how much of modern America speaks. Western New Englanders moved north from the Middle Atlantic states rather than west from Boston. They then were the first to settle the Midwest in great numbers, laying the linguistic foundations for future generations in Ohio, Illinois, Michigan, and beyond.

New England pronunciations shouldn't pose difficulties for first-time visitors, but a number of words and phrases might need explaining.

New England	"American"
Bay State	Massachusetts
frappe	milkshake
frost	milkshake
the Hose	the Red Sox
the Hub	Boston
package store	liquor store
quahog (pronounced "ko-hog")	a hard-shelled clam
rotary	traffic circle
scrod	tender baby cod
ten, quarter of… (telling time)	ten, quarter to…
tonic	soda pop

Media

Newspapers The *Boston Globe* and *Boston Herald* are both dailies, with listings on Thursday and Friday respectively. The *Boston Phoenix* comes out on Saturday and has listings and comments on the city's entertainment. The *Christian Science Monitor*, highly regarded for its unbiased reporting, is published on weekdays and international news.

Hot off the press: this news-stand does brisk business in Harvard Square, Cambridge

Television

Television stations in Boston, Providence, Hartford, and other New England cities link up with the major networks, and a host of UHF and cable stations cater to local interests. Satellite and cable TV are common in the more mountainous and remote areas, where reception has traditionally been poor.

Local stations have long recognized the importance of tourism in the region. Weather reports on the evening news often feature news of peak foliage viewing or of ski reports.

Radio

Local radio derives a great deal of input from the diverse ethnic makeup and from the many colleges and universities in the region. Even commercial FM stations recognize that there is a highbrow audience in this cultural area, so expect to find Berlioz and Bach rubbing shoulders with Bon Jovi on the radio dial.

Politics is a spectator sport in Boston, and listening to AM talk shows is a good way to follow the heated and occasionally witty arguments of local politicians. Professional spectator sports also spawn a number of call-in programs. Expect to hear variations on the following themes: the pitiful state of the Patriots; the glory days of the Celtics and Bruins; and why the Red Sox self-destruct each September.

In rural New England, much of the air time is filled with easy listening, golden oldies, or mainstream pop, but you can also pick up some useful insider's knowledge about upcoming antiques fairs, church bazaars, town meetings, or lobster suppers. If you're lucky, you might even hear about where the trout, striped bass, and bluefish are biting.

Telephones

Find out your hotel's policy on telephones. Local calls are sometimes free, but don't bank on it. Other calls from hotels are usually marked up considerably, so exercise caution. Remember that most state and regional tourist offices have toll-free numbers.

Area codes In New England there is one code per state in most cases, except for Massachusetts, with five, and Connecticut, with two.

- **Boston** 617.
- **Connecticut** 203, 860.
- **Maine** 207.
- **Massachusetts** (western) 413.
- **Massachusetts** (southern and eastern) 508.
- **Massachusetts** (northern) 978.
- **Massachusetts** (Greater Boston, outer areas) 781.
- **New Hampshire** 603.
- **Rhode Island** 401.
- **Vermont** 802.

Overseas call code International calls can be made from any phone. For the international operator, tel: 0. Omit the first 0 if applicable from local area code:

- **Australia** 01161.
- **Canada** no extra code needed.
- **Ireland** 011353
- **New Zealand** 01164.
- **United Kingdom** 001144

261

Weather information

For current weather conditions and forecasts for cities in the United States and abroad, plus the local time and helpful travel tips, call the **Weather Channel Connection** (tel: 900 WEATHER; 95¢ per minute) from a Touch-Tone phone.

Public telephone booth in Boston's Chinatown

Emergencies

Crime

Robert B. Parker and George V. Higgins have put Boston on the crime fiction map, but neither Boston nor New England is swamped by a crime wave. In fact, many parts of the region are charmingly relaxed, with houses and cars left unlocked and bicycles left standing against lampposts.

However, it is wise to be on guard in quiet city areas, particularly at night, to lock your car doors if you are driving, and to be careful about where you park.

Central Boston is generally very safe in daytime, and even its notorious "Combat Zone" (a red-light district between downtown and Chinatown) has had something of a facelift in recent years. Some southern neighborhoods are crime-ridden, but few visitors have reason to go there. There are some other notable no-go areas in the city of Brockton (south of Boston) and in larger cities such as Providence, Hartford, and Bridgeport.

If confronted by a mugger, do not resist him. A wise precaution is to carry a $20 bill separately from other valuables, in the hope that this will satisfy the attacker.

Boston is a safe city but normal precautions should be taken at night

Police There are no county police in New England. Local matters are dealt with by city or town police; state police patrol highways regularly.

Emergency numbers

The best advice is simply to call the operator and explain the difficulty. Boston and Cambridge police can be reached by dialing 911.

Consulates

Boston has consulates dealing with matters involving nationals of the following countries:
● Canada Copley Place (tel: 617/262 3760).
● Ireland 535 Boylston Street (tel: 617/267 9330).
● United Kingdom Federal Reserve Plaza, 25th Floor, 600 Atlantic Avenue (tel: 617/248 9555).

Natural hazards

Deer ticks are tiny insects that can fall on you unawares and burrow into the skin, causing **Lyme disease**, an unpleasant condition that normally starts with a circular rash. It is followed by flu-like symptoms and lethargy, leading in some instances to numbness, tingling, arthritis, meningitis, or heart failure. It is important to get treatment as soon as symptoms occur, as the condition can worsen rapidly. The highest risk areas are Connecticut, Rhode Island, and